Approaches to Teaching Gilman's "The Yellow Wall-Paper" and *Herland*

Edited by

Denise D. Knight

and

Cynthia J. Davis

The Modern Language Association of America
New York   2003

© 2003 by The Modern Language Association of America
All rights reserved. Printed in the United States of America

For information about obtaining permission to reprint material from
MLA book publications, send your request by mail (see address below),
e-mail (permissions@mla.org), or fax (646 458-0030).

Library of Congress Cataloging-in-Publication Data

Approaches to teaching Gilman's "The yellow wall-paper" and Herland /
edited by Denise D. Knight and Cynthia J. Davis.
p. cm. — (Approaches to teaching world literature, ISSN 1059-1133 ; 76)
Includes bibliographical references and index.
ISBN 0-87352-900-6 (acid-free paper) — ISBN 0-87352-901-4 (pbk. : acid-free paper)
1. Gilman, Charlotte Perkins, 1860–1935. Yellow wall-paper. 2. Gilman,
Charlotte Perkins, 1860–1935 — Study and teaching. 3. Gilman, Charlotte
Perkins, 1860–1935. Herland. 4. Feminism and literature — United States.
5. Women and literature — United States. I. Knight, Denise D., 1954–
II. Davis, Cynthia J., 1964– III. Series.
PS1744.G57 Y43 2002
813'.54--dc21   2002154397

Cover illustration of the paperback edition: *Charlotte Perkins Leap*, by
Charlotte Anna Perkins. Watercolor, painted in Ogunquit, Maine, c. 1883.
The painting is owned by her grandson, Walter Stetson Chamberlin.

Set in Caledonia and Bodoni. Printed on recycled, acid-free paper

Published by The Modern Language Association of America
26 Broadway, New York, New York 10004-1789
www.mla.org

CONTENTS

Preface to the Series   ix

Preface to the Volume   xi

Introduction: On Teaching Gilman   xv

PART ONE: MATERIALS *Denise D. Knight and Cynthia J. Davis*

Paperback Editions and Anthologies   3
Further Readings for Students   6
Further Readings for Teachers   9
  Background Studies   9
  Biography   10
  Critical Studies   10
Aids to Teaching   11

PART TWO: APPROACHES

Issues in Teaching Gilman's Works

Texts and Contexts in Gilman's World: A Biographical Approach   17
  Denise D. Knight

Ideology and Aesthetics in Teaching Gilman's Works   26
  Gary Totten

Gilman's Socialism as Background to Her Writings   32
  Mark W. Van Wienen

Placing Gilman in a Context of Intellectual Debate   40
  Michael J. Kiskis

Teaching Gilman in the Context of Her Short Fiction,
    Poetry, and Nonfiction   48
  Michelle N. McEvoy

Teaching "The Yellow Wall-Paper"

Teaching "The Yellow Wall-Paper" through the Lens of Language   53
  Catherine J. Golden

Finding Patterns in the Text: Close Reading
    "The Yellow Wall-Paper" as an Exercise   61
  Michelle A. Massé

The Use of Audiovisual Material as an Aid in Teaching
    "The Yellow Wall-Paper"   67
    Guiyou Huang

A Psychological Approach to Teaching "The Yellow Wall-Paper"   75
    Judith Harris

Using Role-Playing in Teaching "The Yellow Wall-Paper"   84
    Carol Farley Kessler and Priscilla Clement

Teaching "The Yellow Wall-Paper" through French Feminist
    Literary Criticism   90
    Janet Gabler-Hover

Teaching *Herland*

Teaching *Herland* in Context   97
    Melanie V. Dawson

This Land Is *Herland*, This Land Is Our Land? Teaching *Herland*
    in a Course on Community and Identity in American
    Literature   106
    Wendy Ripley

Confronting Issues of Race, Class, and Ethnicity in *Herland*   111
    Lisa Ganobcsik-Williams

The Intellectual Context of *Herland*: The Social Theories
    of Lester Ward   118
    Gary Scharnhorst

Charlotte Perkins Gilman's *Herland* and the Gender of Science   125
    Lisa A. Long

Teaching Gilman in Course Contexts

Teaching "The Yellow Wall-Paper" in an Introductory
    Literature Course   133
    David Faulkner

Teaching the Politics of Difference and "The Yellow Wall-Paper"
    in Women's Literature Classes   143
    Mary C. Carruth

Teaching "The Yellow Wall-Paper" in a Class on Women's
    Autobiography   152
    Kara Virginia Donaldson

Teaching *Herland* in an American Literature Course   159
    Joanne B. Karpinski

Teaching "The Yellow Wall-Paper" in the Context of American
    Literary Realism and Naturalism   166
    Cynthia J. Davis

Notes on Contributors   175

Contributors and Survey Participants   179

Works Cited   181
    Paperback Editions and Anthologies   181
    Books and Articles   181
    Audiovisual Materials   194

Index   195

PREFACE TO THE SERIES

In *The Art of Teaching* Gilbert Highet wrote, "Bad teaching wastes a great deal of effort, and spoils many lives which might have been full of energy and happiness." All too many teachers have failed in their work, Highet argued, simply "because they have not thought about it." We hope that the Approaches to Teaching World Literature series, sponsored by the Modern Language Association's Publications Committee, will not only improve the craft—as well as the art—of teaching but also encourage serious and continuing discussion of the aims and methods of teaching literature.

The principal objective of the series is to collect within each volume different points of view on teaching a specific literary work, a literary tradition, or a writer widely taught at the undergraduate level. The preparation of each volume begins with a wide-ranging survey of instructors, thus enabling us to include in the volume the philosophies and approaches, thoughts and methods of scores of experienced teachers. The result is a sourcebook of material, information, and ideas on teaching the subject of the volume to undergraduates.

The series is intended to serve nonspecialists as well as specialists, inexperienced as well as experienced teachers, graduate students who wish to learn effective ways of teaching as well as senior professors who wish to compare their own approaches with the approaches of colleagues in other schools. Of course, no volume in the series can ever substitute for erudition, intelligence, creativity, and sensitivity in teaching. We hope merely that each book will point readers in useful directions; at most each will offer only a first step in the long journey to successful teaching.

Joseph Gibaldi
Series Editor

PREFACE TO THE VOLUME

Charlotte Perkins Gilman once confessed that "she wrote [. . .] to teach. If it is literature, that just happened" (Black 39). Her statement of pedagogical intent inspires this volume of essays on approaches to teaching Gilman's two most famous fictional works, "The Yellow Wall-Paper" (1892) and *Herland* (1915). Her remark also underscores Gilman's belief that literature's value was primarily instrumental. In this respect, her works lend themselves well to teaching, as they are overtly designed to be teaching documents. But this is not to say that they lack complexity; in fact, their complexity explains the need for this volume.

At least since their reissue, "The Yellow Wall-Paper" and *Herland* have been regularly taught in a variety of courses with a variety of emphases. According to survey participants, the works are widely adopted in introductory surveys as well as advanced seminars in both American and women's literature courses. Other frequently mentioned English courses in which they are taught include American realism and naturalism, feminist theory, composition courses, and classes devoted to particular periods or decades. But part of Gilman's signal appeal is that her work transcends disciplines. "The Yellow Wall-Paper" and *Herland* continue to be adopted in courses in history, psychology, sociology, religion, American studies, and women's studies. They have also been featured in courses in emerging fields, such as literature and medicine or science and technology. At least one survey participant teaches *Herland* in an introductory geography class. One aim of this volume is to give a sense of the myriad cross-disciplinary pedagogical approaches to these works, in the hope of providing teachers at all levels with new insights and new strategies. The overall aim is to offer a practical and valuable resource for teachers who are new to Gilman as well as for experienced teachers looking for novel approaches.

Teaching Gilman offers many rewards. As one respondent stated, "What I love about Gilman is the way she deftly overturns the premises of her society that other writers get wrought up over." In "The Yellow Wall-Paper," Gilman tackles traditional medical and societal views of women, along the way calling into question extant definitions of sanity. *Herland* is designed explicitly to be a countertext to "our land," directly challenging seemingly commonsense assumptions and commonly practiced customs. Each of these works is short and accessible yet still powerful.

But the challenges are also many. According to survey respondents, many teachers have trouble placing these works in their historical contexts and in the context of Gilman's other writings, and they worry over their students' lack of historical consciousness in general. Others have difficulty providing the various feminist readings, especially given students' resistance to feminist inquiry. In many classes, instructors find their students polarized by gender, with the female students loving Gilman and the male students feeling alienated and even insulted. In several instances, teachers must deal with the desire to deny the ideological import of Gilman's fiction as students seek instead to "position the text as personal and idiosyncratic." Still other teachers are troubled over how to introduce students to Gilman's more reactionary views, including her xenophobia and racism, her support of eugenics and her essentialism, without discrediting her entirely. With both works, teachers remain concerned that each provides only a partial picture of Gilman's views and that the part is often taken by students as the whole.

With "The Yellow Wall-Paper" in particular, teachers are anxious to avoid reducing literature to biography. Another problem is making the story new: many students have read it in high school and may have been told that there was only one correct interpretation of the text, especially of its ending. At the same time, lacking historical perspective, many students wonder why the narrator doesn't just leave her husband. Numerous students have difficulty following the narrative shifts and strategies, the stylistic intricacies of Gilman's most complex tale. Finally, students are wont to read "The Yellow Wall-Paper" as simply a ghost story or a story of insanity, and they can be reluctant to comprehend its ideological message.

Herland raises a different set of problems. As one respondent maintained, "Students don't tend to like it as well as 'The Yellow Wall-Paper' and often fail to see the humor in the text and its various subtleties. Its ending also disappoints." Others felt that teaching *Herland* alone would be like teaching only the first half of *Little Women* (Beth lives!)—that is, no true picture of Gilman's intent can be discerned unless one reads the sequel, *With Her in Ourland*. Because *Herland* is often taught in literature courses, Gilman's sustained dialogue in the novel with sociologists including Lester Ward often goes underappreciated. Finally, there is the issue of sex: in particular, getting students to appreciate the novel's power as a depiction of a feminist utopia without obscuring both its heterosexism and the Herlanders' sexlessness.

While the essays contained here do not directly address all these concerns, they do offer ways of dealing with most of them. The volume is split into two sections, each divided into four parts. The "Materials" section consists of an overview of the paperback editions of each work and of anthologies; suggestions for further readings for teachers; suggestions for further readings for students; and suggestions for aids to teaching, including visuals and assignments. The "Approaches" section contains essays by contributors from a variety of fields. An introduction briefly summarizes the contents of the individual essays, which are organized according to the following headings: issues in teaching Gilman's works, approaches to teaching "The Yellow Wall-Paper," approaches to teaching *Herland*, and teaching Gilman in course contexts. The volume concludes with a comprehensive works-cited list.

We want to express our gratitude to Joseph Gibaldi, general editor of this series, for his interest in the project from the first and for his assistance throughout its progress from idea to publication. We also wish to thank the anonymous reviewers of the prospectus of this volume as well as the generous readers of the initial draft. The more than forty scholars who took the time to participate in our survey deserve acknowledgment and credit for their careful and thoughtful responses.

We also thank Elizabeth Holland and Jason Roth of the MLA for their guidance and expertise. Special thanks go to Walter Stetson Chamberlin for supplying the cover art, which was painted by his grandmother, Charlotte Perkins Gilman, in Ogunquit, Maine, in 1883. We also thank our husbands, Michael K. Barylski and John M. Reagle, for their indulgence and support.

INTRODUCTION: ON TEACHING GILMAN

Ever since 1973, when Elaine R. Hedges reintroduced "The Yellow Wall-Paper" to the academic world—a move that helped launch the resurgence of interest in the life and literature of Charlotte Perkins Gilman—instructors have been grappling with how best to teach her works, most notably the widely anthologized story "The Yellow Wall-Paper" and the utopian novel *Herland*. Teaching Gilman almost certainly guarantees a spirited classroom discussion, since students tend to be captivated, intrigued, or puzzled by this rather enigmatic figure. Still, challenges abound for the instructor who seeks to historicize Gilman, to sift through the deep layers of meaning embedded in her texts, or to examine both the satirical elements and the racism that characterize *Herland*.

While providing a wide range of perspectives and backgrounds, the essays in this volume share a similar purpose: to offer instructors, both beginning and seasoned, strategies, techniques, and exercises for approaching Gilman in the classroom. Because Gilman is taught across the curriculum—not only in literature classrooms (which can themselves range from introductory general education courses to graduate seminars in literary criticism) but also in courses in women's studies, philosophy, and the social sciences—the essays are intended to impart practical advice to teachers encountering Gilman in any discipline. Collectively, they seek to situate Gilman in a historical and cultural context, as well as to explore the problems implicit in teaching a writer who was in many ways a study in contrasts: progressive in her activism on behalf of women, yet troublingly conservative in her racial views; an outspoken intellectual, but one with very little formal education; an advocate of social motherhood, who relinquished custody of her own young daughter. Regardless of their theoretical perspectives, the essays should raise new insights about Gilman and her most popular literary works.

The essays on "The Yellow Wall-Paper" cover a number of approaches. Denise D. Knight and Kara Virginia Donaldson examine biographical and autobiographical strands in the story. Michelle A. Massé uses a formalist approach to show how undergraduate students can learn to recognize literary evidence in a text, shape persuasive interpretations, and understand the interdependence of both. Cynthia J. Davis teaches Gilman alongside American realists and naturalists, enabling students to gain a new understanding of the determinisms popular in the Gilded Age. Freudian psychology as a means of exploring "The Yellow Wall-Paper" is discussed by Judith Harris, while Janet Gabler-Hover advocates the use of French feminist criticism. Catherine J. Golden demonstrates how the story's style and grammar can be agents of meaning in literary exegesis. David Faulkner argues that "The Yellow Wall-Paper" can be used as a tool to engage students, especially in introductory courses, to write about that which silences them. Mary C. Carruth's essay addresses issues relevant to classes in women's literature, such as the politics of canon formation, women's literary tradition, and literary aesthetics. Michelle N. McEvoy suggests enhancing students understanding of Gilman's ideological views by bringing some of her other writings into the classroom. Gary Totten emphasizes the intersections between literary aesthetics and culture, while Mark W. Van Wienen demonstrates how socialist analysis informs the perspectives of both "The Yellow Wall-Paper" and *Herland*. Carol Farley Kessler and Priscilla Clement champion the use of role-playing in teaching "The Yellow Wall-Paper," while Guiyou Huang recommends incorporating a wide range of audiovisual materials—including photographs, films, and pictures of nineteenth-century wallpaper—to help contextualize the story for students.

Herland may be the fictional work by Gilman most frequently adopted outside literature classrooms, as the essays included in this volume suggest. Michael J. Kiskis teaches the novel in a core course on modernity and its intellectual traditions. He finds that Gilman's utopia intersects in interesting ways with the writings of Marx, Conrad, Arnold, Achebe, Darwin, Huxley, and Mill, among others. Among the courses in which Lisa A. Long teaches *Herland* is one on science and technology in America; she offers general advice on how to keep students engaged even when the narrative switches from fast-paced science fiction to sociological treatise, and more specific guidance on how to read and teach the novel through its trope of reproduction. Gary Scharnhorst helps students make sense of the novel by calling attention to the often overlooked influence of the sociologist Lester Ward on Gilman's thinking.

Anyone who teaches *Herland* has to deal with the novel's reactionary politics alongside its progressive ones, and it is often tempting to minimize the former while foregrounding the latter. Lisa Ganobcsik-Williams would instead have us recognize that the two are inseparable and that it behooves us to emphasize this inseparability when teaching the novel. Melanie V. Dawson also recommends situating the novel within a larger cultural context and offers numerous examples of teaching aids to help students better understand *Herland's* historical moment.

While the novel clearly lends itself well to interdisciplinary approaches, two contributors offer suggestions for teaching *Herland* in literature courses. Wendy Ripley positions the novel in a thematic course on community and identity, and Joanne B. Karpinski explores the multiple resonances between Gilman's novel and the various literary movements that have governed American literary history and shaped the American literary canon.

Whether Gilman's two works may now be considered canonical remains an open question. If anthologizing is any measure, then surely "The Yellow Wall-Paper" is a serious contender. *Herland* still haunts the margins, taught more often for its historical value than for its aesthetic accomplishments. Yet as canonical standards have shifted over the past several decades—as challenges are mounted to notions of universal, intrinsic value on behalf of a more contingent, functional conception of literary merit—Gilman's fiction increasingly garners attention. Never regarding her work as "literary," Gilman would not be averse to this shift in evaluative standards. As she once claimed, "It is a pretty poor thing to write, to talk, without a purpose" (*Living* 121), a sentiment that might be adopted as the motto for this Approaches to Teaching volume.

A Note on the Text

The word "wallpaper" appears variously in the title of Gilman's story "The Yellow Wall-Paper" as one word (Wallpaper), as two words (Wall Paper), and as a hyphenated word, with both a lowercase and uppercase p (Wall-paper, Wall-Paper). In quoting titles of editions of the book and critical articles, we have retained the spelling as it appears. In general discussion of the story, we have used "Wall-Paper," taken from the original 1892 publication of the story in *New England Magazine*.

Part One

MATERIALS

Paperback Editions and Anthologies

It was in 1973 that Elaine R. Hedges rescued the long-forgotten story "The Yellow Wall-Paper" from literary obscurity. While she was conducting research for her doctoral dissertation at Harvard University, Hedges stumbled across Gilman's now classic tale. The republication of the story in that year by the burgeoning Feminist Press marked a significant step in the reemergence of interest in Charlotte Perkins Gilman that began in 1966 when Carl N. Degler reissued her landmark feminist treatise *Women and Economics*, originally published in 1898. Although the reprinting of "The Yellow Wall-Paper" met an enthusiastic reception during a decade that saw the recovery of dozens of forgotten texts, no one could have anticipated the enormous impact that the story would have. Ongoing debate about the "The Yellow Wall-Paper" resulted in a full-length casebook on the story, a volume providing cultural perspectives, a publication history, dozens of articles and essays in journals and books, countless dissertations, and numerous papers on the subject at literary conferences. The story has been dramatized both on stage and in film. It has been debated and analyzed through virtually every theoretical lens, and the intrigue engendered by the story shows no signs of abating. "The Yellow Wall-Paper" is widely reprinted, appearing in virtually every college literature anthology, and it is taught in a number of disciplines including English, women's studies, philosophy, social sciences, and psychology.

The Feminist Press edition of the story—the version we use here—is an attractive and affordable paperback. Just slightly larger in size than the 1899 Small, Maynard and Company chapbook, it contains the original 1973 afterword by Hedges. We recommend that instructors who use the Feminist Press text adopt the second printing of the revised 1996 edition, published in 2000, which corrects errors in previous printings. This edition, the most popular and best-selling of the press's paperbacks, has just one drawback; the afterword is quickly becoming dated since readings subsequent to 1973 have opened up a wide range of new interpretive possibilities. Without critical apparatus, the edition is somewhat limited. The Feminist Press remedied that shortcoming in part with its 1992 publication of *The Captive Imagination: A Casebook on "The Yellow Wallpaper,"* edited by Catherine Golden, which contains the same uncorrected version of the 1892 *New England Magazine* story originally published by the press in 1973. The edition is useful and engaging in many respects. It includes the three illustrations that accompanied the original 1892 *New England Magazine* printing of the story, features background readings both from Gilman's contemporaries and from modern critics, and contains reprints of some fourteen critical essays, as well as Hedges's retrospective look at twenty years of feminist criticism. This otherwise fine volume contains no index, which makes it less user-friendly than it might be.

The Gilman biographer Ann J. Lane's Pantheon edition, *The Charlotte Perkins Gilman Reader* (1980), was the first anthology to include selections beyond "The Yellow Wall-Paper." Along with the 1892 *New England Magazine* version of that work, the volume contains ten additional stories, including several of Gilman's now popular works, such as "The Unnatural Mother," "Making a Change," and "Turned." It also features representative chapters from seven of Gilman's novels (*The Crux, What Diantha Did, Benigna Machiavelli, Unpunished, Moving the Mountain, Herland,* and *With Her in Ourland*), which are helpful in illustrating Gilman's style and themes. At the same time, the chapter excerpts are of limited use when they are removed from their larger thematic contexts. With the exception of *What Diantha Did*, the novels have since been republished in their entirety by various presses. Lane's volume contains a well-written and informative critical introduction, which was updated in 1999, when the University Press of Virginia reissued the volume.

Bantam's affordable 1989 paperback edition, *"The Yellow Wallpaper" and Other Writings by Charlotte Perkins Gilman*, introduced by Lynne Sharon Schwartz, reprints eight stories, all of which appeared in Lane's anthology. (It should be noted that Gilman published some two hundred stories during her lifetime.) The edition also reprints four chapters from *Herland* as well as selections from *Women and Economics* (1898) and *The Man-Made World; or, Our Androcentric Culture* (1911). The Bantam volume does not contain a bibliography of further readings or any critical apparatus beyond the twenty-page introduction, nor does Schwartz identify the copy text for her selections.

The 1993 Rutgers University Press edition, *The Yellow Wallpaper*, edited and introduced by Thomas L. Erskine and Connie L. Richards, contains just two additional stories, "Through This" (1893) and "Making a Change" (1911), the latter of which also appears in Lane's collection. Along with three brief "background selections," the volume features nine critical essays on "The Yellow Wallpaper," all of them reprints of previously published essays, including five that appeared in Golden's *The Captive Imagination* the previous year. Like Golden's edition, the Rutgers volume contains no index.

Robert Shulman's Oxford edition, *"The Yellow Wall-Paper" and Other Stories* (1995), offers the largest selection of short fiction published to date, featuring thirty-nine stories that span twenty-four years. Shulman has taken Gilman's texts from their original appearances in a variety of sources, including *New England Magazine*, the *Woman's Journal, Kate Field's Washington*, the *Impress, Worthington's Illustrated*, the *San Francisco Call, Physical Culture*, and the *Forerunner*. Also attractive in this edition is a chronology of Gilman's life and two appendixes, including selections from Gilman's "Story Studies," which appeared in the *Impress* in the 1890s, and the short essay "Why I Wrote 'The Yellow Wallpaper'?" (1913). This edition probably offers the best value for students. It is an attractive, affordable volume with a modest bibliography.

The seventy-page Dover edition, *"The Yellow Wallpaper" and Other Stories* (1997), at the cost of a dollar, contains just seven stories, all available elsewhere. Despite its claim that "the introductory Note was prepared specially for this edition" (n. pag.), the note is just a scant two paragraphs. The edition contains no introduction, chronology, or critical apparatus. While it is the most affordable text available, only those instructors who are able to address the inevitable questions that arise during the teaching of "The Yellow Wall-Paper" should use it.

Dale M. Bauer's 1998 Bedford edition, *The Yellow Wall-Paper*, is an excellent resource with much to recommend. It contains a wealth of historical information that helps establish the social and cultural contexts for the story. In addition to reprinting the 1892 *New England Magazine* version of the story, Bauer's volume features several excerpts from motherhood manuals; a section on invalid women; a chapter on sexuality, race, and social control; a section on late-nineteenth-century social reform movements; and a discussion of the period's literary culture. Bauer's edition contains occasional errors, primarily with respect to dates. Missing from this otherwise fine edition is an index.

Julie Bates Dock's slim volume, *Charlotte Perkins Gilman's "The Yellow Wall-paper" and the History of Its Publication and Reception* (Penn State P, 1998), again reprints the 1892 *New England Magazine* version of the story, though Dock does not preserve the story as it originally appeared. Rather, she admits editing the text to "offer the reader my best estimate of the story as Gilman might have expected her first audience to read it" (46). To that end, Dock lists variants found among several printings of the story. Her volume also makes available some new information about the story's reception, most notably by reprinting sixteen reviews of the 1899 Small, Maynard and Company chapbook. Like several others, this volume contains no index.

Of special interest is Shawn St. Jean's forthcoming volume, which will, for the first time, reprint both the manuscript version of "The Yellow Wall-Paper" and the 1892 *New England Magazine* edition. St. Jean has located more than four hundred variants among the texts, and his edition promises to provide the fullest account to date of the publishing history of the story and to interpret the significance of the textual variants.

Instructors and readers will find far fewer options when it comes to selecting an edition of *Herland*. Ann J. Lane's Pantheon edition (1979) was the first reprinting of Gilman's 1915 novel, which originally appeared in serialized form in her journal the *Forerunner*. While it is a popular and attractive edition, with a well-written introduction, the integrity of the volume is compromised by an unreliable text. Spellings have been modernized, words substituted, syntax and punctuation altered, and entire sentences dropped. Other volumes reprinting *Herland*, such as Barbara H. Solomon's 1992 Signet edition, have relied on Lane's transcription, so the errors have been perpetuated. Signet's affordable edition contains a modest critical introduction and twenty stories by Gilman, including a handful not available elsewhere: "My Poor Aunt" (1891), "Her Housekeeper" (1910), "Martha's Mother" (1910), "Making a Living" (1910), "Old Mrs. Crosley" (1911), and "Spoken To" (1915).

Knight's 1999 Penguin edition, Herland, *"The Yellow Wall-Paper" and Selected Writings*, the text used for the essays included in this volume, is based on the original 1915 printing of *Herland* and restores the text to its original appearance in the *Forerunner*. As indicated in her note on the texts, Knight has silently corrected typographical errors and made minor editorial emendations to enhance readability but otherwise has retained Gilman's spelling, punctuation, capitalization, indentations, and italics. The edition also reprints nineteen stories, including four not otherwise available in paperback: "Old Water" (1911), "The Chair of English" (1913), "His Mother" (1914), and "The Vintage" (1916). Unique to this anthology is the inclusion of eighteen poems. The volume also features a critical introduction and suggestions for further reading.

The Modern Library edition, published in 2000, also offers some unique features. Introduced by Gilman's contemporary and friend Alexander Black, whose 1923 essay "The Woman Who Saw It First" opens the edition, the volume reprints "The Yellow Wall-Paper" and ten other stories, all available in other editions. It also features an abridged edition of *Herland*; selections from *Women and Economics*; a note on the text; brief commentaries by Harry Thurston Peck, the *Nation*, William Dean Howells, and Gilman; and discussion questions for reading groups. The biographical introduction is just two pages long, however, and does not offer any social or historical contextualization of Gilman's work.

The Dover edition of *Herland*, available for a dollar, contains a two-page biographical note and offers "an unabridged, slightly corrected republication of a standard edition" (n. pag.). Although the most affordable among the editions of *Herland*, it contains no critical apparatus or suggestions for further reading and is recommended only for instructors who are able to address Gilman's complex social theories on their own.

Further Readings for Students

A good many of the teachers who responded to the MLA survey do not assign secondary readings to their students, often because they want students to develop their own critical insights or simply because they realize that students are already overburdened with assignments. Among those that do, a consensus emerged about what to assign. Leading the list were excerpts from Gilman's autobiography, *The Living of Charlotte Perkins Gilman*, as well as sections from her 1898 treatise *Women and Economics*. Selections from Knight's two-volume edition of Gilman's diaries were also widely recommended. Teachers interested in biographical approaches have assigned parts of Lane's *To Herland and Beyond*, Mary A. Hill's *The Making of a Radical Feminist*, or Gary Scharnhorst's Twayne book. In addition, there are several shorter biographical essays on Gilman that provide students with a more concise life history; those interested should see the works-cited list as well as the biographical section in "Further Reading for Teachers." A number of instructors accompany either work with additional short fictional pieces by Gilman, particularly the stories "Making a Change," "My Poor Aunt," "The Jumping-Off Place," "Through This," "Turned," "An Unnatural Mother," and "With a Difference." Many assign or read aloud at least one of Gilman's poems.

Teachers interested in giving their students a wider sense of Gilman's era may want to assign selections from such primary sources as George Beard's *American Nervousness*, Edward H. Clarke's *Sex in Education: A Fair Chance for Girls*, or Catharine Beecher's many health-related writings (*Letters*; *Physiology*). Those who want to compare relatively contemporary accounts of women's status may want to consider assigning portions of John Stuart Mill's *The Subjection of Women*, Coventry Patmore's *The Angel in the House*, and Mary Wollstonecraft's *A Vindication of the Rights of Woman*. Some teachers have had luck assigning more recent accounts, such as Betty Friedan's *The Feminist Mystique* and Virginia Woolf's *A Room of One's Own* as well as her shorter essays "The Mark on the Wall" and "Professions for Women." Other names widely mentioned as primary sources include Jane Addams, Emile Durkheim, Sigmund Freud, Evelyn Fox Keller, Florence Kelley, Barbara McClintock, Harriet Martineau, Karl Marx, George Herbert Mead, Margaret Sanger, Mari Sandoz, W. I. Thomas, Thorstein Veblen, Lester Ward, the Webbs, and Max Weber.

Secondary sources were also cited as useful in providing historical background: those frequently excerpted for student reading include Ruth Cowan Schwartz's *More Work for Mother*, Barbara Ehrenreich and Deirdre English's *For Her Own Good*, and Carroll Smith-Rosenberg's essays in her *Disorderly Conduct* as well as the essay she co-authored with Charles Rosenberg, "The Female Animal: Medical and Biological Views of Woman and Her Role in Nineteenth-Century America." Barbara Welter's classic essay "The Cult of True Womanhood" has also been assigned to introduce students to nineteenth-century American ideals. Another recommended reading for students was Ann Douglas Wood's "'The Fashionable Diseases': Women's Complaints and Their Treatment in Nineteenth-Century America." Diane Price Herndl's *Invalid Women* provides an overview of fictional treatments of women's illnesses, and portions may provide useful companions to either Gilman work. Many instructors found sections of Sandra Gilbert and Susan Gubar's *Madwoman in the Attic* to be illuminating for students.

Many teachers of both texts assign one or more critical essays from the available edited collections of Gilman criticism, including Golden and Joanna Schneider Zangrando's *Mixed Legacy*, Jill Rudd and Val Gough's *Charlotte Perkins Gilman: Optimist Reformer*, Golden's *The Captive Imagination*, Sheryl L. Meyering's *Charlotte Perkins Gilman: The Woman and Her Work*, and Joanne B. Karpinski's *Critical Essays*.

In addition to recommending many of the works cited above, those who teach just "The Yellow Wall-Paper" assign Gilman's "Why I Wrote 'The Yellow Wallpaper'?" as well as the sections of her *Living* that discuss Dr. S. Weir Mitchell's treatment. A number of teachers regularly ask their students to read actual writings by Mitchell, selected from his medical treatises including *Fat and Blood*; *Wear and Tear*; *Lectures on the Diseases of the Nervous System, Especially in Women*; and *Doctor and Patient*. One respondent recommends Mitchell's own short stories, especially "The Case of George Dedlow." Two helpful overviews of Weir Mitchell's rest cure suggested by respondents were Suzanne Poirier's "The Weir Mitchell Rest Cure" and Barbara Sicherman's "The Uses of a Diagnosis: Doctors, Patients, and Neurasthenia." Selections from the diary of Gilman's first husband, Charles Walter Stetson, published as *Endure* and edited by Mary Hill, also provide a nice counterpoint to the tale. Respondents were almost uniformly delighted with Dale M. Bauer's Bedford Cultural Edition of *The Yellow Wallpaper*, and many use it as an exclusive resource. Others use Julie Bates Dock's thorough and well-documented study.

Several respondents have had success assigning Gilman's short story in conjunction with works by other women writers, including Susan Glaspell's play *Trifles* and stories by Kate Chopin, Mary Wilkins Freeman, and Edith Wharton. For graduate students, one respondent regularly assigns Michel Foucault's "Of Other Spaces," because of its introduction to the concept of heterotopia, which can be useful for conceptualizing the narrator's room. Another recommended Erving Goffman's "The Insanity of Place." Short essays mentioned more than once as further reading for "The Yellow Wall-Paper" include Elaine R. Hedges's "Out at Last?," Richard Feldstein's "Reader, Text, and Ambiguous Referentiality in 'The Yellow Wall-Paper,'" Jonathan Crewe's "Queering 'The Yellow Wallpaper': Charlotte Perkins Gilman and the Politics of Form," Lisa Kasmer's "Charlotte Perkins Gilman's 'The Yellow Wallpaper': A Symptomatic Reading," Annette Kolodny's "A Map for Rereading," Judith Fetterley's "Reading about Reading," Susan S. Lanser's "Feminist Criticism, 'The Yellow Wallpaper,' and the Politics of Color in America," and Paula A. Treichler's "Escaping the Sentence."

When teaching *Herland*, many instructors pair it with its sequel, *With Her in Ourland*, and several with other contemporary utopian works, including Edward Bellamy's *Looking Backward* and William Dean Howells's *Altrurian Romances*. Selections from Carol Farley Kessler's and Polly Wynn Allen's books on Gilman were also mentioned, as was Dolores Hayden's book, in which Gilman's kitchenless homes are discussed. One respondent recommends assigning articles from the same or other issues of Gilman's the *Forerunner*, where the novel was first serialized. For general introductions to the novel, teachers recommend Ann J. Lane's introduction to her edition of *Herland*, Mary Jo Deegan's introduction to her edition of *With Her in Ourland*, and Minna Doskow's introduction to her collection of Gilman's utopian novels. Among the essays recommended were Gilbert and Gubar's "Fecundate! Discriminate!," Gough's "Lesbians and Virgins," and Thomas Galt Peyser's "Reproducing Utopia."

For additional reading suggestions, see the next section. For ideas for assignments as well as teaching aids, see the section "Aids to Teaching."

Further Readings for Teachers

Respondents to the MLA survey offered numerous suggestions for readings for teachers who are new to Charlotte Perkins Gilman. A number of these readings have already been discussed in the above section on readings for students, and we advise teachers to peruse both "Further Readings" sections.

Gilman herself was a prolific writer: in her lifetime she published some 1,490 works of nonfiction, 185 pieces of fiction, and 490 poems, and she wrote at least 7 dramas and dialogues. In addition, she kept a diary nearly all her life and was a dedicated letter writer. Gary Scharnhorst has prepared a nearly exhaustive bibliography of Gilman's writings, and it is highly recommended as the first stop. Larry Ceplair has prepared a nonfiction reader that includes important lesser-known pieces by Gilman. Denise D. Knight edited an edition of Gilman's later poetry, and there are a number of available collections of Gilman's fiction (see "Paperback Editions and Anthologies" in the works-cited list). But there is more to teaching Gilman than simply reading Gilman. Additional suggestions follow.

Background Studies

Critical editions of both texts—especially Dale Bauer's Bedford edition, *The Yellow Wall-Paper*—come highly recommended by our survey participants as good places to start when looking for background information. Most of the primary sources providing background for Gilman's works are listed in the section "Further Readings for Students." One respondent felt that those who teach Gilman should familiarize themselves with Thorstein Veblen's *Theory of the Leisure Class*, especially since Gilman's *Women and Economics* predates it by one year (though she knew of Veblen's work) and it is interesting to compare them. For general overviews of gender roles during the period, our survey participants consistently mentioned such secondary sources as Elizabeth Barnes's *States of Sympathy*, Gail Bederman's *Manliness and Civilization* (esp. ch. 4, which focuses on Gilman), Ehrenreich and English's *For Her Own Good: 150 Years of the Experts' Advice to Women*, Eva Figes's *Patriarchal Attitudes*, Sheila Jeffries's *The Spinster and Her Enemies: Feminism and Sexuality, 1880-1930*, and Smith-Rosenberg's *Disorderly Conduct*. Those interested in illness in Gilman's era should consult Smith-Rosenberg's text as well as George Frederick Drinka's *The Birth of Neurosis* and Herndl's *Invalid Women*; these works nicely complement primary sources such as Beard's *American Nervousness*, Clarke's *Sex in Education*, and Mitchell's medical treatises.

Studies of women writers and characters cited by survey participants as useful reading for teachers include Elizabeth Ammons's *Conflicting Stories*, Gilbert and Gubar's *The Madwoman in the Attic*, Susan K. Harris's *Nineteenth-Century American Women's Novels*, Ellen Moers's *Literary Women*, and Elaine Showalter's *A Literature of Their Own*. A very helpful introduction to feminist theory is Showalter's edited collection *The New Feminist Criticism*.

Biography

Gilman wrote her autobiography, *The Living of Charlotte Perkins Gilman*, in the last decade of her life, and it is a fascinating if not always fully reliable resource. The two-volume edition of *The Diaries of Charlotte Perkins Gilman* provides a wealth of biographical information. Also of interest is Mary A. Hill's collection of Gilman's letters to her second husband, *A Journey from Within*, as well as *Endure*, her edition of Charles Walter Stetson's diaries, with an introduction by Hill providing biographical information particularly relevant to "The Yellow Wall-Paper."

There are currently three book-length Gilman biographies: Hill's *The Making of a Radical Feminist*, which covers Gilman's life up to 1896; Lane's *To Herland and Beyond*, which focuses primarily on Gilman's relationships; and Scharnhorst's literary biography, *Charlotte Perkins Gilman*. Survey respondents mentioned two other book-length studies of Gilman as biographical resources: Allen's *Building Domestic Liberty* and Kessler's *Charlotte Perkins Gilman: Her Progress toward Utopia*. Critical introductions to various editions of Gilman's works, both fiction and nonfiction, also provide useful biographical information. Many respondents recommended shorter biographical sketches. The several collected in Karpinski's volume of critical essays include anonymous portraits; tributes by such friends and contemporaries as Alexander Black, Harriet Howe, and Amy Wellington; and a compelling biographical essay by Carol Ruth Berkin. One respondent found that Wilma Mankiller and others' *The Reader's Companion to U.S. Women's History* contains interesting tidbits about Gilman in a wider context.

Critical Studies

An upsurge of interest in Gilman over the last three decades has produced an abundance of criticism on both "The Yellow Wall-Paper" and *Herland*. Many of the best articles are collected in editions devoted exclusively to Gilman, namely Golden's *The Captive Imagination*, Golden and Zangrando's *The Mixed Legacy of Charlotte Perkins Gilman*, Karpinski's *Critical Essays*, Meyering's *Charlotte Perkins Gilman: The Woman and Her Work*, Val Gough and Jill Rudd's *A Very Different Story: Studies on the Fiction of Charlotte Perkins Gilman*, and Rudd and Gough's *Charlotte Perkins Gilman: Optimist Reformer*.

Another useful resource is Knight's *Charlotte Perkins Gilman: A Study of the Short Fiction.*

Participants who regularly teach "The Yellow Wall-Paper" particularly recommend the following authors' articles: Jonathan Crewe, Julie Bates Dock, Richard Feldstein, Judith Fetterley, Juliann Fleenor, Janice Haney-Peritz, Elaine R. Hedges, Mary Jacobus, Lisa Kasmer, Annette Kolodny, Susan S. Lanser, Loralee MacPike, Suzanne Poirier, Conrad Shumaker, Paula Treichler, and William Veeder; Walter Benn Michaels's first chapter of *The Gold Standard* is also recommended (full citations are in the works-cited list).

Teachers of *Herland* have learned much from the following: Knight's introduction to the Penguin edition of the novel, Lane's introduction to the Pantheon edition, Gilbert and Gubar's essay in Rudd and Gough, Gough's own essay in *Anticipations*, and Thomas Galt Peyser's work. One participant suggests that those interested in examining *Herland* from a sociological perspective should read Mary Jo Deegan's introduction to *With Her in Ourland*, Patricia Madoo Lengermann and Jill Niebrugge-Brantley's *The Women Founders: Sociology and Social Theory, 1830-1930* (esp. 105-48), and Minna Doskow's introduction to *Charlotte Perkins Gilman's Utopian Novels.*

Aids to Teaching

MLA survey respondents were more forthcoming about, and more apt to use, audiovisuals when teaching "The Yellow Wall-Paper" than when teaching *Herland*. Many at least show photographs of Charlotte Perkins Gilman, and when teaching "The Yellow Wall-Paper" especially, they also include pictures of her first husband, Charles Walter Stetson, and her one-time doctor, S. Weir Mitchell. For both works, teachers frequently show their students sketches and pictures found not only in the Gilman biographies and critical editions but also in studies such as Allen's *Building Domestic Liberty* and Hayden's *The Grand Domestic Revolution.*

There are several film versions available of "The Yellow Wall-Paper"; while none are perfect, the version directed by John Clive is most preferred (for more specific discussion of the films and other audiovisuals for the short story, see Huang's essay in this volume). At least one teacher plays songs about mental disorders by Dorrie Previn and Suzanne Vega. A number of respondents find supplementary materials through the World Wide Web, and searchers might want to start with the Charlotte Perkins Gilman Society Web site (http://www.cortland.edu/Gilman).

Historical documents provide excellent resources when teaching "The Yellow Wall-Paper." Many respondents bring in the original illustrations by Jo H. Hatfield for the story's 1892 publication in *New England Magazine* (reprinted in Golden's and Bauer's critical editions). Others circulate dress reform diagrams, documents on neurasthenia and hysteria, studies on the proper way to raise a child, and books on interior decoration from the period, such as *Hints on Household Taste*, by Charles Eastlake. One respondent particularly recommends *The Woman's Book, Dealing Practically with the Modern Conditions of Home-Life, Self-Support, Education, Opportunities, and Everyday Problems* (1894). Another creative instructor has amassed a collection of artifacts from the Victorian age: periodicals, clothing, jewelry, cookbooks, fans, art, needlework, and "hidden pictures" and puzzles of all kinds, so that her students "can put themselves in the place of the narrator studying the pattern and color of the paper as she had nothing else to read." Contemporary periodicals such as *Godey's Ladies Book* and *Petersen's Magazine* provide a rich array of materials, with articles on household organization and medical treatment for women, illustrations including portraits of the Gibson Girl, and advertisements geared toward or depicting women.

Many teachers turn to other writers to help teach Gilman's short story. A number assign Harriet Beecher Stowe's writing on her difficulties as wife, mother, and writer (see Stowe; Hedrick), as well as sections from *Uncle Tom's Cabin* and Beecher and Stowe's *American Woman's Home* to set up the expectation of ideal womanhood. Others regularly partner "The Yellow Wall-Paper" with tales by Poe, Chopin, Freeman, Faulkner, and Shirley Jackson. One instructor recommends Janet Beer's *Kate Chopin, Edith Wharton, and Charlotte Perkins Gilman* for those interested in teaching the short fiction of these three writers together.

Art figures prominently among the preferred audiovisuals. One respondent uses David Lubin's book on Thomas Eakins and John Singer Sargent to introduce realistic art to students; others bring in examples of art nouveau as well as Pre-Raphaelite portraits of women. Yet another instructor recommends Rozsika Parker and Griselda Pollock's *Old Mistresses*, which addresses the role of the woman artist from the Middle Ages to the early twentieth century. Other teachers use art in less conventional ways, including handing out crayons, pastels, chalk, markers, or pencils in shades of yellow and having students draw the wallpaper; one has them draw on the blackboard and then asks for a student volunteer to creep along in front; afterward students are asked to discuss their feelings and perceptions about the process.

When teaching *Herland*, one respondent uses film clips from *The Wizard of Oz*, *The Matrix*, and *The Handmaid's Tale* as "a contemporary way to help [students] understand utopian/dystopian worlds." Another shows George Cukor's screen adaptation of Lillian Hellman's play *The Women*, which, she points out, "has an all-women cast but its plot is still dictated by absent men because of economics and heterosexual imperatives." Others use photocopies or slides depicting how *Herland* originally appeared in the *Forerunner*.

Respondents who teach *Herland* have provided their students with information on birth control movements; books or articles about the eugenics movement; documents about women in World War I; newspaper articles about electrification, motor cars, indoor plumbing, and the like; documents from the socialist movement; and newspaper reports about the Wright brothers or subsequent plane flights. One survey participant highly recommends handbooks such as *The Woman's Book: Contains Everything a Woman Ought to Know* (1911), as well as books on women and education such as *The College Girl of America and the Institutions Which Make Her What She Is*, by Mary Caroline Crawford (1904).

When it comes to assignments, many respondents who teach both works ask their students to write papers on genre. During class discussion of "The Yellow Wall-Paper," one participant asks students to free write about the moment in the narrative when they began to question the narrator's reliability. Other assignments on the short story include asking students to discuss the influence of Gilman's life on its composition, to compare and contrast the story with works by other female authors, and to assess female invalidism as a form of feminist resistance. One instructor assigns Virginia Woolf's *A Room of One's Own* and asks students whether the narrator gets her own room in the end and at what cost. Another has her students seek out sociology texts, both current and contemporary, and use them to explore Gilman's critique of marriage in the story. Those who also show a film version sometimes have students compare the story with the film. Creative assignments include asking students to discuss whether John is an abusive husband, in the narrator's time or in ours; to write about what happens after John wakes up; to envision what happened in the nursery before the narrator got there; or to rewrite the story from John's viewpoint.

Possible paper assignments for *Herland* include asking students to create alternate endings; to take the role of Ellador and then critique social phenomena in Herland and Ourland and in the real world today; to find a contemporaneous cultural text and compare it to Gilman's treatment of that topic in the novel (e.g., dress reform or air warfare); to write their own utopia or dystopia; and finally, to compare Gilman's utopian vision in *Herland* with another utopian or dystopian vision of choice.

Part Two

APPROACHES

Texts and Contexts in Gilman's World:
A Biographical Approach

Denise D. Knight

One of the first things that invariably occurs when I teach "The Yellow Wall-Paper" at the undergraduate level is the nearly universal curiosity among students about the woman who wrote this "very strange story." While students generally find "The Yellow Wall-Paper" an engaging work and can identify its central metaphors, explicate passages, and discuss conflicts and themes, they typically have little knowledge of Gilman's biography, aside from the brief summary offered in a prefatory headnote. Yet an introduction to Gilman's background provides readers with a fuller understanding of the social theories she espoused throughout her career in her essays, poems, and fiction. And with respect to "The Yellow Wall-Paper" in particular, familiarity with Gilman's biography enables students to explore additional layers of meaning and to become more astute observers of the story's intriguing subtext. I have found it effective to supplement a general analysis of the literary elements in "The Yellow Wall-Paper" with a discussion of relevant experiences from Gilman's private life so that students can better comprehend the story's tensions. I also often assign two additional short readings: the short essay "Why I Wrote 'The Yellow Wallpaper'?," originally published in the October 1913 issue of the *Forerunner* magazine, and a short story by Gilman titled "Through This," published in 1893. (Depending on how many class periods instructors can devote to "The Yellow Wall-Paper," students might also be directed to read excerpts from her autobiography, *The Living of Charlotte Perkins Gilman*, in which Gilman describes her breakdown and maintains that "the real purpose of the story was to reach Dr. S. Weir Mitchell," the physician who treated her for nervous prostration at the age of twenty-six, "and [to] convince him of the error of his ways" [121]. Pages 90–98 and 118–21 are particularly illuminating.)

Before commencing a discussion of Gilman's biography, I usually remind students about the obsequious status of bourgeois women in the nineteenth century stemming from their lack of legal rights. I point out that throughout the nineteenth century, women in most states were considered the legal property of their husband and that once a woman married, she relinquished all legal entitlement to her accumulations, including her own income and even the clothing that she wore. The husband was considered the legal guardian of the children and was awarded custody in the event of a divorce. Students can usually make the connection between the absence of legal rights in society and the forfeiture of personal freedoms experienced by the protagonist of "The Yellow Wall-Paper." I also review nineteenth-century medical practices and their effect on women, and I have found Dale M. Bauer's edition an excellent resource for such discussions. For example, some medical authorities argued that casual reading by women, particularly of novels, not only could corrupt the female reader but also could be physically dangerous and cause potentially serious medical problems. According to Dr. John Kellogg, for example, "Reading [. . .] may produce or increase a tendency to uterine congestion, which may in turn give rise to a great variety of maladies, including [. . .] weak backs, painful menstruation, [and] leucorrhoea," a whitish vaginal discharge (qtd. in Bauer 160). Gilman's own physician, Dr. Mitchell, went even further by contending that education in general was dangerous for women, who, he believed, were intellectually inferior to men. A proponent of Edward H. Clarke's *Sex in Education* (1874), which posited the health risks of higher education for women, Mitchell opined that it would be far better if the brains of women "were very lightly tasked" because the "overworked brain" is a "serious evil to women" (qtd. in Bauer 140–41). He maintained that women too often "collapsed under the strain that higher education imposed on their physical, [intellectual] and emotional state" (qtd. in Lane 118) and that "we expose [women] to needless dangers when we attempt to overtax them mentally" (qtd. in Bauer 141).

Advice and medical manuals were also full of misinformation. For example, Susan Power, author of *The Ugly-Girl Papers; or, Hints for the Toilet* (1874), argued that women's breasts are irreparably "injured by nursing children" and that at all costs a baby must "be taught not to pinch or bite its mother" since "a baby's bite has more than once inflicted [breast cancer] upon its mother" (qtd. in Bauer 85). With this dangerously distorted depiction of the perils of motherhood, it is little wonder that late-nineteenth-century fictional protagonists such as Kate Chopin's Edna Pontellier and Gilman's unnamed narrator rejected their maternal roles. Many doctors believed, too, that the loss of menstrual blood each month "diverted energy from the brain, rendering women [temporarily] idiotic" (Schneider and Schneider 10). Women were also instructed not to engage in sexual intercourse, except for the purpose of reproduction, an attitude that prevailed until the early twentieth century.

After a brief overview of nineteenth-century medical practices, I go on to examine Gilman's private life, focusing on her reluctance to marry, her post-partum depression, and her experience in undergoing the rest cure for nervous prostration.

One key to understanding the poignancy and the complexity that character-izes the narrator's condition in "The Yellow Wall-Paper" is, in fact, the bio-graphical dimension and particularly Gilman's fear of marriage. Gilman herself obscures the role that marriage played in her breakdown, however, by insisting that the purpose of the story was to convince Dr. Mitchell that his treatment of nervous prostration was misguided at best. But through an examination of Gil-man's biography, three primary images that emerge in the text—the "hysteri-cal" woman, the insurmountable walls that entrap, and the paper itself—assume greater significance. Moreover, it becomes clear that identifying Mitchell and his treatment of nervous prostration as the real impetus for the story was done, in part, to deflect direct criticism away from her first husband, Charles Walter Stetson, whom Gilman held equally accountable for her break-down. The act of writing the story can be viewed as a way for Gilman to pro-vide closure on the complex psychological and emotional entanglements that had their origin in her turbulent engagement and subsequent ten-year mar-riage to Stetson.

While the various theoretical approaches to the text—psychoanalytic, lin-guistic, new historicist, deconstructionist, reader response, and the like, which are summarized by Elaine R. Hedges in her insightful essay "'Out at Last'? 'The Yellow Wall-Paper' after Two Decades of Feminist Criticism"—tend to isolate the text and to engender debates about infantile regression, referential-ity, and triumph or defeat, it is important to note that for Gilman, the process of writing the story was a major act of empowerment, a therapeutic form of self-preservation, an act both defiant and personally triumphant. Whether the narrator of "The Yellow Wall-Paper" is victorious or defeated at the story's end is not as significant as the fact that the writer who gave birth to the story tri-umphed by exposing the deleterious effects of work deprivation on intelligent women. One question that we tend to overlook is whether Gilman would have written the story merely to condemn the treatment of her illness, or even the practitioner who administered it, rather than to expose one of the primary causes of that illness. Mitchell is, after all, mentioned only briefly in the story, and the imbalance of power in the conventional marriage is as much at issue as are the dangers of the cure. When even a few snippets of Gilman's background are introduced to students, they often independently draw the conclusion that Gilman is not holding Mitchell alone accountable; rather, she is implicating her first husband as well.

Students should be introduced to the following relevant biographical facts: During her teenage years, Gilman [then Charlotte Perkins] made a pact with her close girlhood friend Martha Luther never to marry, so as not to compro-mise the independence that they had come to treasure. Martha, however, eventually met a young man, fell in love, and married. Devastated by what Gilman perceived to be Martha's betrayal, she immersed herself in work and planned to devote her life to public service. Soon after Martha's marriage, however, Gilman was introduced to Charles Walter Stetson, a young and handsome Rhode Island artist, who proposed marriage just twelve days after they met. Gilman promptly declined. She explained her reasons in a letter to Stetson: "You *must* believe that I love you. [. . .] But much as I love you, I love WORK better, & I cannot make the two compatible" (Hill, *Endure* 63). Stetson pursued the subject of marriage for two years, and finally, though exceedingly apprehensive, Gilman agreed to marry him. Her fears of subjugation were recorded in her diary just four months before her wedding:

> With no pride, with little hope, with uncertain occasional happiness, with no glad energy and living power; with no faith or nearly none [. . .] I begin the new year.
> Let me recognize fully that I do not look forward to happiness; that I have no decided hope of success. So long must I live.
> One does not die young who so desires it. [. . .]
> I am weak.
> I anticipate a future of failure and suffering. Children sickly and unhappy. Husband miserable because of my distress; [. . .]
> I think if I woke, dead, and found myself unchanged—still adrift, still at the mercy of passing waves of feeling, I should go mad. (*Diaries* 246–47)

On 2 May 1884, Charlotte Perkins married Walter Stetson. Within weeks, she discovered she was pregnant, and the depression to which she was already susceptible deepened. After the birth of her only child, Katharine, the following year, Gilman became even more despondent. Eventually, when Katharine was a year-and-a-half old, Gilman traveled from Providence, Rhode Island, to Pasadena, California, leaving husband and child behind, to spend the winter months resting at the family home of her old friend Grace Ellery Channing. Her recovery was swift, and believing herself cured, Gilman returned home only to discover that her spirits had reached a new low. At the urging of a friend, she entered a Philadelphia sanitarium, where she sought treatment from Dr. Mitchell, the nation's preeminent nerve specialist. There she underwent the rest cure, a rigid program requiring enforced bed rest, inactivity, isolation from friends and family, and the consumption of a high-fat diet. As Mitchell describes in his book *Wear and Tear; or, Hints for the Overworked* (1871), patients undergoing the cure were allowed neither physical exertion nor intellectual activity of any kind and typically endured spoonfeeding as a part of the therapy. After a month, Gilman was pronounced cured by Dr. Mitchell and sent home with this prescription: "Live as domestic a life as possible. Have your child with you all the time. [. . .] Lie down an hour after each meal. Have but two hours' intellectual life a day. And never touch pen, brush or pencil as long as you live" (Gilman, *Living* 96). Gilman tried to adhere to the mandate for several months and subsequently suffered a complete breakdown. She finally garnered the courage to separate from her husband and to move with her daughter to Pasadena, where her career as a writer and lecturer flourished. It was in California that she wrote "The Yellow Wall-Paper," in 1890, which was published in 1892 in *New England Magazine*. In 1894, Gilman divorced Walter Stetson and voluntarily relinquished custody of Katharine to him. Stetson married Gilman's old friend Grace Ellery Channing a few weeks later.

This thumbnail sketch of Gilman's biography often provides the foundation for a spirited classroom discussion, but a few additional details usually ensure an even livelier exchange. Students are intrigued to learn that Walter Stetson claimed to understand Gilman's reservations about matrimony, and he therefore promised that he "should not object" if she supported herself by writing (Hill, *Endure* 69). Stetson's promises, however well intended, were short-lived, and he complained bitterly in his diaries about his wife's desire for intellectual freedom. "It is sin—surely sin: anything that takes woman away from the beautifying and sanctifying of home and the bearing of children must be sin. [. . .] She little knows what she does" (Hill, *Endure* 148). Although a kind, tender, and loving husband, Stetson was ultimately a product of a society that embraced the cult of domesticity for women. The more he insisted that Gilman adhere to conventional roles, the more she withdrew. Stetson's demand that she forfeit her desire to serve humanity, coupled with Dr. Mitchell's later admonition not to write, left Gilman resenting the patriarchal imperative that sought to silence women.

As various critics of "The Yellow Wall-Paper" have observed, the fictional narrator, deprived of the freedom to write, inscribes her experiences on the wallpaper, which serves as the "text," in that large attic "nursery." To compensate, perhaps, for the disempowerment that Gilman herself suffered during marriage, she created a protagonist who projects her conflicts, fantasies, and deepest anxieties onto the paper in a bizarre configuration that "slaps you in the face, knocks you down, and tramples upon you. It is like a bad dream" (25). In addition, we are told that the wallpaper is "lurid" (13), "irritating" (18), "infuriating" (25), "foul" (28), and "bad" and that "the pattern is torturing" (25), descriptors that can all be applied to her marriage to Stetson. (It is important that students know, however, that while Gilman's story is based on her own breakdown, Gilman herself never suffered from the hallucinations that plague her narrator.) Moreover, the protagonist asserts that "there are things in that paper that nobody knows but me, or ever will" (22). In reality, however, the paper is transformed into a tableau depicting both an amalgam of frightening emotional entanglements and the torment suffered at the hands of her oppressive warden-physician-husband. The statement, then, that "there are things [. . .] that nobody knows" is an intentional fallacy of sorts, since Gilman makes certain through the discourse of the text that everyone will know the secrets of the narrator's marital entrapment. The reader, in fact, is enticed into "reading" into that particularly enigmatic statement, into "reading" the patterns in the wallpaper, and particularly into "reading" the merger between fact and fiction.

Students are also interested to learn that just six months before her wedding, Gilman painted a "lugubrious picture of 'The Woman against the Wall'" (*Diaries* 233). Her fiancé immediately recognized the work as a troubled self-portrait: his diary described the painting "as a wan creature who had traversed a desert and came, worn out, to an insurmountable wall which extended around the earth. It was powerful. [. . .] I know it was a literal transcript of her mind" (Hill, *Endure* 244). Forty-two years later, Gilman searched for that painting, hoping to include it in her autobiography. She never found it. But worn-out women and wall imagery would figure significantly in "The Yellow Wall-Paper," penned just six years after she created the painting.

In the months following her marriage, Stetson became far less inclined to honor his prenuptial pledge to allow Gilman certain freedoms, including the freedom to write. In his diaries, he reviled the drudgeries of housework and revealed a double standard that mimics the source of much of the tension found in "The Yellow Wall-Paper":

> There is housework to do and though [Charlotte] does what she can, I find enough to tire me and make me feel sometimes that I am wasting my energy, power that should be applied to my art. [. . .] For love's sake, one must bear all things. [. . .] But I feel certain that other work is not so well done because of it. I cannot let my mind roam in sweet fancy's field now. It is utterly impossible. [. . .] I cannot afford, nor would it be right for me, to give up all my time and strength to such things [as housework].
> (Hill, *Endure* 276)

Not surprisingly, Gilman's own sentiments toward the need to indulge her fancies—toward her need to accomplish meaningful work—mirrored those recorded in her husband's diary. The theme of work, and her earnest desire to indulge her need to work, is foregrounded in "The Yellow Wall-Paper." "[I] am absolutely forbidden to 'work' until I am well again," laments the narrator. "Personally, I disagree with their ideas. Personally, I believe that congenial work, with excitement and change, would do me good" (10). The emphasis on the personal nature of the issue underscored the narrator's and the author's attempts both to emerge with an independent, singular voice and to take control of her own life by subverting that which was "prescribed" for her by Walter Stetson. His diary entry for 13 March 1884 reveals his attitudes toward his future wife's illness. He writes, "My love is sad: she has been very happy; and [is] now correspondingly depressed. *I* think she is unwell" (256). And then he adds his own prescription: "I think a cure will come with marriage and *home*." Home, for Gilman, was analogous to prison, a parallel she expounded on at length in her landmark feminist treatise *Women and Economics*, published in 1898, and in *The Home: Its Work and Influence* (1903).

Although Walter Stetson tried to accommodate his wife's desire to write, he was exceedingly conventional in his advocacy of a gender-based division of labor, a practice that Gilman emphatically rejected on both philosophical and ideological grounds. (It is likely, in fact, that Gilman's outrage at Stetson's conventional notions inspired her to write *Women and Economics*, just three years after their divorce became final.) "The Yellow Wall-Paper," then, actually served as a way for Gilman to encode her rage toward Stetson over a host of matters: his broken promises, the loss of personal freedom following the birth of Katharine, her enforced economic dependence, her obsequious status and entrapment in the marriage, and even the pressure Stetson exerted on her to marry. Compounding her mounting dissatisfaction with her husband was the particularly acute form of postpartum depression that Gilman suffered after her daughter's birth, a condition that was neither diagnosed nor acknowledged in the late nineteenth century. Rather, the medical community labeled the symptoms of postpartum depression as a form of hysteria.

Gilman's resentment at being coerced into assuming the role of wife and mother not only emerges in diary entries and in the painting depicting a defeated woman literally up against a wall encircling the earth—a potent symbol of her unattainable quest to serve humanity should she marry—but is also embedded deep within the framework of both "The Yellow Wall-Paper" and a short sequel of sorts, titled "Through This," published just a year later, in 1893. Significantly, wall imagery recurs in this story, serving as a metaphorical representation of isolation and entrapment. Taken together, the stories reveal much about the marital patterns and power struggles that are embedded in the text.

Gilman reincarnates the oppressed "Wall-Paper" narrator in the short story "Through This" but makes one dramatic change: the new Jane has undergone a metamorphosis and is transformed into the doting wife that John tried to invoke in "The Yellow Wall-Paper." Gilman reassembled nearly the entire "Wall-Paper" cast: John, Jennie, Mary, Jane's brother, and a male first-born child all either appear or are alluded to. Although the reincarnated Jane does not seem to succumb to "a false and foolish fancy" ("Wall-Paper" 24), which John found objectionable in his "Wall-Paper" wife, she shows subconscious signs of frustration, resentment, and anger toward her roles of wife and mother. Beneath her gracious veneer lies an enormously conflicted woman. Although she is allowed the freedom to write, unlike the earlier Jane, her duties within the home deprive her of the opportunity; by the end of her day, she is so debilitated by fatigue that she cannot muster the energy to compose even a letter. The loss of the ability to compose—to become in a sense "discomposed"—parallels the emotional disintegration that she is just beginning to experience. At the end of the story the weary protagonist is left staring at the "evening shades creep[ing] down [her] bedroom wall," which recalls not only the "lugubrious picture" of the wan, worn-out creature against an insurmountable wall but also the throngs of creeping women in "The Yellow Wall-Paper." Taken together, then, the stories reveal a discernible pattern. Although the protagonists would appear to be mirror opposites, the endings of each story underscore the futility of the women's condition. But the stories also served a therapeutic purpose for Gilman. Both became devices through which she could simultaneously retaliate against her oppressor, restore a sense of power, and ultimately practice the very craft that she had been for so long denied.

One in-class assignment that often yields effective results is to set aside fifteen to twenty minutes (after discussion of "The Yellow Wall-Paper" has concluded) and to ask students to analyze similarities in style, imagery, symbolism, and narrative technique between "The Yellow Wall-Paper" and "Through This." This exercise can be followed by a discussion about how each story might enhance our understanding of Gilman's own conflicts. Not only are students able to generate a comprehensive list of fictional elements shared by the two stories, but they also typically leave class with a much stronger understanding of the concept of fictionalized autobiography.

After the class discusses Gilman's biography, it is often illuminating to ask students to analyze the narrator's enigmatic assertion at the end of "The Yellow Wall-Paper," where she remarks, "I've got out at last [. . .]! And I've pulled off most of the paper, so you can't put me back!" (36). In looking for a parallel to this declaration of independence in Gilman's own life, we are reminded of a pivotal moment described in her autobiography when after "crawl[ing] into remote closets and under beds—to hide from the grinding pressure of that profound distress" (*Living* 96), she gradually reclaimed an identity independent of the conventional one thrust on her by Walter Stetson. Students often recognize the empowerment implicit in one's "coming out of the closet"—which evokes images of suffocation, constraint, and secrecy—by exposing to the world the truth about one's private life.

While Gilman took pains to deflect direct blame away from Stetson, there is little doubt that Stetson recognized the thinly disguised husband in "The Yellow Wall-Paper" as a portrait of himself. He was decidedly disconcerted by what he read. Gilman, however, seemed curiously satisfied by his reaction. In a letter to Martha Luther Lane, she urged, "When my awful story 'The Yellow Wallpaper' comes out, you must try & read it. Walter says he has read it four times, and thinks it is the most ghastly tale he ever read. [. . .] But that's only a husband's opinion" (letter, 27 July 1890). As an unintended but ironic commentary on their relationship, Gilman described the story to Martha—with its depiction of her marriage encoded in its text—as "highly unpleasant." But to paint Walter Stetson as the villain rather than Dr. S. Weir Mitchell would have been a blatant violation of fair play, a move that Gilman obviously recognized. She was, after all, still married to Stetson when the "The Yellow Wall-Paper" was first published, and an open attack against him would have been unnecessarily cruel and personally embarrassing. The indictment of Mitchell, therefore, can be read as a psychological maneuver on Gilman's part: by deflecting conscious criticism away from Stetson, she also avoided confronting the vulnerable part of herself that had submitted to a marriage of servility against her better judgment. It also served a therapeutic purpose. The act of writing an exposé of her temporary loss of sanity—the price exacted for succumbing to the pressure to marry—helped restore a sense of control and power.

As a postscript, students are often intrigued to learn that Gilman eventually remarried and found happiness in her thirty-four-year marriage to her first cousin, Houghton Gilman, which ended with his death in 1934. The following year, Gilman committed suicide, not because of depression but because she was battling inoperable breast cancer and could no longer contribute anything meaningful to society. As she remarked in her autobiography, "When all use-fulness is over, when one is assured on unavoidable and imminent death, it is the simplest of human rights to choose a quick and easy death in place of a slow and horrible one. [. . .] I have preferred chloroform to cancer" (*Living* 333–34).

Familiarity with Gilman's biography, then, establishes a context for the student, which can be useful in exploring additional layers of meaning in the story. It serves another purpose as well: students not only tend to remember the story "The Yellow Wall-Paper" but learn to appreciate Charlotte Perkins Gilman, the survivor, as well.

Ideology and Aesthetics in Teaching Gilman's Works

Gary Totten

Although the rise of cultural studies has infused literary criticism with energy and fresh insight, some scholars worry that this trend threatens our ability to appreciate aesthetic technique. This fear speaks to the tendency in English studies to position culture and aesthetics at opposite ends of the critical spectrum. The recent interest in aesthetic criteria in criticism, characterized as the literary alternative to cultural studies, complements rather than conflicts with cultural criticism. It allows students to appreciate literary aesthetics while considering the ideological relations between texts and culture. To regard cultural and aesthetic criticism as irreconcilable is to ignore the fact that, as Fredric Jameson observes, "the production of aesthetic or narrative form is [. . .] an ideological act in its own right" (79). In the critical space between viewing texts as what George Karnezis terms "cultural propaganda," on the one hand, and resorting to a "hermeneutics of adoration," on the other (B10), lies a valuable but relatively unexplored critical approach that provides a useful pedagogical framework for teaching Gilman's work. Gerald Graff and James Phelan argue that "[c]ritical dialogues that are clear, pointed, and well-focused [. . .] should lead [students . . .] *into* the intricacies of literary works rather than away from them" (10). Addressing contemporary critical debates, as Graff and Phelan note, not only facilitates discussion but also provides "models of argumentation on different sides of the question" (13).

When I teach Gilman's "The Yellow Wall-Paper" to undergraduates—both in an American literature survey course and in an introductory literature course designed to acquaint students with literary approaches—I emphasize the intersections between literary aesthetics and culture, not only to turn students' attention to the pleasures and distinctive (and, thus, ideological) nature of literary language, but also to introduce them to contemporary critical debates. This approach leads students into the intricacies of Gilman's text and involves them in the critical conversations surrounding it.

Sustained attention to both culture and aesthetics is a particularly appropriate (and timely) approach to teaching Gilman's work. Recent critical editions of Gilman's work edited by Catherine Golden, Thomas Erskine and Connie Richards, Dale Bauer, and Julie Bates Dock collect cultural documents and critical essays to illuminate the text's cultural context but devote less attention to literary aesthetics. Bauer excerpts selections from William Dean Howells's *Criticism and Fiction* and Henry James's *Notebooks* in a brief concluding chapter titled "Literary Responses and Literary Culture," and some critical essays in both the Golden and the Erskine and Richards editions address aesthetics. For example, Paula Treichler's "Escaping the Sentence," Mary Jacobus's "An Unnecessary Maze of Sign-Reading," Richard Feldstein's "Reader, Text, and

Ambiguous Referentiality in 'The Yellow Wall-Paper'" Judith Fetterley's "Reading about Reading," and Marianne DeKoven's "Gendered Doubleness and the 'Origins' of Modernist Form" all consider aesthetics. However, the primary focus of the material and criticism in these editions is cultural context. Dock's discussion of the "legends" of the text's reception documents how reference to the aesthetic in critical considerations of Gilman's work has often been used to explain the need for more cultural criticism of the text. To illustrate the inaccuracy of reception legends, Dock refers to Jean Kennard's 1981 essay in *New Literary History*, in which Kennard argues that our understanding of the sexual politics in "The Yellow Wall-Paper" required a change in literary convention accomplished through the rise of feminist theory (Kennard 78). Dock observes that Kennard echoes Elaine Hedges's observation, in the afterword to the 1973 Feminist Press edition of "The Yellow Wall-Paper," about the story's initial audience: "no one seems to have made the connection between the insanity and the sex, or sexual role, of the victim, no one explored the story's implications for male-female relationships in the nineteenth century" (Hedges 41). Dock directs our attention to contemporary reviews of the story to argue that the text's first readers, even male critics such as Henry B. Blackwell in the *Woman's Journal*, recognized the story's ideological intent (19–20; 107). I share with students Dock's argument regarding the text's reception to emphasize how recent scholarly work privileges culture over aesthetics.

To introduce students to the current debate between culture and aesthetics, I have them read Scott Heller's article "Wearying of Cultural Studies, Some Scholars Rediscover Beauty," which provides a brief but useful introduction to the arguments in favor of a return to aesthetic criticism. William Cain's article "A Literary Approach to Literature: Why English Departments Should Focus on Close Reading, Not Cultural Studies" also alerts students to the recent movement to reclaim the aesthetic. There generally is not time in a literature survey course to have students read many secondary sources, but I at least make them aware of several more essays including George Levine's introduction to his collection *Aesthetics and Ideology*, "Reclaiming the Aesthetic," and Michael Bérubé's response to Levine, "Aesthetics and the Literal Imagination," both (Levine's in abbreviated form) reprinted in David Richter's *Falling into Theory*. While I may not have students read these selections, I draw on Levine's and Bérubé's arguments during class discussion. Richter's volume also contains excellent essays arguing for the necessity of cultural criticism, which I can summarize for students in a handout or brief lecture or refer to during class discussion as appropriate (e.g., Barbara Hernnstein Smith's "Contingencies of Value" and Lillian S. Robinson's "Treason Our Text: Feminist Challenges to the Literary Canon"). Other useful instructor resources include Eugene Goodheart's *Does Literary Studies Have a Future?* (particularly ch. 1, "Casualities of the Culture Wars") and James Soderholm's *Beauty and the Critic: Aesthetics in an Age of Cultural Studies*.

Once students understand the nature of the debate between culture and aesthetics, I ask them to perform a careful close reading of Gilman's text. At this point, I do not discuss the historical, biographical, and cultural contexts of the story. Because many students, especially in my introductory literature courses, are not familiar with close reading, I explain how such a reading is performed, provide them with sample essays, and explain how the concept of close reading was created in conjunction with the rise of New Criticism in the first half of the twentieth century. Lois Tyson's *Critical Theory Today: A User-Friendly Guide* has an excellent chapter on New Criticism, very accessible for undergraduates, with a clear, yet complete, definition of close reading and fine sample essays demonstrating the approach. I supplement Tyson with an excerpt from Terry Eagleton's chapter in *Literary Theory* "The Rise of English" (also excerpted in Richter), where Eagleton describes the rise of the New Criticism and the establishment of the journal *Scrutiny* in 1932. Eagleton emphasizes how close reading served as a response to specific historical circumstances and fulfilled certain ideological needs, including the desires to establish English as a legitimate discipline, "roll back the deadening effects of industrial labour," and avert the "philistinism" of the popular press and mass culture (34). Familiarizing students with this background demystifies literary analysis and allows me to introduce them to the ideological nature of aesthetic criticism.

I may ask students to produce a written close reading of "The Yellow Wall-Paper" or work in small groups in class to construct close readings of particular passages. We discuss the text's formal and aesthetic aspects, including point of view, structure, pace, figurative language, setting, characterization, and so forth. I begin by asking the students questions such as the following: How does the narrator describe the setting? How is this description elaborated on as the narrative progresses, and what does this tell us about the narrator's mental state? How is the narrative organized? How does the diary form affect the narrator's ability to construct and articulate a self-identity? How does the narrator represent her relationship with her husband? How does she represent her husband's attitude toward her and her illness? What do these representations reveal about the narrator's point of view? With these questions in mind, how does the narrative style change as the story progresses? Students observe how the narrative pace quickens as the story progresses, moving from longer, more developed paragraphs to short disconnected sentences. They also note that the narrator's reflective tone and passive attitude give way to a more frantic tone (indicated by her word choice, shorter sentences, and increased use of exclamation points) and assertive attitude. Initially, she expresses her willingness to submit to John's treatment, stating that "[h]e is very careful and loving, and hardly lets me stir without special direction" (12). Even later, she reveals that "[i]t is so hard to talk with John about my case, because he is so wise, and because he loves me so" (23). However, she eventually takes control of her actions, and of the narrative, with declarative sentences such as "I have locked the door," "I don't want to go out," "I want to astonish him," and "I am getting angry enough to do something desperate" (34).

Next, we turn our attention to the wallpaper. I ask students to consider questions such as the following: What does the wallpaper symbolize? How does the narrator's representation of and attitude toward the wallpaper change as the narrative progresses? What do the figures in the wallpaper represent? How does the narrator's attitude toward the women in the wallpaper change as the narrative progresses? Students recognize the connection between the wallpaper and the narrator's mental state and observe that while the narrator refers to her writing as "dead paper" (10) at the beginning of the narrative (and, in the process, recording her distrust of John's medical diagnosis), near the end of the story her paranoid attitude toward John and Jennie, and any potential audience of her writing, leads her to state, "I have found out another funny thing, but I shan't tell it this time! It does not do to trust people too much" (31). Students link the narrator's increasing paranoia to her obsession with, and even dependence on, the wallpaper and conclude that this paranoia prompts her to invest her own instincts for self-preservation into her narration. They suggest that the wallpaper pattern represents the oppressive social conventions the narrator is trying to break through, such as gender roles, motherhood, and medical attitudes toward women's health. Students also suggest that the pattern in the wallpaper parallels the writing of the narrative and represents the narrator's writing of self. As the narrator emerges triumphant from these various patterns that oppress her, she is able to write her true self. Some students read the ending as an indication that all screens between the narrator's self and her expression of that self have fallen away, allowing her to express her genuine identity undistorted by social and gender constraints.

When we discuss the narrator's relationship with the wallpaper, students often find themselves referring to cultural context, which allows us to discuss the difficulty of maintaining a purely aesthetic reading. I ask whether a purely aesthetic reading or a purely cultural studies reading is possible, and if so, what would either look like? Has the rise of cultural studies made it impossible to perform the kind of purely aesthetic reading that might have been possible several decades ago? Students in sophomore survey courses, in particular, have already been exposed to cultural criticism and asked to perform cultural readings in other literature courses, and they often find it difficult to disregard culture to concentrate solely on aesthetics. Students require instruction in aesthetics, culture, and changes in critical approaches (and, in this case, even the experience of several literature courses) to recognize the state of their own critical perspectives, suggesting the important role of pedagogy in negotiating these intersections between culture and aesthetics.

Once the question of culture arises, I present students with information about the cultural contexts of Gilman's story. I draw on the compelling assortment of cultural documents that illuminate the text to demonstrate how it coincides with turn-of-the-century discourse on women's mental and physical health, writing, sexuality, motherhood, and consumer culture. I have found Dale E. Bauer's Bedford Cultural Edition of the text to be very helpful in this regard. Having provided students with this cultural context and having apprised them of the current debate between culture and aesthetics, I ask them to consider how aesthetic technique illuminates cultural issues in Gilman's text; how aesthetics produce ideology (instead of simply being informed by ideology) and construct, as Jameson suggests, imaginative or "formal 'solutions' to unresolvable social contradictions" (79). As I noted, students are willing to accept that the wallpaper symbolizes the narrator's oppression, and when the narrator begins to imagine dim shapes behind the wallpaper pattern, students read this as a manifestation of her desire to resist patriarchy, medical opinion, or prescribed gender roles. To emphasize how attention to both culture and aesthetics allows insights denied by separating the two, I ask students to consider how the pattern of the narrative itself reproduces this struggle, allowing both Gilman and the narrator to imagine and create, through aesthetic form, "solutions" to the narrator's social dilemma. I place students in small groups to consider questions such as the following:

> How are the narrator's acts of writing represented in the text, and what does this representation tell us about her ability to resist her situation? Track the nature of her acts of writing over time in the text. How does her ability to express herself sustain or challenge contemporary attitudes toward women and writing?
>
> How does the narrator's "reading" of the wallpaper empower or disempower her? How do these descriptions change as the narrative progresses, and what do these changes reveal about late-nineteenth-century attitudes toward gender?
>
> How does the narrator's representation of and reference to her self change as the narrative progresses? What does this reveal about a woman's ability to construct an identity in the late nineteenth century?
>
> How does the narrator manipulate her description of the setting to imaginatively solve the problem of her confinement in particular and women's oppression in general?
>
> How does the ending reveal an (aesthetically) formal solution to an unresolvable social contradiction? Is the narrator's (and Gilman's) resorting to insanity the only formal solution to her unresolvable social dilemma? Is the story's ending only achievable through the aesthetic? As an aesthetic solution to a social problem, how does the text's ending produce ideology?

These questions allow students to recognize the text not only as a specifically aesthetic object but also as an object contributing to the production of ideology within a prescribed set of possibilities defined by culture. I find that students are eager to discuss Gilman's artistic choices in the light of what they now know about the cultural context. In their small groups, students generate important insights into how aesthetics and culture interact in the text. Since they have already noticed how Gilman allows the narrator to invest her own instincts for self-preservation into the narrative's language, structure, and style and since they are now armed with specific information about cultural movements, students are able to formulate a more complete analysis of the narrative's changing style and the narrator's attempts to hold onto an identity even as it slips into the oblivion of cultural oppression. In the progressively terse style and combative tone, the narrative itself becomes a battle zone and constitutes a central aspect of the narrator's resistance to culture. The narrative reflects her attempts to create a "scientific hypothesis" (27)—in this case, structure and sense through narrative—to explain her experience despite the wallpaper's "lack of sequence" and "defiance of law" (25). The students' ability to see narrative as ideology develops in a manner similar to the narrator's growing awareness of the "dim sub-pattern" in the wallpaper (26). The narrator tells us that she stares at the wallpaper for hours, trying to determine if the front and back pattern "move together or separately" (25). Immersed in the spectacle of the wallpaper, the narrator discovers that the front pattern moves because "[t]he woman behind shakes it" (30); immersed in the text's aesthetic patterns and cultural context, students discover not only that ideology "moves" or invests narrative patterns but also that narrative patterns produce ideology. The narrator breaks free of the wallpaper by literally "writing her way out," and despite the incoherence of self that results, she still retains a degree of self-possession because she has utilized narrative to resist the containment of culture. In this case, Gilman chooses to formally solve the narrator's social dilemma through insanity, an artistic solution that relies on the unconventionality of insanity to allow the narrator to transgress conventional boundaries and liberate herself, while at the same time utilizing conventional ideology about women and insanity to critique women's oppression. This discussion allows students to consider how the writer makes aesthetic choices in response to culture.

By taking students through Gilman's text using two critical approaches that have been traditionally considered diametrically opposed, I am able to alert students to the possibilities of interpretation, apprise them of new directions in literary criticism, and expose them to the ideological nature of our critical poetics. I want students to recognize that culture influences not only Gilman's aesthetic choices but also the reception and ongoing criticism of the text. Our discussion of the text's contexts (both cultural and critical) demonstrates that we can only see what our critical lenses, as influenced by our contemporary critical culture, permit us to see. Our analysis of the text demonstrates that attention to both aesthetics and culture expands our critical options and enriches our understanding of Gilman's work.

Gilman's Socialism as Background to Her Writings

Mark W. Van Wienen

On the strength of "The Yellow Wall-Paper" and *Herland*, Charlotte Perkins Gilman is seen principally—and justly—as a notable feminist activist and writer. Yet Gilman's career, especially in the important formative decade of the 1890s, was dedicated equally to socialist causes. Initially involved in the Nationalist movement inspired by Edward Bellamy's utopian novel *Looking Backward, 2000-1887*, Gilman subsequently campaigned for the Populists and worked for the American Fabian Society, and throughout her life she described herself as an advocate of socialism as well as women's rights (Gilman, *Living* 187). Through this essay, I would like to facilitate two different approaches for teachers to incorporate Gilman's socialism into their classroom discussions. First, by examining some of the speeches and journalistic and sociological writings that were the primary vehicles for Gilman's socialist advocacy, I hope to entice teachers to select these as supplemental readings to the canonical literature. Second, by considering how specifically socialist analysis informs the perspectives of both "The Yellow Wall-Paper" and *Herland*, I would like to encourage teachers to incorporate Gilman's socialism into their discussion of these works.

To begin this exploration, teachers can introduce students to the interconnections between socialism and the publication history of "The Yellow Wall-Paper." The critical issue usually highlighted in this history—William Dean Howells's and Horace Scudder's inability to recognize the genius of the story (Dock et al. 62)—skims over the preliminary question of just how Gilman, then a neophyte professional writer, came to have the self-assurance to seek Howells's assistance in the first place. By August 1890, when Gilman completed the story and began to seek a publisher, both she and Howells were active in the Nationalist movement, a nationwide network of clubs—numbering 158 by 1890 (Hill, *Making* 170)—that had been inspired by Bellamy's socialist vision and were dedicated to bringing it into reality through political action and education. Howells had been a charter member of the first Nationalist Club to be formed in the country. In April 1890 a poem of Gilman's, "Similar Cases," had been published in the Nationalist party organ and had won such wide recognition that it led to a steady series of paying lecture dates at Nationalist Clubs throughout California (Scharnhorst, *Gilman* [Twayne] 20). Howells, too, had read the poem and written Gilman a letter of praise. It was on the strength of this commendation that Gilman wrote to Howells to request assistance in placing "The Yellow Wall-Paper." In other words, Gilman was calling on Howells out of a shared commitment to contribute to the transformation of the American political-economic system.

As a Nationalist, Gilman endorsed Bellamy's particular brand of socialism, in which collective ownership of industry takes the form of "nationalization or

municipalization" and under which "economic equality" is taken to be "the ultimate and ideal social condition" (Bellamy, "Socialism"). Although his scheme
applied to society generally, Bellamy also wrote specifically about how economic inequality enslaved women and how Nationalism would liberate them.
In a series of fictional dialogues between a newly converted Nationalist and
various skeptics appearing in the *New Nation* for 1891, one of the interlocu-
tors, a woman's rights advocate, complains bitterly about her economic plight:
"You can't tell us women anything we do not already realize as to the humiliation of pecuniary dependence, either as daughters or wives" ("Talks" 192). Bellamy also provides a prescription to cure this ill, as his Nationalist speaker
promises that under Nationalism women will, "through life, be not only economically equal with every man, but absolutely independent of any man"
(192). However we trace the lineaments of patriarchy in "The Yellow Wall-
Paper," the kind of economic dependency that Bellamy describes may be read
as fundamental to the narrator-protagonist's predicament. While middle-class
status is conferred on the narrator by virtue of her marriage, it is clear that her
husband, "a physician of high standing," is the breadwinner (10). His professional and economic status, in turn, gives him the authority to keep his wife
locked away for the summer and the arbitrary power to rebuff her when she
asks him to "take me away" (23). While the only way out for the narrator of the
story appears to be madness, Gilman, like Bellamy, purported to see "the way
up" for women—the title of a lecture she gave in the fall of 1891. That "way"
was "pecuniary freedom" ("Way" 12), and between 1890 and 1894 she saw the
possibility of its realization through the Nationalist movement.

Also like Bellamy, Gilman saw economic oppression as permeating society.
Economic subjugation like that faced by the narrator in "The Yellow Wall-
Paper" is portrayed as a widespread and longstanding social condition in Gilman's very first public lecture, preceding the composition of the story by a few
weeks. In her lecture "On Human Nature," delivered to the Nationalist Club of
Pasadena in June 1890, Gilman observes, "[A] small portion of the world grow[s]
fat on the foolishness of the rest. The same human power and human smartness,
the same beastlike weakness and folly, that [allow] one man to send a hundred
thousand to fight and die for they know not what, [enable] one man to count his
gold by carloads while a hundred thousand live and die in hopeless want" (23).
But Gilman's account reveals not only a widely distributed problem but also a
comprehensive solution, a solution grounded in the malleability and the con-
structedness of human society. "Here we all are today," cajoles Gilman, "suffering from this and suffering from that and suffering from the other, and calling it
'the common lot of humanity'! Lot indeed!" But human beings, Gilman asserts
through her metaphor, are not "trees" or "houses"; they are gardeners, who can
"dig and ditch and plow and plant until that lot is a garden of Eden," who can
"so alter that lot that the former owners would not recognize it" (25).

One problem with this early formulation of the people's power to remake
their "lot" is that it lacks a suitable political instrument permitting the masses

to work in concert with one another; the Nationalists, after all, were mostly middle-class intelligentsia rather than labor or political activists. But after the 1892 Nationalist convention voted to support People's Party candidates (Painter 98), Gilman's work for Nationalism led to advocacy of Populism, and Populism—however unwieldly its assemblage of southern and western agrarian groups, labor unions, and smaller reform parties (Goodwyn xviii-xix; Painter 61, 69)—did have potential as a mass political organization. In her speech "What the People's Party Means" delivered on 9 June 1893, Gilman counters the argument of more radical socialists that cross-class coalitions are impossible by defining "socially productive work" far more broadly than does classical Marxism. While Marxists see the industrial occupations of proletarians as singularly real labor, Gilman maintains that both the working and middle classes are socially productive, leaving as their common adversary only a "handful" of rich who are "helpless nonproducers" (22). From this ground, Gilman can further contend with more militant socialists who "talk of necessary bloodshed." As she explains, "The people, the poor people and the middling people, are so large a majority that they have only to decide on their course and take it" (23).

In her ready embrace of Nationalism and Populism, Gilman may seem vulnerable to the criticism of Thomas Peyser that she, like "many members of the middle class," sought "therapeutic diversion" in radical politics ("Reproducing" 1). Indeed, here the debate over Gilman's radicalism intersects with a central issue in recent interpretations of both "The Yellow Wall-Paper" and *Herland*: Gilman's attitudes about class and race. By now it has been acknowledged that Gilman had problems with both. Mary A. Hill observes that Gilman, however "theoretically [. . .] egalitarian," was "sometimes a racist and a snob" (*Making* 172). Susan S. Lanser similarly argues that "The Yellow Wall-Paper" reveals the classism and enthnocentrism of a white professional woman, a sense of "white Protestant supremacy" that belies Gilman's supposed "socialist values" (429). Like Peyser, both critics suggest that Gilman was middle class, and hence her attitudes about race and class are anchored in a presumption of racial and class difference. Hill remarks pointedly, "Though Charlotte had seen hard times, she was not working class" (172).

But page through Denise D. Knight's edition of Gilman's *Diaries*—ask your students to read through portions written between 1890 and 1900—and consider just how secure Gilman's hold on middle-class status was. To be sure, the *Diaries*' detailed record of expenditures certainly reveals a middle-class lifestyle: $10.50 for two dresses (2: 462), 50 cents for having her silver cleaned (465), $5 for new shoes (475, 516, 524), $6 to visit the dentist (477), even $2 to hire a gardener (529), and an unspecified amount for a "Chinaman" who "comes to clean" (546). And yet, between 1890 and 1895, when she was trying to maintain a household, the *Diaries* make clear that Gilman lived mostly on credit and gifts from friends and relations, not on her earnings from either speaking or writing. During a good month, January 1893, Gilman reports having completed "fifteen pieces of salable work" for which she had earned $40

(2: 515). Yet by the evidence of a speech written little more than a year earlier, at $40 a month Gilman was making no more than "the common laborer, the hod carrier, the digger and lifter and breaker of stones" ("Our Domestic Duties" 17). Under these circumstances, Gilman could hardly be above accepting charity from others; she was usually delighted when help came, as in an 1892 entry reporting that "Mr. Andrews, Socialist, calls, as a committee. He had heard that I was 'destitute,' and was sent to offer assistance[.] Good for my people!" (*Diaries* 2: 506).

In class, students can be asked to report on the evidence they find in the *Diaries* about Gilman's finances and lifestyle, particularly in the years between 1889 and 1894 when she was attempting to support herself, her daughter, and (for much of the time) her mother. When they discover how hard-pressed Gilman often was for money and how frequently she spent that money on what must have been borderline luxuries, they can be asked what this economic pattern suggests about Gilman's perception and experience of class, a question that likely will, and should, draw on students' own various experiences as money earners, consumers, and economic dependents. There are, of course, scholarly resources that can be introduced by the instructor into this discussion. Gilman's social and economic status during these years represents a conundrum of class definition aptly described by Raymond Williams, in which subjects perceive their social status as middle class while at the same time experiencing an economic situation no more elevated than that of unskilled, manual laborers (65–66). Moreover, research into racial and ethnic conflict suggests that overt prejudice such as Gilman exhibits is less commonly a marker of middle-class elitism than of competition between rival work-class groups (see Asher and Stephenson). Students should not—and probably will not—see Gilman's precarious class position as excusing the racist and ethnocentric statements that recur in her work. But they are also likely to understand Gilman's aspiration to achieve middle-class status and the insecurity—sometimes directed outward as hostility—that arises from lacking the present means actually to earn that status. The issue of Gilman's socioeconomic identity raises a further question of particular importance because of her involvement in socialist politics: to what extent does she speak on behalf of either working-class or middle-class people? Students will likely have a variety of responses, some maintaining that she speaks for neither group, some asserting that she speaks for both. The best compromise in this discussion is probably that Gilman did have opportunities to act as a mediator between the two groups, though she was not always able to seize on them. At this point in the discussion, additional noncanonical texts from the 1890s can be brought into play.

In the weekly newspaper the *Impress*, for instance, which Gilman edited and in large part wrote in late 1893 and early 1894, we can find Gilman playing precisely the role of social intermediary more than once. One editorial quotes and then responds to a *New York Tribune* article on female garment workers then on strike: having earned "from $3 to $5 a week, working from

7 in the morning until 6 in the evening," these workers "have been driven to lives of shame to keep from starving." I quote Gilman's scathing commentary in full:

> Whose is the shame? Does it not redden your cheeks, you women of respectability and refinement, who are always eager for bargains, and you men who buy "cheap" shirts, without a thought of the wages paid to the makers of them? And you merchants, who think you are doing a clever thing when you can increase your profits some five or ten percent, regardless if the increase is squeezed out of the life and soul of the sewing woman,—is not her blood on your hands? But who of us is not partaker in this guilt? Who of us can plead not guilty to the charge: "These are the images ye have made of me!" And what are you going to do about it? Read the line again—*have been driven to lives of shame to keep from starving.*   ("What We Are Doing" 1)

Gilman thus squarely faces the consequences of her middle-class audience's— and her own—consumer behavior. Confronting the disjunction between working-class and middle-class interests, she seizes on the need for middle-class citizens to take responsibility for reforming their behavior.

The Populist movement was meteoric, as political movements go; by 1896 the People's Party agenda had been largely coopted by the Democratic presidential candidate William Jennings Bryan. The Nationalist movement petered out around the same time, its Bellamy-edited organ the *New Nation* discontinuing publication in 1894. Neither development disillusioned Gilman in her socialist faith, however. In 1896 she attended the International Socialist and Labor Congress in London, where she formed almost immediate and strong ties with the English Fabians Beatrice Webb and Sidney Webb, socialists distinguished for their commitments to the democratic transformation of society and to women's rights (see Beilharz and Nyland, chs. 3 and 5). On her return to the United States, Gilman joined the staff of the *American Fabian*; she proved so committed to the journal that eighteen of the twenty-four poems and articles she published in 1897 appeared there (Scharnhorst, *Bibliography*). Significantly, this period of intense socialist activity was also the period when Gilman was drafting *Women and Economics*.

Hence it should come as no surprise that *Women and Economics*, Gilman's most famous work until the author's literary rediscovery in the 1970s, should be thoroughly informed by socialist analyses and argumentative strategies. Of particular relevance to teachers of Gilman, however, are two strands: the echoes in *Women and Economics* of Marx and Engels and the book's anticipation of *Herland*, especially in its analysis of the sexual-economic institution of marriage.

The two strands are, as it happens, often intertwined. For example, Gilman's consideration of the economic basis of social reality is centered not on the distribution of material goods but rather on the impact of modes of production on social being: it is not just the amount of a worker's wages that matters, but also the worker's autonomy in the productive process, the conditions of the workplace, and the ownership of the product of labor. Thus Gilman writes in the opening chapter of *Women and Economics*, "Under all the influence of his later and wider life, all the reactive effect of social institutions, the individual is still inexorably modified by his means of livelihood: 'the hand of the dyer is subdued to what he works in'" (3). So, too, the high quality of life in *Herland* is defined not just by material comfort but by the variety, quality, and level of satisfaction the Herlanders enjoy in their work. Labor among the Herlanders is decisively unalienated. A whole range of products—books, statues, houses, furniture, dishes—are signed by their individual creators, both gratifying their pride and permitting users "to know to whom to be grateful" (76). The point is perhaps clearest to students when considered in contrast to the decidedly consumerist utopia outlined by Bellamy in *Looking Backward*, a novel that works superbly preceding *Herland* on a course syllabus. Certainly, Gilman's definition of production is far more multifaceted and progressive than Peyser's identification of it with "nostalgia for the natural place of women as mothers, or rather for a society in which a woman's place as producer of children, instead of consumer of goods, will be judged natural" ("Reproducing" 14).

Women, Gilman's central line of reasoning goes, have been grotesquely stunted because their livelihood consists solely of offering sex in exchange for material support. The "virtuous" woman, especially, forbidden by moral edict to trade her sexual services on an open market, makes a bargain for life with one man and henceforth becomes utterly dependent on him and vulnerable to his later whims to renegotiate their contract. Gilman explains, "Although marriage is a means of livelihood, it is not [. . .] labor without shame, but a relation where the support is given outright, and enforced by law in return for the functional service of the woman, the 'duties of wife and mother'" (*Women* 89). Indeed, economically speaking, there is little to separate marriage from prostitution, as Gilman remarks with withering irony, "The transient trade we think evil. The bargain for life we think good" (64). The parallel to Marx and Engels could hardly be more exact. As they write in *The Communist Manifesto*, "The bourgeois sees in his wife a mere instrument of production," and consequently bourgeois gender relations amount to little more than "prostitution both public and private" (488).

The one point on which *Women and Economics* parts ways with classical Marxism is on proletarian as opposed to bourgeois gender relations. For Marx and Engels proletarian women are exploited when brought into the factories, but they experience something like a domestic idyll when their family's financial security allows them to engage in "free labour at home within moderate limits for the support of the family" (*Manifesto* 404). Gilman, with subsequent sociological research into gender relations across cultures and classes firmly on her side, argues that women regardless of class are, typically, both economically dependent on the men in their household and socially subordinate to them (*Women* 7). As for the bourgeois woman and her family, Gilman concurs with Marx and Engels that her emancipation is impossible under the sexual-economic institution of marriage. They all, indeed, agree that marriage as currently constituted impedes not just the free development of women but the collectivization of society as a whole. In Engels's late work *The Origin of the Family, Private Property, and the State* (based on notes Marx left at his death), we read that "[the] modern individual family is based on the open or disguised enslavement of woman; and modern society is a mass composed solely of individual families as its molecules" (744). Gilman is more expansive on the destructive linkage between the two, arguing that the socioeconomic unit of marriage

> has affected the economic relation of society by bringing into it a tendency to individualism with sex-advantage, best exhibited in the frequent practice of sacrificing public good to personal gain, that the individual may thereby "support his family." We are so used to considering it the first duty of a man to support his family that it takes a very glaring instance of bribery and corruption in their interests to shake our conviction; but, as a sociological law, every phase of the prostitution of public service to private gain, from the degradation of the artist to the exploitation of the helpless unskilled laborer, marks a diseased social action.
>
> (*Women* 106–07)

In championing the public good, in criticizing individualism, in looking past traditional families to broader and more inclusive social formations, Gilman's criticism forecasts the social vision of commonwealth in *Herland*. On the level of individual characters as well, Gilman's economic analysis explains much about what happens in *Herland*. The error of Van and his fellow sojourners in Herland in believing that women will naturally play the part of the coquette is based not simply on a difference of social and sexual conditioning but on a fundamental economic difference: women in Herland do not depend on men for their maintenance; with no economic reason to pursue a role submissive to men, they have no social or "natural" cause to either. Van presently recognizes that "those 'feminine charms' we are so fond of are not feminine at all, but mere reflected masculinity—developed to please us because they had to please us" (60). Ultimately, Terry attempts to rape his Herlander wife and is banished because he cannot see women other than in terms of sex-attraction (130–31). Accustomed to a world that makes sexual access of a husband to his wife a moral and legal right, he cannot adjust to a society that sees woman as man's equal rather than his property.

Whether Gilman's *Herland* is a "nowhere" land, a utopia in the root sense of the word, or a realizable vision, a "pragmatopia," is a central issue in criticism of the novel (Kessler, *Gilman* 4). In either case, the linkage of Gilman's work to socialism proves significant, both because it establishes important common ground for comparing *Herland* to a substantial tradition of socialist utopian literature, including Bellamy's *Looking Backward* and William Dean Howells's *Altrurian Romances*, and because it brings *Herland* in closer contact with long-standing socialist debates over utopianism (and its merits or demerits; see Kumar; Beilharz) As a part of these debates, students should be invited to discuss whether they find Gilman's social vision in the novel feasible—or, for that matter, desirable. Placing *Herland* in the context of Gilman's socialism as well as her feminism, particularly as they are combined in *Women and Economics*, may actually suggest that Gilman herself saw Herland as neither practicable nor ideal. *Women and Economics* ends with a clear hope, though a heavily conditioned one, that society might indeed provide the context for the free and equal development of all human beings: "Where our progress hitherto has been warped and hindered by the retarding influence of surviving rudimentary forces," Gilman writes, "it will flow on smoothly and rapidly when both men and women stand equal in economic relation" (340). But just what are the chances that men and women would stand in equal economic relation any time soon? Gilman cites as hopeful portents the current revolts of women and the "laboring classes"; these social movements, she asserts, "mean but one thing,—the increase of social consciousness" (138). Notably, although the focus of *Women and Economics* is on women's economic subordination, Gilman sees the labor movement as an equal partner with the women's movement; she speaks of them as "the twin struggle that convulses the world to-day" (138). In 1898, at any rate, Gilman continued to see the cause of the people as part and parcel with the cause of women and saw the militancy of these causes as evidence that society might be transformed.

After 1900 Gilman became less active as a socialist, stepping back from the newly formed Socialist Party of America under the impression that the party was too divisive, too ready to countenance violence. At the same time, her 1909 *Forerunner* article "Why We Honestly Fear Socialism" reaffirms her commitment to socialist principles. In 1915 *Herland* reasserts Gilman's support for socialism, but her choice of a remote and improbable setting may indicate her doubts about the commitment of the current socialist standard-bearer—and also of the current women's movement—to a radically egalitarian society. Insofar as the women of *Herland* have formed their ideal society exclusive of masculine input, it would seem that by the time Gilman wrote the novel she had judged the labor movement incapable of recognizing that its revolution must demand economic equality for women as well as for labor. It is also possible, however, that through Herland's isolation, stasis, and sheer implausibility—parthenogenesis having replaced sexual reproduction—Gilman is critiquing the women's movement for failing to see the kinship of their interests with those of others, including male proletarians. While it is important to develop in our students sympathy for Gilman's social critique and social vision, students who are dubious about the practicality or appeal of Herland may be responding to Gilman's own historically specific discontent over the lack of feminist thinking in American socialism and the lack of socialist thinking in American feminism.

Placing Gilman in a Context of Intellectual Debate

Michael J. Kiskis

I have introduced Charlotte Perkins Gilman to students frequently in recent years in survey discussions of post–Civil War American literature or with more intense focus in a course devoted to American women writers. My decision to include *Herland* in the reading list for the course The Female Voice in American Fiction placed Gilman in good company, and an examination of the tradition of women's writing in America's eighteenth, nineteenth, and twentieth centuries invited Gilman's clear voice. Not surprisingly, the students in that class were all women, many of whom were reluctant to consider their beliefs in equal rights for women as feminist. While often critical of Gilman's leanings toward polemic and explicit and (they thought) heavy-handed social criticism, my students were generally willing to suspend their disbelief as well as their expectation of complex plot and character design to entertain Gilman's utopian (or, as I argue, dystopian) vision. Their reaction to Gilman overall was positive. Because *Herland* drew students into that discussion so effectively, I decided to include the novel again when I was asked to teach in Elmira College's Core Program—all third- and fourth-year students are required to take COR 3000, which carries the title Evolution of Modern Times.

Four major movements shape the reading list—liberalism, Marxism, Darwinism, and globalism-imperialism. All faculty members include Marx and Darwin, though the selections vary (especially for Darwin). My reading list included (in alphabetical order) Chinua Achebe's *Things Fall Apart*, Matthew Arnold's *Culture and Anarchy*, Joseph Conrad's *The Heart of Darkness*, Charles Darwin's *The Voyage of the Beagle*, Margaret Fuller's *Woman in the Nineteenth Century*, Charlotte Perkins Gilman's *Herland*, Aldous Huxley's *Brave New World*, Karl Marx and Frederick Engels's *The Communist Manifesto*, John Stuart Mill's *On Liberty* and *The Subjection of Women*, Henry David Thoreau's "Resistance to Civil Government," and Mark Twain's *Pudd'nhead Wilson*. I asked students to read the complete texts of all these works. I started students with the heaviest reading, assigning Mill, Fuller, Thoreau, and Arnold back-to-back in the opening weeks. Gilman's tale came along in the last third of the course, after discussion of Darwin, Twain, and Huxley and within a (more or less) chronologically linked section that featured Marx, Gilman, Conrad, and Achebe.

During our discussion of *Herland*, it became increasingly important for me to become proficient at an academic version of "the electric slide" so that students were consistently reminded of material already covered or yet to be read. Sliding around our reading list was even more necessary in this class because of the variety of academic backgrounds represented: students came from a cross-section of disciplines and majors, including biology, art, English (only three of twenty-one students), nursing, psychology, environmental studies, elementary education, and management. Even given the junior-senior level of the course, I had to acknowledge that a good number of my students were not versed in methodologies of literary or historical or cultural analysis. Students were likely to become either passive or ambivalent (there is a difference) if confronted with a conventional, formalist literary pedagogy based on a Socratic method prone to a simple call and response. Unlike the earlier course dedicated to women writers, this class was composed of male and female students (eight were men), and I anticipated a different classroom dynamic. Most students who responded and took the lead in discussion, however, were women, several of whom were majoring in the sciences.

Teaching *Herland* has both physical and intellectual sides. As we consider the complications within Gilman's novel—complications most clearly demonstrated in the conversations that take place among Terry, Jeff, and Vandyck and their "teachers" Moadine, Zava, and Somel and "mates" Alima, Celis, and Ellador—it is worthwhile to note the symbiosis that exists between conversation and the setting in which it takes place. In the novel, Gilman is careful to reinforce the criticism of Van's "Ourland" (which is very much *our* land) through conversation descriptions of, and comments on, a variety of ergonomic innovations. From the functional dress of the Herlanders to the basic design of living space to the cultivated and abundant gardens, Gilman stresses how a community's use of physical space is influenced by, and dependent on, its intellectual traditions. The Herlanders' theology of a maternal pervading power affects the design of schoolrooms as well as whole communities.

It is possible to demonstrate this link between philosophy and physical setting by considering our classrooms as extensions of the intellectual tradition that we aim to explore. We can highlight the philosophical and theoretical discussion by the way we set up, live in, and use classroom space. For example, I introduce students to the rules of conversation, as well as the impact of the physical and intellectual space of the classroom itself on that conversation, by using John Stuart Mill's statement of belief in the primacy of debate:

> But the peculiar evil of silencing the expression of an opinion is, that it is robbing the human race; posterity as well as the existing generation; those who dissent from the opinion, still more than those who hold it. If the opinion is right, they are deprived of the opportunity of exchanging error for truth; if wrong, they lose, what is almost as great a benefit, the clearer perception and livelier impression of truth, produced by its collision with error. (*On Liberty* 20)

Against Mill's notion of complete openness, I ask students to think about Matthew Arnold's opposition of anarchy to culture (order) as another way to juxtapose liberty against social stability. Arnold writes:

[W]ithout order a revolution cannot accomplish itself by due course of law. So whatever brings risk of tumult and disorder [. . .] our best self, or right reason, plainly enjoins us to set our faces against. It enjoins us to encourage and uphold the occupants of the executive power, whoever they may be, in firmly prohibiting them. But it does this clearly and resolutely, and is thus a real principle of authority, because it does it with a free conscience.   (65–66)

Arnold's interest in order hints at a conservatism (social and political) that both Mill and Gilman reject. Spotlighting Mill presents challenges for the physical space of the class meetings as well as the specific discussion of Gilman's work. In essence, we cannot focus on the power of dissent and the value of challenging dominant beliefs, which is what Mill certainly offers and what Gilman so clearly practices (and why both run afoul of Arnold), and then run our classrooms as physical or intellectual boxes. Students pushed into ordered rows all facing an instructor who appears a strangely morphed entity (part human, part lectern) understand the kind of authority that is prized: we cannot insist on our intellectual authority by restricting the use of physical space. Our students will deconstruct that kind of hypocrisy either through open resistance or, more likely, through silent revolt. They will tell us what they know we want to hear and then laugh behind out self-assured backs. We should let students sit wherever they want as long as they face the center of the conversational space. Whether they are in desks, in chairs, on the floor, on pillows, on bean bags or thick pads borrowed from the theater department, what matters is that they see one another and have their gaze directed to the reading and at whomever happens to be speaking—student or teacher or author. With freedom of movement and possibility of comfort come the possibility of looking at ideas and matching an out-of-the-box physical arrangement with out-of-the-box thinking. I am reminded of bell hooks's comment on the value of engaged pedagogy: "Our solidarity must be affirmed by shared beliefs in a spirit of intellectual openness that celebrates diversity, welcomes dissent, and rejoices in collective dedication to truth" (*Teaching* 33). An open setting will enhance honest thinking and communicating.

One necessity of hooks's "collective dedication to truth" is that we work to relate the reading to the world outside the story. This task is especially important when we approach Gilman. We must be clear that not all of Gilman's ideas are attractive. As with many ideas that are bound by their times and contexts, as well as the writer's personal agenda, some of Gilman's do not translate well. Her emphasis on the Aryan characteristics of Herland's citizens is troublesome: Van tells us early in his visit, "[T]here is no doubt in my mind that these people were of Aryan stock, and were once in contact with the best civilizations of the old world. They were 'white,' but somewhat darker than our northern races because of their constant exposure to sun and air" (55). Another oversimplification is Gilman's too facile separation of male characters into types: the rake

(Terry, equated at the opening of the tale with the devil himself: "we used to call him the Old Nick, with good reason" [3]); the poet (Jeff); and the sociologist (Van). Each carries in him the seeds of his and Herland's destruction. Gilman's sharp criticism of a patriarchal system dominated by inconsistencies between philosophy and practice resonates well in our own times.

Herland is, in fact, more accessible and attractive to students once they place it in relation to other works. Debate is the primary tool of culture building. In the prologue to *The American Adam*, R. W. B. Lewis offers a definition of culture that is germane:

> Every culture seems, as it advances toward maturity, to produce its own determining debate over the ideas that preoccupy it: salvation, the order of nature, money, power, sex, the machine, and the like. The debate, indeed, may be said to be the culture, at least at its loftiest levels; for a culture achieves identity not so much through the ascendancy of one particular set of convictions as through the emergence of its peculiar and distinctive dialogue. (2)

Gilman's contributions to feminist ideology and definitions of social justice become clearer when students read *Herland* critically and within an intellectual context. Once Gilman is introduced, it is necessary to look back and ahead to demonstrate both her debt to those who come before and her connection to those who come along after. Unless we proactively locate Gilman within the broad conversation of nineteenth-century intellectual inquiry, her work will be seen by students in atomized form—*Herland* will be a single work hanging outside history.

This approach works particularly well if we juxtapose Gilman with Margaret Fuller on the one hand and with Darwin, Marx, Conrad, and Achebe on the other. Let me be more explicit. Gilman's concern with women's issues and the possible evolution of a specifically female perspective on the world is underscored when students are asked to recall the ideas of Margaret Fuller, whose foundational work in *Woman in the Nineteenth Century* sets a direction for Herlandian society. Fuller's philosophical and moral conviction that "the gain of creation consists always in the growth of individual minds" (12) is essential to our understanding of Gilman's perfect society. Fuller's warning, "Accursed be he who sins in ignorance, if that ignorance be caused by sloth" (13), seems to guarantee the Herlanders' patience with the male invaders. Terry's exile is foretold in these few words. His entire demeanor toward Herland is an echo of Fuller's indictment, "there exists in the minds of men a tone of feeling toward women as toward slaves" (17). Terry thinks of home as a place designed for male comfort. Home for Fuller and for Gilman is a place to nurture the individual self. "A house is no home," Fuller writes, "unless it contain food and fire for the mind as well as for the body" (19). Her tale of Miranda, a young woman brought up in an environment that kindled that fire, is instructive (21–22).

Miranda could be a child of a Herland home, a child who "[f]rom the first memory [. . .] knew Peace, Beauty, Order, Safety, Love, Wisdom, Justice, Patience, and Plenty" (Herland 101). Or so Fuller wanted. She also wanted men simply to stop holding women back and for women to gain a stronger sense of their souls. In *Herland*, Gilman gets men out of the way by an act of God. Even her essential ambivalence at the end of the novel marked by the dawn of "The New Motherhood" (137)—which is ironically the restoration of fatherhood—can be tied to Fuller's earlier worry:

> I have urged on woman independence of man, not that I do not think the sexes mutually needed by one another, but because in woman this fact has led to an excessive devotion, which has cooled love, degraded marriage, and prevented either sex from being what it should be to itself or the other.
>
> I wish woman to live, *first* for God's sake. Then she will not make an imperfect man her god, and thus sink into idolatry. Then she will not take what is not fit for her from a sense of weakness and poverty. Then, if she finds what she needs in man embodied, she will know how to love, and be worthy of being loved. (117)

Fuller was not sure whether women would be able to create this kind of inviolate self. Though she very much hoped and argued and prayed for this outcome, she understood the challenge: "The lot of woman is sad. She is constituted to expect and need a happiness that cannot exist on earth. She must stifle such aspirations within her secret heart, and fit herself, as well as she can, for a life of resignations and consolations" (105). Years later, Mill would assert that "the inequality of rights between men and women has no other source than the law of the strongest" (*Subjection* 124). Men's physical and economic strength ensures their dominance. Gilman understood.

Seemingly optimistic about the integration of Jeff into Herland (he is the one male allowed to procreate; his partner, Celis, is the one female) and the emotional and psychological connection between Van and Ellador, Gilman nonetheless remains concerned that the insertion of an alien element (men) will undo the balanced ecology of Herland. Gilman's concern about male power has at its heart an observation that Charles Darwin made in *Voyage of the Beagle*. Darwin noted a potential for mischief when new species are introduced into a territory; for example, of Rio de Janeiro, Darwin writes:

> We see here in two distinct countries a similar relation between plants and insects of the same families, though the species of both are different. When man is the agent in introducing into a country a new species, this relation is often broken: as one instance of this I may mention, that the leaves of the cabbages and lettuces, which in England afford food to such a multitude of slugs and caterpillars, in the gardens near Rio are untouched. (69)

The docility of a water hog at Malonado was another instance: "This tameness may probably be accounted for, by the Jaguar having been banished for some years, and by the Gaucho not thinking it worth his while to hunt them" (78).

Darwin thus notes the social changes that take place when the species introduced is man, and in so doing he offers a warning to the previously cloistered Herlanders. In a stinging passage Darwin describes the effect of General Rosas's presence in Bahia Blanca (situated north of Rio de Janeiro):

> I think there will not, in another half-century, be a wild Indian northward of the Rio Negro. The warfare is too bloody to last; the Christians killing every Indian, and the Indians doing the same by the Christians. [. . .] Not only have whole tribes been wholly exterminated, but the remaining Indians have become more barbarous; instead of living in large villages, and being employed in the arts of fishing, as well as of the chase, they now wander about the open plains, without home or fixed occupation.   (113)

Darwin's comments reveal his ability to translate his wonder at how new species corrupt ecological systems to European incursions into South American social, ethnic, and racial systems. Gilman evinces concern over man's corruption in Herland, but elsewhere she also prejudicially reverses Darwin's trajectory of racial incursion.

The analogous character of biological and social and economic systems tied Darwin to Marx, with a line of relation running directly to Gilman. Marx considered economic brutality and exploitation exports of the European bourgeoisie. He saw the modern state as inherently dangerous: "It has resolved personal worth into exchange value, and in place of the numberless indefeasible chartered freedoms, has set up that single, unconscionable freedom—Free Trade. In one word, for exploitation, veiled by religious and political illusions, it has substituted naked, shameless, direct, and brutal exploitation" (Marx and Engels, *Manifesto* 57–58). Marx believed that those in power worked most energetically to create the world in their own image: "The ruling ideas of each age have been the ideas of its ruling class"; and "Political power, properly so called, is merely the organized power of one class for oppressing another" (73, 75). Mill extends these beliefs to gender relations: "But was there ever any domination which did not appear natural to those who possessed it?" (*Subjection* 129). Gilman agreed and emphasized such class hegemony in Terry's last words to the Herlander tribunal that will exile him: "The first thing I'll do is to get an expedition fixed up to force an entrance into Ma-land" (143). These are the words of a quintessential imperialist.

With imperialism in focus, I want, finally and briefly, to suggest comparisons among characters in *Herland* to those in *The Heart of Darkness, Things Fall Apart,* and *Brave New World.* Gilman's recognition of class and gender hierarchies and of the battle for dominance (imperialism on both a personal and global scale) links her at once to the predecessor Conrad and the successors

Achebe and Huxley. To understand the pulse of intellectual life, it is helpful to consider characters who act as observers of their own and other cultures. That role as participant-observer links Gilman's Van and Conrad's Marlow and suggests the deeply rooted ambivalence each feels for the actions of his home society. Van is often embarrassed at the excesses of his modern world and, in fact, colludes with Jeff and Terry to withhold information about their home:

> [W]e three, in our constant talks and lectures about the rest of the world, had naturally avoided the seamy side; not so much from a desire to deceive, but from wishing to put the best foot foremost for our civilization, in the face of the beauty and comfort of theirs. Also, we really thought some things were right, or at least unavoidable, which we could readily see would be repugnant to them, and therefore did not discuss.   (137)

Van sees value in the communal lives of Herland but will never appreciate the compassion that is at the heart of Herland society. He sees Herlanders as the other and will never reconcile himself to their ideals; even his relationship with Ellador is compromised. Like Conrad's Marlow, Van is a sensitive outsider who remains convinced that his worldview should prevail. The racism that is at the base of Marlow's inability to accept the trauma of the Congo (his lie, after all, leaves intact the missionary zeal that serves as cover for genocide) echoes in Van's willingness to exit Herland for the psychological safety of his world's social hierarchy. That he rationalizes Terry's attack of Alima and is clearly ready to leave underscores his allegiance to his home society.

On a more profoundly disturbing level, Gilman's Alima and Achebe's Okonokwo are clearly targets for exploitation. Okonokwo, the main character in Achebe's *Things Fall Apart*, commits suicide when faced with European domination. He is shamed by the West's increasingly virulent attack on his people's beliefs; he is driven to kill a representative of the colonial government out of frustration and humiliation; and he takes his own life in violation of ethical and religious beliefs of his own people. Alima, schooled in "Peace, Beauty, Order, Safety, Love, Wisdom, Justice, Patience, and Plenty" is so shaken by Terry's physical attack that, "in a cold fury" (131), she wants him killed! Both characters suffer as they face the power of an invading force, and both can deal with the onslaught only with violence, a violence that is antithetical to their and their people's interests. Darwin, it seems, was clearly on to something.

Perhaps most disturbing of these pairs, however, is Gilman's Ellador and Huxley's John Savage. Huxley's Savage is schooled by Shakespeare's tragic characters, such as Lear and Othello; once removed from the reservation, he is unable to reconcile his vision of honor and chivalry with the abandon and excess of the new world. During a charged conversation with The Controller late in the book, Savage goes so far as to say, "I am claiming the right to be unhappy" (246). He dies finally because his Shakespearean intensity cannot survive in a mechanized world of artificial emotion awash in sex. Gilman's

Ellador is also Shakespearean. She is positioned for tragedy. In a direct maternal line back to Margaret Fuller, Ellador is Miranda. Unlike Fuller's Miranda,
who managed to gain a sense of self and a reliance on her own soul, Ellador at
the end of *Herland* is more rightly the child of Prospero, whose magic in *The
Tempest*—the source of Huxley's title—has schooled her, protected her, and
finally found her a mate. Throughout *Herland* Ellador wants nothing more
than to travel with Van to the new world and to meet Van's mother. She is
entranced and naive. As she alights in Van's new world, we might imagine her
quoting Shakespeare's Miranda: "O, wonder! / How many goodly creatures are
there here! / How beauteous mankind is! O brave new world / that has such
people in't!" (5.1.211–14). Like Prospero, we might look solemnly at her and
respond, "'Tis new to thee" (5.1.215). In *With Her in Ourland* Gilman shows
us Ellador's experience in the new world. It is not the wonder that she deeply
desires.

Linking Gilman with so varied a collection of writers and works challenges
student assumptions about nineteenth- and twentieth-century thought and
introduces them to the complex cultural conversation about civil and human
rights and obligations that continue to shade and shape our contemporary
intellectual scene. In a twist that takes us back to Mill's ideal of intellectual
freedom, Robert Scholes states that we need "a reorientation of courses
around the work of students. [. . .] It is not what is covered that counts but what
is learned. It is not what students have been told that matters but what they
remember and what they can do" (113). This sentiment is echoed by hooks:
"maybe the material I most want them to know on a given day is not necessarily what learning is about" (*Teaching* 156). Given the chance, our students are
capable of driving this process of discovery: ask students to share excerpts from
the assigned works they find compelling (or strange or upsetting or beautiful)
and they more often than not will identify pivotal and poignant passages. Tying
Herland to a broad selection of radical (both liberal and conservative)
approaches to social relations offers students an opportunity to place Gilman
within a debate that echoes into the twenty-first century. Students will more
easily understand Gilman not as a lone singer in the wilderness but as an
activist whose voice gives resonance to the conversation that is our culture.

Teaching Gilman in the Context of Her Short Fiction, Poetry, and Nonfiction

Michelle N. McEvoy

Charlotte Perkins Gilman never apologized for the didactic nature of her writing, in whatever genre. "I have never made any pretense of being literary," she declares in an oft-quoted passage of her autobiography. "As far as I had any method in mind it was to express the idea with clearness and vivacity so that it might be apprehended with ease and pleasure" (*Living* 284-85). For Gilman, "the idea" was usually related to her vision for comprehensive social reform, which included the emancipation of women and men from stereotyped gender roles, radical changes in child care and education, and the restructuring of society along communitarian lines. Although we most often teach her as a feminist writer—an angle well suited to both "The Yellow Wall-Paper" and *Herland*—Gilman's conception of her ideas and advocacy was significantly broader. By bringing her other writing into the classroom, we can make more of that ideological scope available to our students in Gilman's own words, while enlarging their understanding of the strategies she employed as a didactic writer.

Gilman was prolific across the genres, publishing in her lifetime hundreds of poems, short stories, and essays in addition to numerous short reviews and commentaries, several dramatic dialogues, eight novels, seven book-length works of sociological nonfiction, and her autobiography. These texts take a multitude of forms, ranging from creepy Gothic stories (a common form in her early short fiction) to articulations of complex social theory. They embrace a wide array of topics as well, including the roles of women in society and their underappreciated intelligence and abilities, the importance of good sanitation and health education, the desirability of professionalizing housework and child care, the need for full, forthright sex education for both girls and boys, and every person's need and right to grow personally and contribute socially. Most of her writing reiterates, from a variety of angles, the basic tenets of Gilman's feminist reform Darwinism, aiming to demonstrate how people might improve the world by adopting new modes of thought and action.

Conscious of her adopted role as a public educator, Gilman often uses stories and poems to illustrate principles for which she argues carefully and thoroughly in her nonfiction. These shorter writings can introduce students to important concepts in Gilman's reform program while also inviting discussion about the methods she adopts "to express the idea." As Catherine J. Golden has pointed out, both Gilman's early volume of poetry, *In This Our World* (1893), and her most influential nonfiction book, *Women and Economics*, address the "sexuo-economic relation" that, according to Gilman, prevents women from leading satisfying, productive lives and thereby impedes the progress of the human race ("Recalling" 246). However, where the reform treatise may be long-winded and repetitive, the poetry presenting the same ideas is brisk, pointed, and often witty.

Students can appreciate the mocking irony of a poem like "The Holy Stove," in which Gilman attacks the glorification of the stove as "The Altar of the Home" (line 10) and wryly concludes, "The Holy Stove is the altar fine— / The wife the priestess at the shrine— / Now who can be the god?" (lines 38–40). This poem debunks the cult of domesticity more succinctly than her polemic nonfiction does. It also provides students with a cultural framework in which to consider the implicit critique of women's restricted roles in marriage that lurks, like the woman behind the pattern, in "The Yellow Wall-Paper," as well as the more overt polemic in *Herland*. Moreover, the humor of the poem, like that of Gilman's first major success, "Similar Cases," raises the issue of Gilman's strategies for disarming resistance to her message. Humor is one of her most effective tools, and the Gothic qualities of stories like "The Yellow Wall-Paper" and "The Giant Wistaria" may also be seen as literary cloaks wrapped around Gilman's serious ideas.

The poem "Similar Cases" also introduces students to Gilman's reform Darwinism through its narrative of intentional evolutionary progress despite the mocking objection *"You would have to change your nature!"* (line 75). In the same way, "To Man" describes the shift from prehistoric equality between the sexes to gendered patriarchal society—an idea Gilman derived from contemporary theories about prehistoric humanity. This kind of long-term, evolutionary thought clearly structures how Gilman imagines Herland; reading such poems encourages students to think of the utopia as an alternative history. Other poems in the collection encourage mothers to care for the whole world for the sake of children ("Mother to Child"), women to contribute to society not simply as mothers and wives but as "Human Being[s]" ("We, as Women," line 19), and girls to develop themselves as exemplars of the "strong and free" ("Girls of To-Day," line 23) people men ought also to become, because, as Gilman argues in *Women and Economics*, stunted mothers cannot raise powerful sons. "Females" reiterates the idea that women, like men, are first and foremost human beings, using the same examples from the animal kingdom that Gilman offers in *Women and Economics* to demonstrate that most females mate and bear young without becoming dependent on males—a tactic that reflects both her humor and her evolutionary thinking.

For classes reading "The Yellow Wall-Paper," the poem "She Walketh Veiled and Sleeping" may prove especially conducive to discussion because of its use of the word "creeping." The poem posits that "the Woman" comes to the present hour "Slow advancing, halting, creeping [. . .] / For she knoweth not her power" (lines 6–9). This context for the verb that dominates the conclusion of "The Yellow Wall-Paper" emphasizes Gilman's sense of the untapped capabilities of women—a subtext of the short story and a major theme in Gilman's work. All these ideas are essential to Gilman's social theories, and while they may be implied in "The Yellow Wall-Paper" and are explicitly addressed in *Herland*, the short poems offer a context to discuss the fictions and allow us to impress on our students that these were ideas Gilman pondered at length and theorized in detail.

Gilman's nonfiction is valuable for demonstrating her conviction that reform was actually achievable. Students familiar only with "The Yellow Wall-Paper" and *Herland* may reasonably conclude that Gilman wrote primarily fantastic fiction—tales that draw on the supernatural or speculative to offer social critiques but no manageable program for real-world reform. However, Gilman's idealism was closely tied to what she hoped for from her own society. Such essays as "Why Cooperative Housekeeping Fails," which addresses and dismisses the obstacles to Gilman's proposals for professionalizing domestic chores, or the New Year's piece "Reasonable Resolutions," which lists what Gilman hopes her readers will do "*now—this year,*" articulate her objectives in terms of actual and imminent change. A striking example of this ideology can be found in the essay "Feminism or Polygamy," which appeared in the October 1914 issue of the *Forerunner*, two months after World War I began and one month before Gilman announced her plan to publish *Herland* as the serialized novel for the 1915 *Forerunner*. "Feminism or Polygamy" predicts that many of Europe's women, left without hope of monogamous marriage after the slaughter of men in the war, will turn their energy to social work and service. From this assumption, Gilman goes on to present an agenda of social and political reforms these European women should undertake that is strikingly similar to the programs and methods employed by the fictional women of Herland. Regular readers of Gilman's magazine, coached by the earlier essay, would have read the serialized novel with the knowledge that Gilman hoped similar progress would be made in the actual world in the not-so-distant future. This kind of contextualization invites class discussion about Gilman's individual optimism as well as about wider cultural contexts, such as the nineteenth century's various reform movements and the nation's narratives of self-improvement at both the individual and the collective level.

Offering a selection of Gilman's short fiction is another way to help students better understand her preoccupations and patterns of thought and theory.[1] Among the stories that have been anthologized are several that can illuminate students' readings of *Herland* or "The Yellow Wall-Paper." "Dr. Claire's Place" (1915) provides an excellent counterpoint to "The Yellow Wall-Paper" in its description of a woman doctor's treatment of patients suffering nervous or psychological disorders. Dr. Clair's method encourages patients to develop interests and skills and become involved with other people as members of a community—a treatment that is diametrically opposed to the famous rest cure for hysterical women that Gilman critiques in "The Yellow Wall-Paper." Another story, "Through This" (1893), offers a day in the life of a young wife and mother as she labors through the domestic duties that leave her too tired and distracted to enjoy the beauty of the day or to act on her many interrupted dreams about contributing to the world outside her home. As Denise D. Knight has pointed out, this protagonist is an alter ego to the suffering mother in "The Yellow Wall-Paper," "a woman who can carry out the mission [she] intended but abandoned" (*Study* 43). Although the narrator retains her sanity, her exhaustion and frustration indict the same predetermined roles found in "The Yellow Wall-Paper." Teaching either or both of these stories as companions to "The Yellow Wall-Paper" invites discussion of the differences and relations between critique (the mainstay of the earlier stories) and proposals for reform (which dominate Gilman's later short fiction) as elements in didactic fiction. Students may be asked to assess the relative strengths and weaknesses of each approach and to contemplate why Gilman might have adopted each in different phases of her life and career.

In a class that has explored the autobiographical nature of "The Yellow Wall-Paper," these stories can also spark discussion of the ways in which Gilman extrapolated from her own experience and of the advantages and risks of that approach. Such a discussion also provides an opportunity to introduce some of the serious flaws in Gilman's thought, as it becomes evident that Gilman is addressing only the situation of white women in the upper and middle classes.

Other stories that may contribute to students' understanding of Gilman's preoccupations as a feminist and reformer include "Making a Change" (1911) and "Turned" (1911), in which women of varying situations form alliances in rejection of patriarchal expectations and abuses; "His Mother" (1914) and "The Unnatural Mother" (1916), in which Gilman challenges the prevailing idea that women should be devoted above all to their own children and suggests, instead, that caring for one's offspring should be understood in the context of one's duty to the larger society; and "Mrs. Beazley's Deeds" (1911) and "Mrs. Elder's Idea" (1912), in which women who have been oppressed by their husbands for years strike out on their own with enterprising plans to support themselves and their families. This last theme is common in Gilman's fiction; in many *Forerunner* stories (as well as the first *Forerunner* novel, *What Diantha Did* [1909–10]), Gilman devotes considerable narrative attention to women's calculations and plans for businesses that will support them while also contributing important services to the community. Comparing any of these stories with *Herland* may— as with reading it against *Forerunner* nonfiction—help students see how Gilman's utopian vision relates to her ideas about the real world.

"Mrs. Beazley's Deeds" is also a fine example of a narrative tactic Gilman frequently employed to emphasize the unrecognized capabilities of women. The story focuses on the wife of a surly man who has systematically sold the property she inherited from her father to finance ill-fated moneymaking schemes. She regains her independence with the help of a clever female attorney who shows her how to capitalize on the fact that he has deposited most of his assets in her name to protect himself from debt collectors. The end of the story finds him expelled from the family and shut out of their business. He is baffled and humiliated at being outsmarted by women. This particular type of surprise ending, in which women triumph over men who have underestimated them, appears even in some of Gilman's earliest short fiction. In "The Unexpected" (1890) a young husband is startled to discover that his new bride is the famous artist he has admired and imitated in his own career. These surprise endings set the stage for the pattern of disbelief and discovery that repeats throughout *Herland* and can provoke class discussion about the much debated conclusion of "The Yellow Wall-Paper" as well. Gilman could have written a less terrifying story with a positive surprise ending, such as the completion of a novel in the solitude of the nursery, but doing so would have yielded a far less compelling plot. Considering such a possibility can help students think about why "The Yellow Wall-Paper" works so well and what choices—or sacrifices—Gilman made in her fiction in the service of her didactic objectives.

Given the range of Gilman's writing, it can be interesting to combine a variety of forms in reading assignments, bringing together samples of her poetry, fiction, and nonfiction as Gilman herself did in the *Forerunner*. Students can thus gain an understanding of Gilman the reformer and educator (rather than simply the writer) as they explore her use of literary forms as weapons in her "armory" (Gilman, "Thoughts" 114). Just as we know that varied pedagogical strategies can engage a wider audience of students than one method alone can, Gilman undoubtedly recognized that varying the vehicles for her message would widen her reach. Teaching either "The Yellow Wall-Paper" or *Herland* within the context of Gilman's other writing allows us to re-create something of that method. It also allows us more effectively to teach Gilman as she perceived herself: a "Social Inventor" ("Summary" 287) using literature to educate and encourage others in building a better world.

NOTE

[1]The short stories mentioned in this essay are in Knight's Penguin edition of *Herland*.

Teaching "The Yellow Wall-Paper" through the Lens of Language

Catherine J. Golden

Gilman's landmark short story of a woman undergoing the "rest cure" for nervous depression invariably prompts spirited debate in the college classroom. The story reflects the sexual politics confronting American women in the late nineteenth century. The fate of the nameless narrator crawling in circles over her swooning husband defies one reductive explanation. In a historical overview of the story entitled "'Out at Last'? 'The Yellow Wallpaper' after Two Decades of Feminist Criticism," Elaine R. Hedges notes that critics have offered "a dazzling and significantly disparate array of interpretations" and endlessly debated the richly ambiguous ending (319–20). Echoing the more extreme voices of literary critics over the last several decades, my students' interpretations of the narrator's fate typically cluster at opposite ends of this spectrum: liberation versus entrapment, triumph versus defeat.

Usually over half of the class sees the narrator as destroyed at the end of the story. To these students, the narrator regresses to an infantile or animalistic state: she is groveling on the floor, ripping wallpaper from the walls, and creeping over her husband, who has fainted at the sight of her. About a fourth of the class argues just the opposite. The narrator emerges as a liberated figure, having torn down the restrictive bars of her Victorian world that are encoded in the wallpaper pattern. At least temporarily, she has outwitted her husband, John, the antagonist of the story. And in identifying with and freeing both the woman and that part of herself trapped by her patriarchal world, the narrator finds a measure of freedom. Only a few students see both sides of the argument; they conclude that the narrator has a dubious victory. Her freedom comes at the cost of madness.

The discussion becomes less lively when I ask students to support their reading of the narrator as a tragic versus an inspirational figure. Those students who argue for the narrator's victory seem to have more trouble supporting their views than those who claim her defeat. Students who see the narrator as destroyed, however, often experience difficulty understanding the opposite point of view. I regularly assign students to write a paper taking a position on the narrator's fate, using textual evidence for support. These papers, which serve as the basis for class discussion, offer students new ways to support their position and encourage them to consider alternative viewpoints (e.g., crawling as rebirth versus regression, madness as a higher form of sanity). Although students use criticism to advance their position, they must assert an argument and defend it with the text. While students always turn to theme, characterization, and plot to support their interpretation of literature, they rarely consider a prime source of evidence—language.

Students commonly think of style and grammar as a matter of correctness in writing. They may have some knowledge of basic grammar and syntax gleaned in introductory composition and foreign language courses. Yet they rarely recognize that style and grammar can be agents of meaning in a literary text. Before introducing this approach, however, I present short lessons on the grammatical and stylistic elements we examine in the story.

In approaching "The Yellow Wall-Paper" through the lens of language, students engage many of the seminal issues confronting the narrator—patriarchal repression, infantilization, escape, and madness. Language, or style, comprises elements such as passive versus active construction, pronoun usage, word choice, word placement, and syntax. Each time I reread and debate "The Yellow Wall-Paper" with colleagues and students, I am continually impressed by how the form and language of the story lead the reader into the complex psyche of the narrator. When I teach "The Yellow Wall-Paper" to first- and second-time readers (a few students have encountered it in high school), I want them to perceive how the writing of the story offers clues to support a diverse array of interpretations. In focusing on language, students often find evidence not only for their own ideas but also for alternative views they have previously not considered.

"The Yellow Wall-Paper" is artistically superior to Gilman's other, often hurriedly written, fiction. Critics have explored the diary format, word choice, and discourse of diagnosis as well as the ambiguous presentation of the main symbol of the story, the wallpaper. Given its first-person narration, diary format, style, and brevity, Gilman's story lends itself to linguistic analysis. For example, in "Escaping the Sentence: Diagnosis and Discourse in 'The Yellow Wallpaper,'" Paula Treichler argues that the narrator increasingly writes her sentences with a defiant language to escape the medical sentence of patriarchy. By looking at features of the narrator's language that change as the story progresses, students can support an interpretation not only of defiance for the narrator, as Treichler argues, but also of madness or a dubious victory. In turn, analyzing the linguistic features of "The Yellow Wall-Paper" allows students to uncover the ambiguities of Gilman's text.

The narrator chronicles her stay at a secluded ancestral hall through twelve undated diary-like entries, each separated in the revised 1996 Feminist Press edition by a row of asterisks. The short, blunt sentences and one- and two-sentence paragraphs reveal the narrator's agitated mental state. The namelessness of the narrator further contributes to our sense of her fragmentation. The format of the story, written in the first person, also leads us to question whether the narrator is the protagonist of the tale or the author of her own story, a view that denies any disjunction between the narrator and narrated.

The narrator herself is an inventive language user. Many linguistic features invite exploration in the classroom. I direct my students to three specific areas: the narrator's heightened linguistic definition of the woman trapped behind the wallpaper; the narrator's increased use of nominative-case pronouns ("I"), replacing her initial reliance on "John"; and the narrator's placement of pronouns referring to herself and John within the boundaries of a sentence. While I have chosen these three elements for analysis, those who teach this work may select other linguistic features that, likewise, inform a reading of the sociocultural situation confronting women in the late nineteenth century.

Students arguing that the narrator succumbs to madness can trace how the muted figure of the woman trapped behind the bars of the wallpaper gains more definition for the narrator as the story progresses. The narrator's room— a former nursery with bars on the windows and a bed nailed to the floor—can be interpreted as a microcosm of the narrator's restrictive patriarchal world. Her doctor-husband John—who administers her rest cure and forbids her to write—infantilizes the narrator, calling her his "blessed little goose" (15) and addressing her as "little girl" (23). The narrator, who prefers a room that opens onto the piazza with roses over the window and chintz hangings, comments frankly, "I never saw a worse paper in my life" (13), when she first sees the room John chooses for her. She describes the pattern as "flamboyant" and notes its "repellant" color: "a smouldering unclean yellow" with "dull yet lurid orange in some places, a sickly sulphur tint in others" (13). But the narrator, who has "imaginative power" and a "habit of story-making," soon becomes fascinated by "that horrid paper" (15). Its dominant front pattern, in time, comes to signify the repression of women within her patriarchal world.

The changes in the wallpaper occur gradually, requiring students to read the text closely. As early as the second entry, the narrator personifies the wallpaper, noting, "This paper looks to me as if it *knew* what a vicious influence it had!" (16). In the eighth entry, the wallpaper gains odor, seeps around the house, and "gets into my hair" (29). In the final entry, when the narrator seems most delusional, she comments that the front pattern of the wallpaper laughs at her (33).

Although the narrator sees in the paper "two bulbous eyes" (16) and "a broken neck" (16) and describes the pattern as "a kind of 'debased Romanesque' with *delirium tremens*" (20), she admits, with ambivalence, in the third entry:

> I'm getting really fond of the room in spite of the wallpaper. Perhaps *because* of the wallpaper.
> It dwells in my mind so!   (19)

Just before she makes this confession, the narrator recognizes a subpattern in the wallpaper: "I can see a strange, provoking, formless sort of figure, that seems to skulk about behind that silly and conspicuous front design" (18). Those who argue that the narrator is destroyed at the end of the story can pin-point this moment as the beginning of her hallucinations, which eventually compromise her sanity.

As the story continues, the narrator notes that the figure or subpattern she sees, or imagines, is "like a woman stooping down and creeping about behind that pattern" (22) and that the "faint figure behind seemed to shake the pattern, just as if she wanted to get out" (23). Although the color of the paper remains "hideous" to the narrator and the pattern "torturing" (25), in the sixth entry the figure of the woman trapped behind the front pattern gains real definition for the narrator. Simile drops away from the narrator's language to reveal a certainty. She concludes, reflectively, "I didn't realize for a long time what the thing was that showed behind, that dim sub-pattern, but now I am quite sure it is a woman" (26).

Those students who believe the narrator to be totally insane at the end of the story can trace the increasing clarity in the narrator's description of her hallucinations to argue their case. The narrator's delusions translate into actions of madness during the final four diary entries when she attempts to free the trapped woman seemingly born of her own hallucinations. The narrator observes that the woman gets out from behind the paper in the daytime to creep by daylight. She ponders, "If only that top pattern could be gotten off from the under one! I mean to try it, little by little" (31). At the opening of the final entry, the narrator, by moonlight, comes to the aid of the trapped woman to help her escape from the restrictive top pattern: "I pulled and she shook, I shook and she pulled, and before morning we had pulled off yards of that paper" (32). I always point out the linguistic identification between the narrator and the trapped woman that occurs in this sentence. The narrator, "I," and the woman behind the paper, "she," join together as "we." The narrator comes to see and identify with this woman and the figures of many women creeping within the ancestral hall: "I wonder if they all come out of that wall-paper as I did?" (35). Refusing to be "put [. . .] back" (36), the narrator declares, "I've pulled off most of the paper, so you can't put me back!" (36). The lens of language enables students to conclude that, in obsessively reading the pattern of the wallpaper that she vows to figure out, the narrator gives way to her active imagination and loses touch with her social reality.

In contrast, those arguing for the narrator's liberation or for a dubious victory can trace how her language gains strength and boldness precisely at the point when she dramatically creeps on the floor, tears the paper from the walls, and seemingly condemns herself to madness. By comparing the pronouns of self-definition that the narrator uses in the first and final entries, for instance, students can find ample evidence to support an argument that the narrator gains a forceful sense of self and defies the restrictions imposed on the role of a perfect, submissive Victorian wife and mother.

In the opening sentence of the story, the narrator writes, "It is very seldom that mere ordinary people like John and myself secure ancestral halls for the summer" (9). This is one of four references to John by name in the first paragraphs of the story alone. In contrast, the narrator remains nameless until the very end of the story, where she hints that her name may be Jane. This reference can signify the narrator's respectable "Jane" self, of which she is now seemingly free. She first refers to herself, however, as "myself." The reflexive-case pronoun "myself" reads more cumbersomely than the objective-case pronoun "me," which more typically follows a preposition. Reflexive pronouns may follow prepositions. Because they are heavier in English than in other languages (e.g., French and German), the tendency is to drop away the reflexive pronoun (used, for instance, when the subject and object of a sentence are identical) if no ambiguity exists. In presenting herself to the reader through a pronoun case noted by linguists for its cumbersomeness and expendability, the narrator indicates a poor self-perception of her place in society at large (Jespersen 11–12). Even if the narrator and John are "mere ordinary people," the narrator suggests that she is not on equal footing with John.

Equally disturbing in the opening entry is the helpless refrain—"what is one to do?" (10)—that the timid narrator utters following her frustration that John laughs at her, forbids her from writing, and does not even believe she is sick. The narrator refers to herself as "one," a pronoun the linguist Otto Jespersen calls "a kind of disguised *I*" (150). When the narrator refers to herself as "I," she frequently qualifies it with "perhaps" and "personally," stereotypical features of women's language. For example, in the opening entry, she uses "I" timidly when expressing her discontent with John: "John is a physician, and *perhaps*—(I would not say it to a living soul, of course, but this is dead paper and a great relief to my mind—) *perhaps* that is one reason I do not get well faster" (9–10). In this sentence, "I" appears once in parenthesis, diminishing its importance. Twice the narrator qualifies, and weakens, her assertion with "*perhaps*," emphasized through italics. The narrator also couches her own opinions: "Personally, I believe that congenial work, with excitement and change, would do me good" (10). The narrator's qualified statements reveal a hesitant and uncertain voice, shy of the definitiveness of traditionally masculine judgment.

In contrast, in the final entry, at the point where the narrator's actions seemingly condemn her to madness, she speaks in a forceful, at times impertinent, voice. Gone is her deference, qualification, and hesitation. She openly defies John. The threefold use of "I" in the following two paragraphs conveys boldness:

> I don't want to go out, and I don't want to have anybody come in, till John comes.
> I want to astonish him.   (34)

In fact, the narrator does astonish John, who faints straightaway—a point that leads some students to argue for the narrator's temporary victory, at least until John regains consciousness.

In the final entry, the narrator's use of pronouns in the nominative, objective, and demonstrative cases to refer to her doctor-husband weakens his position further. The narrator, who refers and defers to "John" four times in the opening paragraphs of the story, uses his name only once in the closing paragraphs. She calls John "he," "him," and "that man" in the final paragraph, where her own linguistic power grows most forceful. The narrator declares of her husband, "Now why should that man have fainted? But he did" (36). Unlike "this," the demonstrative pronoun "that" lends a sense of detachment. "That man" makes her husband unfamiliar, distances the narrator and the reader from John, and diminishes an authority to which the narrator herself initially submitted.

Placement of pronouns, the third linguistic feature I analyze with my students, even more forcefully conveys the narrator's rejection of her former submissive state and a reversal of power in gender dynamics. As the story progresses, the narrator not only increasingly uses but also prominently places the nominative-case pronoun in the defiant sentences she writes. The first and last words of a sentence typically receive most emphasis. In the opening entry, "John" appears as the first word, introducing three successive short paragraphs that assert John's views or facts about him:

> John laughs at me, of course, but one expects that in marriage.
> John is practical in the extreme. He has no patience with faith, an intense horror of superstition, and he scoffs openly at any talk of things not to be felt and seen and put down in figures.
> John is a physician, and *perhaps*—(I would not say it to a living soul, of course, but this is dead paper and a great relief to my mind—) *perhaps* that is one reason I do not get well faster.   (9–10)

The word "John" usurps power through syntactic placement and repetition. But the narrator rejects this pattern of deference in the fourth entry and syntactically inverts the dynamics of gender. She begins three one-sentence paragraphs with "I" and a fourth with "And I":

> I don't know why I should write this.

> I don't want to.
> I don't feel able.
> And I know John would think it absurd. But I *must* say what I feel and think in some way—it is such a relief!   (21)

No longer writing under the disguise of "one," the narrator conveys a forceful fictionalized self through pronoun choice and placement. "I" appears seven times in these sentences along with an emphatic italicized *"must"* and an exclamation point. Those who argue for the narrator's liberation can pinpoint this sequence as the beginning of her rebellion against John's prescription for sanity and the oppressive authority John represents. Those who advance the narrator's debatable victory can argue that her sense of self emerges just at the point where she begins to have delusions that eventually lead her to tear the wallpaper from the wall to free both the woman and her own repressed self.

Pronoun position is also crucial to interpreting the often-quoted final paragraphs of "The Yellow Wall-Paper":

> "I've got out at last," said I, "in spite of you and Jane! And I've pulled off most of the paper, so you can't put me back!"
> Now why should that man have fainted? But he did, and right across my path by the wall, so that I had to creep over him every time!   (36)

The narrator here, and elsewhere, repeats "I" in close proximity. Just a few paragraphs earlier she notes, for instance, "'I can't,' said I" (36), where "I" occupies the two most forceful positions of a sentence. Beginning and ending sentences with "I," the narrator rebels against a patriarchy that has fragmented her identity. Whether "Jane" signifies the narrator's restrained self or her sister-in-law, Jennie (whom she describes as "a perfect and enthusiastic housekeeper" [17]), the narrator pairs "Jane" with "you" (her husband) and identifies the name as a repressive force. The narrator asserts the dominance of her new personality by grammatically surrounding "you" and "Jane" with "I."

In the final clause of the last compound sentence—"so that I had to creep over him every time!" (36)—the narrator moves into the subject place, which she initially reserved for John. No longer privileged, the now swooning John is reduced to an object of a preposition ("him"), a syntactical position that is both nonessential and powerless. Ruled only by the preposition "over," the objective-case reference to John could even be dropped from the final sentence to read, "I had to creep every time!" Even those who remain convinced that the narrator's actions reveal her madness at the close of the story cannot help appreciating the force and boldness that punctuate the writing in the final lines of the once timid narrator. Patriarchy may be skirted, and not destroyed, but the narrator has at least moved John to the periphery of her own sentence.

A linguistic approach to "The Yellow Wall-Paper" opens up multiple readings of a work that puzzles, intrigues, and captivates new and seasoned readers of Gilman. Exploring "The Yellow Wall-Paper" through the lens of language, students discover how to support various interpretations about the fate of the narrator, who is undeniably "out at last." Much like Gilman's determined narrator who vows to figure out the perplexing pattern of the wallpaper, students become better readers of Gilman's complex text as they examine its linguistic patterns and learn a valuable lesson in language as well.

Finding Patterns in the Text:
Close Reading "The Yellow Wall-Paper"

Michelle A. Massé

This essay is about how, through analysis of "The Yellow Wall-Paper," undergraduate students can learn to recognize literary evidence in a text, shape persuasive interpretations, and understand the interdependence of both. There are uncanny parallels between those tasks and mine here, which is to identify actual teaching activities, set forth a pedagogical rationale that will be convincing to other teachers, and articulate the interrelations of theory and praxis. Teachers and students also share a risk of parading generalizations that we want to believe are profundities or, conversely, presenting strings of citations that we think have explanatory force in and of themselves. Ideally, however, we develop ever-finer calibrations of analytic balance between cosmic musings and summary.

When I first assigned "The Yellow Wall-Paper," it was primarily because of its themes, its quasi-canonical status, and its providing historical coverage in courses such as Introduction to Fiction or Survey of Women and Literature. I have my own understanding of the story, which I have written about elsewhere, but I found that it "taught" beautifully because students quickly develop their own interpretations. The exact relations of students' responses to the specific language of this text or others often remained murky, however: both their writing and their discussion frequently showed confusion over what constitutes textual evidence and what it means to read a text.

In trying to address this quandary, I began to present "The Yellow Wall-Paper" as a chapbook for interpretation and to move its positioning in the semester. It is now the first text read in most of my undergraduate courses, because I have found that Gilman's compact and complex story can act as a prelude to almost any form of literary investigation. A series of intense close reading exercises serve as a review of or introduction to an understanding of form and technique as integral to interpretation and underscore the significance of textual evidence. Through dedicating a class or two at the beginning of the semester to "The Yellow Wall-Paper," I can establish general expectations for students' daily journal entries, class discussion, and the more extensive and formal acts of interpretation they will develop in their essays.

Most students respond intensely to "The Yellow Wall-Paper" and are often certain they know what it means. First-time readers usually decide that it is a ghost story or a tale about a crazy woman; readers already familiar with the text or particular methodologies will confidently proclaim that it is about postpartum depression, hysteria, or the oppression of women. When asked to explain their conclusions, students give responses ranging from de facto sureness ("Well, of course she's insane! What kind of person would see things in wallpaper?") through deductive generalizations ("All women used to be oppressed") to extraliterary considerations ("Gilman had to see a doctor, too") or imaginative exercises of the how-many-children-had-Lady-Macbeth ilk ("John was going to town a lot and probably having an affair").

Precisely because students engage so readily with "The Yellow Wall-Paper," it is an ideal text through which to discuss critical interpretation and methodology. The students' assignment for the first full day of classes is to read the story and to write the first of their daily journals. In some courses, such as Critical Strategies (an introduction to theory), I also have them read definitions of core terms such as *diction, imagery, narrator, point of view, setting, style,* and *tone.*

At the beginning of class, I talk briefly (no more than ten minutes) about evidence and interpretation in the literary text and about how both are necessary to experiment with ideas in daily journals as well as in discussion or essays. I explain that we are going to do a simple review exercise in three parts that will work for anything they read and tell them the rules of the game. In part 1, students in a circle take turns reading aloud a brief passage from "The Yellow Wall-Paper." The reader is the first commentator; others can add comments afterward. I ask questions, but I usually do not add to the commentary. The ground rules limit discussion to the language of the passage and whatever precedes it; students cannot refer to later material. I also emphasize that the first commentator is just getting things rolling (to lessen pressure and to ensure that students do not feel that general discussion only happens when someone doesn't get the "right" answer), urge students to chip in (in part so that others will do so in turn), warn them that our discussion will take far more time than they might expect (because in-depth analysis always does), and tell them that I am particularly interested in any form of repetition they can identify.

The beginning of the exercise is usually somewhat halting and calls for a few reminders about the protocol: it is not fair, for example, to say, "She uses 'haunted house' because she finds out that there's a ghost." It also takes a few turns before students realize that we really are going to talk about each word. And so, we move (or creep) through the beginning, phrase by phrase.

The first repetition noted is usually imagery: the cluster of "ancestral halls," "colonial mansion," "hereditary estate," and "haunted house" (9) is readily identified. Deliberating what country, period, or class these phrases might suggest (without using knowledge gleaned from external sources) is more difficult, as is speculating about the meaning of such a setting or the significance of a summer stay (the ultimate vacation? isolation?). Someone will almost inevitably comment on the stylistic repetition of the adjective-noun pairings, which lets me ask how "romantic felicity" (9) fits in as the last term of the second sentence. One student will postulate that the narrator is looking forward to a really happy and romantic summer; another will wonder whether "romantic" has a different meaning in this context (and if one doesn't, I will ask, "Has anyone read Romantic poetry yet?").

"Romantic felicity," conjoined with "mere ordinary people" and *"secure ancestral halls"* (emphasis added) lets me ask, "What about the narrator's lan-

guage? Would you tell us you had 'secured' an apartment for the semester?"
My question allows students to see that there is something strained about both
the speaker's diction and style. At that point, I will usually ask for a volunteer
to read the first five paragraphs aloud quickly and dramatically. Those with
good ears will comment on the exclamatory chirpiness and febrile intensity
(well, not perhaps in quite those terms) of voice and tone; others will note the
choppiness of the style and its paragraph breaks.

The inevitable comment "She's just weird!" leads to discussion of "Who is
'she'?" and an explication of how or why she is weird. I will probably be the one
to ask, "Who is the speaker, and to whom is she speaking?"; we will agree that
we know she is female and married but nothing more. She has no name, someone will point out, and we already know that there is a "John," though it clearly
isn't John to whom she is speaking. A practical soul will confess to calling her
"Sue" in that day's journal entry, which is the prompt to my asking why we are
so uncomfortable with her not having a name and flat-out stating that we
expect one in first-person intimacy with a confidante.

Although it might seem that the weirdness issue is so major that it would be
hard to localize in discussion, in fact some of the strongest precise commentary
comes from addressing that issue. That the narrator thinks having a haunted
house "would be asking too much of fate" (9) and that she will *proudly* declare
that there is something queer about it" (9; emphasis added) is usually considered very strange reasoning but in line with her longing for the "romantic felicity" of a "haunted house." I usually have to ask directly, though, about the
sentence, "John laughs at me, of course, *but* one expects that in marriage" (9;
emphasis added). The first response is usually content-based ("It's not right for
a husband to laugh at his wife"); it takes a second look before someone comments on "of course" and on the dissonance caused by the conjunction. But
whether I or a student-interpreter raise the last point, someone else will chime
in with a comment about how the repeatedly emphasized, putative nonlogic of
"John is a physician, and *perhaps*— [. . .] *perhaps* that is one reason I do not
get well faster" (9–10) actually marks a strong causation.

The infamous "but one expects that in marriage" also prompts notice about
the use of "one" in writing (and, alas, usually a quick pedantic comment by me
about not being pedantic) and about the triple variation in a brief span of the
phrase, "what is *one* to do?" (10; emphasis added). The escalating intensity of
the first two uses of that phrase, which impel the segue into personal information (her brother's status as a reprise of her husband's; her health regimen), the
eruption into the correctively redundant "Personally, *I* . . . ," and the subsid-
ing into the last "what is *one* to do?" have a rhythm that is inescapable.

That this emotive extravaganza ends with "So I will let it alone and talk about
the house" (11) is, as most students note, the narrator's talking about something
that is safe. They will usually recognize that this shift happens again and again;
I am ordinarily the one to point out the importance of this kind of structural
repetition: *how* the story is told has a good deal to do with *what* we conclude.

Finally, after our more slow-paced hairsplitting, I will again ask for a volunteer to read aloud, beginning with the first, exploratory "And what can one do?" to the final, dispirited discussion of the house (10–11). The oral rendition helps to reunite the fragments of our analysis.

This first part of our exercise takes us a bit more than two pages into the text—a fact that consistently amazes students, given that discussion usually moves fairly quickly. Usually, only seven or eight readers have had turns at this point (enrollment runs twenty-five to thirty-five students), and we are fifty minutes into an hour-and-twenty-minute class (including the ten minutes of introductory comments). In this part of the exercise, students begin to see textual repetition of diction, images, and structure as a flag for meaning. Whether the reiteration is "What is one to do?," the narrator's description of setting, or her rapid shifts from discussion of her own life to "objective" external events, it becomes clear that our impressions about the text are actually produced through very specific techniques.

If class discussion of "The Yellow Wall-Paper" has to be completed in one day, I then break the last half-hour into two fifteen-minute whirlwind overviews; if we are going to work on the text for two days, I do only the second half of the exercise and hold the third part for the next class meeting (for which I often have them read Susan Glaspell's *Trifles* (also known as "Jury of Her Peers") as the next, thematized step in discussing textual evidence).

I explain to students that we are going to begin talking and working more quickly and ask them to brainstorm their verbal responses, with first right of response going to the students who haven't read aloud. I note how much we have discovered through identifying stylistic repetition in stage 1 and tell them that what we are next going to review is recognizing and grouping structural elements that may not be as easily detected. Our purpose is to garner evidence that will let us convince someone who disagrees with a conclusion without our having to fall back on "Well, that's your opinion."

I usually offer a premise for them to begin with. For example, during the first part of class, the odds are that someone has commented on the narrator's passivity. I refer to that comment and ask that students argue instead for her activity and initiative through textual evidence. Working in groups, they collectively assemble a quick catalog of substantiating material, such as her desire to choose her own room, her clandestine writing, her wish to have company, and her attempts to tell John what she is feeling. John's role in the text frequently prompts much discussion, and, here too students can quickly identify elements of plot and episode that argue for John's authority and control. They also see that linguistic elements (such as the repetition of "John says" or his use of "little" in referring to her) bolster an argument that would otherwise be baseless assertion. We can usually construct no more than two of these clusters in fifteen minutes.

As we begin the last quarter-hour of class, I resketch our progress: we have moved from the smallest units of interpretation through ever-widening spheres of internal structure to, finally, the contexts and methods of interpretation. Even in classes that do not focus on critical theory, I then ask students to provide evidence for a specific methodological focus. I rapidly list several—feminist, psychological, Marxist, reader-response, cultural studies, deconstruction— and ask them to choose one and to briefly explain the premise of that method. This question always halts our until now rapid progress, but some intrepid student will tentatively offer a statement we can work with, such as "Women are oppressed by patriarchy." (Feminist and psychological theories are always the most popular.)

I then ask students to begin supporting that argument. My questioning is the most directive during this stage, both in defining the relation of the story to the specific method being discussed and in suggesting limitations or problems. With the example given, for instance, I would comment on the hard time I would have writing an essay with a thesis that, if true, is true for all texts. How could I say anything specific about any one text? How could I answer the question "So what?"? What would my working definition of patriarchy be? of oppression? How could I begin to refine such a large statement in such a way that it fit "The Yellow Wall-Paper," and how could I answer the reader who says "John's a great guy! It can't be easy taking care of a crazy wife"?

There is often some uncertainty at this stage, because I have told my students on the first day of class that my own work is feminist and psychoanalytic. So some will wonder why I am skeptical about their diagnosis of the narrator's problem or their proposal to work deductively from a universal statement about women. They soon begin to see that the issue is that of argumentation and interpretation itself, however, and that many of the words and concepts used to speak for a text in fact need explanations *Webster's* isn't going to supply (e.g., "crazy," "oppressed"). We can then agree that we will talk about, say, a psychological interpretation but that we still need to demonstrate every point made through the text itself.

An important part of this phase is identifying the limitations of a method in relation to a given text, as well as our own limitations as interpreters. We will agree, for example, that historical—or new historicist—analysis works in just about every instance but that we ourselves often don't know enough to employ it. Thus claims such as "in the nineteenth century, people believed $\underline{x}$" don't reinforce an argument but instead cast doubt on everything else said. And sometimes, the limits are not ours but those of the method. If I ask the students to start putting together an analysis of "The Yellow Wall-Paper" based on class status, for example, they stall out fairly quickly. As we note, it isn't that the text doesn't represent class implicitly and explicitly throughout but rather that, for most readers, it doesn't seem the primary lens through which the text can be best viewed.

Lastly, I at least briefly mention that, just as a theory may help us understand a text, so too may a text clarify or even correct a theory. Psychology is, of course, the easiest example in "The Yellow Wall-Paper"; my students readily understand that gendered concepts about mental health are central to the story.

When we conclude this intense class period, I give students a specific journal assignment: they are to write down one sentence that sets forth the central argument of their first journal entries (already handed in). They then are to reread the story (and here I insert a plug for textual underlining and annotation) and to find evidence to support their claim. Finally, they are to write a new journal entry that includes both analysis and evidence, followed by a brief commentary on whether they had to change or narrow the argument, what they saw or responded to differently on rereading, and what they think about any changes.

These revised journals will be the starting point of the next class, whether as a segue to discussion of a new text or as the prelude to a second-day discussion of critical methodologies. Several students will read their entries aloud, and I will ask that they, along with the rest of the class, talk about how they would revise if they were writing an essay on the proposition set forth. The class collectively and quickly supplies validating material or sagely notes the major textual contradictions lying ahead. Students thus model how journals can succeed best, as well as begin to think about revision as something they will be doing throughout the semester.

Whether in critiquing the use of evidence in sample journal entries or in earlier discussion, students' responses to learning or reviewing critical analysis through a close reading of "The Yellow Wall-Paper" are excellent. The exercise becomes something of a game in which they can quickly establish proficiency, and it helps establish ease in classroom discussion early in the semester. The question "But where's the textual evidence?" becomes a common classroom question (sometimes asked of me as well), and students vigorously defend or debate given propositions by excitedly flipping through pages of a text so that they can prove someone right or wrong.

I believe that other instructors will find this exercise useful and that "The Yellow Wall-Paper" is an ideal text for it. Early, intensive analysis of Gilman's tale helps to demystify the perennial conundrum of "What does the teacher want?" and to turn attention instead to what the text wants from its readers.

The Use of Audiovisual Material as an Aid in Teaching "The Yellow Wall-Paper"

Guiyou Huang

The narrator of "The Yellow Wall-Paper" suffers a nervous breakdown that results in her inability to control both the environment and her mental condition; she is thus considered a mental patient by medical professionals such as Dr. S. Weir Mitchell (by implication), by her brother, and by her husband, John. In writing this autobiographically inspired story challenging biased medical views, Gilman uses visual, olfactory, and tactile imagery in a masterly manner throughout the narrative: the narrator imagines the existence of a woman struggling behind the pattern of the wallpaper in her room (visual); she claims that she smells the smoldering yellow color (olfactory); and in the end she literally tears down the hideous wallpaper (tactile), accomplishing the act of self-liberation from an asylum-like house.

The story spans a period of three months, during which time the reader witnesses the protagonist's gradual descent into madness. The narrator characterizes the wallpaper as possessing two salient properties: patterns that resemble iron bars on prison windows that trap and suppress whatever is behind them (in this case an imaginary woman) and the odor of the paper that the narrator describes as "yellow" (13). Despite questions about the state of the narrator's mind, the story is truly poetic because of the use of metaphoric language to express feelings and emotions. Yet the structure of the story, largely reflecting the narrator's unstable mental health, poses difficulty to students who may find it hard to follow the choppy style that the narrator employs. It therefore follows that in teaching this short masterpiece the instructor and students will both be well served by the use of audio and visual materials to enhance students' understanding of the social and cultural dynamics in the story.

This essay considers the following materials: three film versions of the story; pictures and drawings of asylums for the insane; illustrations and photographs of women's fashions; pictures of nineteenth-century wallpaper; and photographs of Gilman and her first husband, the artist Charles Walter Stetson.

Like the narrative itself, the International Instructional Television production of "The Yellow Wall-Paper," directed by John Robbins, utilizes the protagonist to narrate her story to a presumed audience. For most of the film's fifteen-minute duration, the narrator delivers a monologue commenting on her predicament in confinement, on other characters, and on her immediate physical surroundings: the room and its yellow wallpaper and the outside world represented by the seeable but unreachable green garden. Because students may look for differences between the written text and film representations—for instance, changes or alterations in the plot or the characters' appearances—the instructor may emphasize the film as one of many interpretations of the story.

For example, two important visual aspects that the film depicts effectively are the layout of the room, formerly a nursery, in which the narrator is confined and the design and surface appearance of its wallpaper.

The woman in the Robbins film cries a lot from hysteria, caused by what we would now call postpartum depression (one might remind students that the word *hysteria* originates from the Latin word for "uterus"). The wallpaper and the path in the garden are two things she obsesses over during the three-month rental of the colonial mansion. She also alludes to "some legal trouble [. . .] about the heirs and co-heirs" (11), which suggests male dominance both in the ancestral house and in history. The tedium of a confined stay in a room with a bolted-down bed—symbolizing the narrator's immovable and inflexible situation—contrasts sharply with the variety of the wallpaper patterns in yellow and orange that the narrator despises. The principle of wallpaper design, about which the narrator claims to "know a little" (19), does not seem relevant, because the pattern is pointless, an observation the narrator makes repeatedly in both the film and the story. This pointlessness is perceivable, however, only to the obsessed narrator. Her husband, John, and his sister, Jennie, do not seem to be bothered by the alleged lack of design principle. It is only the narrator who casts it as pointless, just as she views Dr. Mitchell's rest cure as pointless, and, more important, male dominance as pointless.

Male dominance manifests itself symbolically, and specifically, in the bars surrounding the narrator: bars on the windows, bars created by the moonlight on the wallpaper, and bars on the banister. These visual images clearly work more concretely and immediately on the film viewer than their textual descriptions do on the reader; the instructor should thus point them out while screening the film for the students, in order to stress their symbolic significance. I recommend connecting these images to the oppressive power of male-dominated social and familial structures that not only severely limit women's physical freedom but also restrict the exercising of their imaginative faculty. The narrator is prohibited from writing by her husband, a restrictive rule implemented with the help, ironically, of another woman, Jennie, who in the film is represented as a tall, serious, and stern figure.

John Clive's film, often used in the classroom, has three distinct characteristics: it is a full-length film that runs ninety minutes, longer than any other film adaptations of "The Yellow Wall-Paper"; it relocates the story to England, to a village outside London, with characters who speak British English; and it changes the personages or names of several characters and adds new ones. For example, the protagonist is called Charlotte (Lotta), which reflects the autobiographical nature of the original story; and taking the place of the actual historical figure, Dr. Mitchell, is a Dr. Charles Stark, who is depicted as a condescending man. Among the other new characters are the couple's son, James, and a little girl (the gardener's daughter) riding a bicycle. Jennie's characterization is also noteworthy: unlike her counterpart in the story, who is content with her role in life, Jennie in the end of the Clive film begins to question her brother's treatment of her sister-in-law and seems on the verge of a rebellion.

Using this film, the instructor may want to point out that unlike other film versions and the story itself, Clive does not overemphasize the function of the wallpaper. Instead, special attention is given to a golden yellow dress that John bought for Charlotte in Rome and that Charlotte believes was worn by a woman who is now somewhere in hiding. Also highlighted is the recurring sound of rustling, to suggest the creepiness and perhaps Gothic aspects of the haunted house. The rustling, caused either by someone tearing at the wallpaper or someone crawling on the leafy ground, taps Charlotte's imaginative faculties. John is presented largely along the lines of the original story, though in the movie he appears to be very ambitious and is more concerned with his professional success than with his wife's mental health. Because of his frequent absences, Charlotte suffers intense boredom, which contributes to her descent into madness. Contrasting her boredom is the freedom that the gardener's daughter enjoys riding her bicycle on the garden path: her freedom emphasizes Charlotte's lack of it, signified by the barred windows of the nursery on the top floor, by the repetitive patterns of the yellow wallpaper, and by the yellow dress worn by the woman behind the wallpaper, who emerges to meet and merge with Charlotte, who now appears insane.

The third film, Tony Romain's, is considerably different from the previous two in a number of ways. First, this twenty-six-minute film juxtaposes the story of a woman writing the narrative with images from the actual story of the nineteenth-century character she is creating. It also endows the principal characters with full names; the original unnamed woman narrator becomes Kathy Parker, her husband is called John Parker, and Kathryn is the name given her fictional creation. Another difference is that it emphasizes the abusive relationship that Kathy has with John (she is seen with a large bruise on the side of her face). Jennie is presented as a vibrant small woman in her twenties, conspicuously different from Robbins's much older, taller, and sterner counterpart or Clive's artistic and questioning figure. Also noteworthy are Dr. Mitchell's brief visit and appearances of the couple's child, who is not featured in Robbins's film. While Robbins's film seems to follow the original story more closely, Romain's seems to capture its spirit.

Just as an understanding of the story can be enhanced with the use of films, both the films and the story may be better appreciated with other visual aids, such as pictures of insane asylums. Few readers would argue with the idea that Gilman chose to describe the nursery as emblematic of a nineteenth-century insane asylum. Four books with many illustrations of insane asylums and hospitals are thus particularly useful as instructional aids. David J. Rothman's *The Discovery of the Asylum: Social Order and Disorder in the New Republic* addresses two major issues: why America in the Jacksonian era suddenly began to build institutions for deviant and dependent members of the community and why since 1820 so many penitentiaries, insane asylums, almshouses, orphan asylums, and reformatories for delinquents were constructed all at once (xiii). Rothman writes, "The first postulate of the asylum program was the prompt removal of the insane from the community" (137), suggesting that such persons constitute a threat to the social order. Hence "the charge of the asylum was to bring discipline to the victims of a disorganized society" (138). In Gilman's story the narrator journeys to the old colonial house to undergo a version of the rest cure. Rothman inserts twenty-one illustrations of mostly nineteenth-century prisons, asylums, penitentiaries, hospitals, and almshouses in New York, Boston, and Philadelphia, including two insane asylums in Pennsylvania and two in Massachusetts (44, 139, 140, 267). Using these illustrations in class offers the students an opportunity to compare insane institutions with prisons and jails and with Gilman's depiction of the rental house. Gilman writes of the house, "The most beautiful place! [. . .] It makes me think of English places that you read about, for *there are hedges and walls and gates that lock*, and lots of separate little houses for the gardeners and people" (11; emphasis added). Students can draw parallels between the common function of asylums and the colonial house. Because mental patients are perceived as dangerous, imprisoning or confining them is a measure taken to prevent social disorder. One of Rothman's illustrations of a "houselike colonial jail" in Philadelphia (241) suggests that Gilman's narrator received no better treatment than a criminal who was jailed and deprived of freedom.

Gerald N. Grob's *Mental Institutions in America* also includes a considerable number of illustrations of mental hospitals from colonial America to 1875, when Gilman was fifteen. Grob traces the historical development of America's mental institutions, mainly in New England, including asylums established in Providence, Rhode Island, Gilman's birthplace, where the first mental institution, the Butler Hospital for the Insane, was erected and opened in 1847 (74– 75, 350–51). Grob points out that many of New England's mental hospitals were meant for the indigent, a class to which neither Gilman nor her narrator belonged. The narrator's upper-middle-class status, in fact, may help explain John's decision to rent a colonial house as a place for his "mentally ill" wife to receive private care. Of much instructional value are Grob's vivid illustrations of asylums; a picture of Isaac Ray (1807–81), "probably the most influential nineteenth-century American psychiatrist [and] Superintendent of the Maine Insane Hospital and the Butler Hospital for the Insane in Providence" (146); and a facsimile of the cover of Isaac H. Hunt's pamphlet *Three Years in a Mad-house!* that shows Dr. Ray giving a patient "poisonous medicines" with a notation that says, "There is nothing given you but what is for your good" (265), a statement not unlike the authoritarian one John makes to his wife: "I am a doctor, dear, and I know" (23–24). The instructor may use this last illustration to show that just as Hunt wrote *Three Years in a Mad-house!* to criticize mental hospitals in the early 1850s, Gilman wrote "The Yellow Wall-Paper" to attack both the medical profession and male dominance.

Perhaps the most meaningful illustration in Grob's book is the one titled "Kidnapping Mrs. Packard" (266), in which the "kidnapped" woman is helplessly taken to an insane hospital by force while a large crowd look on. Mrs. E. P. W. Packard, charging that she had been committed to the Illinois State Hospital for the Insane for three years by her husband, eventually launched one of the first freedom crusades for persons committed involuntarily to mental hospitals. It is obviously helpful for students to consider the parallels between Mrs. Packard's and Gilman's situations: both were confined for alleged mental instability, and, after they regained physical freedom, both wrote to condemn man-caused imprisonment. Packard's own book, *Modern Persecution; or, Insane Asylums Unveiled,* published in 1875, is an autobiographical account of Packard's heart-wrenching hospital experience, illustrated with nearly twenty drawings of key events and characters during the author's three years of incarceration. Students will learn the dark side of nineteenth-century treatment of the allegedly insane as well as of the marriage institution during the time period. Packard's book closes with a plea for married women's emancipation made before the Connecticut Legislature in the Hartford State House: "Should the husband's power over the wife become an oppressive power, by any unjust usurpation of her natural rights, she shall have the same right to appeal to the Government for redress and protection that the husband has" (406). This same plea is made more subtly in "The Yellow Wall-Paper."

Thomas S. Kirkbride's *Construction, Organization, and General Arrangements of Hospitals for the Insane*, published in 1880, just two years before Charles Walter Stetson began courting Charlotte Perkins, is another relevant source on insanity and its treatment: it not only offers detailed discussion of the physical aspects of an insane asylum, but it also contains twenty-three illustrations of actual asylums, including the layout of mental hospitals (plans of cellar, basement, kitchen, main floor, and so on). Kirkbride's book, dealing with mental hospitals established from 1840 to 1880 in Philadelphia, where Dr. Mitchell was living, provides insights into the practice of managing asylums and treating mental patients in the middle and late nineteenth century. It therefore offers students a professional's views of insanity and its treatment. (Kirkbride served as physician-in-chief and superintendent of the Pennsylvania Hospital for the Insane at Philadelphia and as president of the Association of Medical Superintendents of American Institutions for the Insane.)

Pictures of nineteenth-century women are also useful for teaching Gilman's story. The films and the story's original illustrations for its *New England Magazine* publication (reprinted in Bauer's Bedford edition and Golden's *The Captive Imagination*) make it clear that how the narrator looks serves as a commentary on women's social and domestic status as well as their expected behaviors of the day. Therefore a knowledge of women's dress codes and fashions during the period in which the story is set offers insights into women's roles in marriage and society. One might begin by examining photos of Gilman herself at the time. A good number of photographs of the Stetsons exist: pictures of

Charlotte Perkins, Charles Walter, and their daughter, Katharine, can be found scattered in books such as Gilman's autobiography, *The Living of Charlotte Perkins Gilman*; her first husband Stetson's *Endure: The Diaries of Charles Walter Stetson* (Hill); Ann J. Lane's biography of Gilman, *To* Herland *and Beyond*; and Polly Wynn Allen's *Building Domestic Liberty*. These photographs give students a visual sense of Gilman from a child of two to a woman in her sixties. It is noteworthy that of the many available photographs and drawings of Gilman, one can rarely find a picture that shows her smiling; in fact, most of them present her as either pensive or meditative or merely quiet. The only published photo that portrays her as genuinely happy and broadly smiling was taken in 1927 with her second husband, George Houghton Gilman (Ho) and her two grandchildren, Dorothy Stetson Chamberlin and Walter Stetson Chamberlin (see *Living* 314).

One telling photo that Gilman did not use to illustrate her autobiography but that can be found in Ann Lane's biography shows a sad-eyed, emaciated, tight-chinned Gilman in a tight-collared jacket, with Gilman's own chilling notation that reads, "This is what my breakdown did" (122). Also in Lane's book is Robert William Vonnoh's portrait of Dr. Mitchell (114). Of course, the instructor might show students photographs of other persons as well, such as those of Grace Ellery Channing, Charlotte's confidante who later married her first husband, Stetson, and those of Stetson himself.

Many pictures of Gilman show her wearing flat- or high-collared dresses reaching down to the ground, common in women's fashions in the Victorian era. To better understand the dress codes of the late nineteenth century, the instructor may refer students to Douglas Gorsline's illustrated book *What People Wore: A Visual History of Dress from Ancient Times to Twentieth-Century America*, part 3 of which surveys American costume in different regions of the country in the latter half of the nineteenth century. *Dressed for the Photographer: Ordinary Americans and Fashions, 1840-1900*, by Joan L. Severa, is a more detailed study illustrated with photos that give students a historical sense of attire worn by late-nineteenth-century men and women.

Another illuminating study of the history of Western dress is Phyllis Tortora and Keith Eubank's *Survey of Historic Costume*, which examines the significance of dress in connection to social cultures, morality, values, and behavior, among other things. Tortora and Eubank point out that in the nineteenth century, "the term 'middle-class morality' is often applied to a code of behavior that stressed obedience, male authority, religious piety, thrift, hard work, and sexual morality" (255); fashions for women tended to reflect these values, "particularly those fashions that tended to confine and hamper women" (256). During the so-called bustle period (1870–90), roughly the two decades before the publication of "The Yellow Wall-Paper," "the confining nature of women's clothing, the heavy draperies and long trains, encumbering bustles, and the tight corseting necessary to achieve the fashionable silhouette prompted intense activity on the part of those promoting dress reform" (328).

One often-voiced concern motivating women's dress reform was the effect of contemporary garments on the health of women. Tortora and Eubank include some early 1890s comments on the "long, heavy, disease-producing skirts" of the bustle period; Dr. Emily Bruce is quoted as saying, in 1894, that the long, heavy skirt impedes free and graceful movements and picks up and carries home "all sorts of evil things from the street" and that the skirt "aids the wicked bodice in compressing the waist, and drags upon spine, hips, and abdomen, producing a state of exhaustion very conducive to the development of disease" (329). This does not mean that the dresses that Gilman's narrator wore were responsible for her disease, but it does make one think it's no wonder the narrator often feels exhausted, wearing the kind of dress she does (Charlotte rejects a blue bustle handed to her by Jennie in Clive's film). Clearly, these illustrations contribute to students' understanding of the narrator's physical constriction, if not her mental status.

Clothing, however, does not affect the narrator's state of mind as immediately as does the yellow wallpaper. Students will therefore benefit greatly from photos and drawings of wallpaper from the late nineteenth century, a pedagogical purpose served perfectly by Lois Katzenbach and William Katzenbach's richly illustrated book *The Practical Book of American Wallpaper*. Readers of Gilman's story well know that what bothers the narrator is the wallpaper's color and design. The Katzenbachs consider color and design as wallpaper's two most important elements and point out that yellow, along with peach and red, is a warm color (6). This book indicates that Gilman's choice of the color yellow may have been no accident. Paintings before the Italian Renaissance were largely religious, and the church prescribed certain colors to represent the various virtues and vices; yellow represented glory and power (102). The yellow of Gilman's wallpaper may have been seen as symbolizing control and power—specifically, on the familial and social level, the power of the narrator's husband and the male-dominated culture represented by Dr. Mitchell; thus tearing the paper down constitutes an act of protest and rebellion against patriarchal rule and male dominance.

The Katzenbachs write, "Wallpaper is made for the wall, and its colors, like its design, should stay quietly on the wall and not appear to dance or jump about on it. Like its design, the colors in a wallpaper should have a pleasant rhythm and 'cover space simply but eloquently' without the overpunctuation of contrasting spots" (105). A pleasant rhythm is what Gilman's paper lacks: hers is "stripped off [. . .] in great patches all around the head of my bed" (12), "and when you follow the lame uncertain curves for a little distance they suddenly commit suicide—plunge off at outrageous angles, destroy themselves in unheard of contradictions" (13). In other words, the pattern has no eloquence; instead it has the power to drive one crazy.

"Iron bars" (stripes and straight lines) are a property of many wallpapers, and, according to the Katzenbachs, "their angle and their arrangement on a wall can either imprison or release one" (10). In the narrator's case, the design imprisons. The breadths in the wallpaper connect diagonally while the whole thing goes horizontally, adding to confusion (20); as a result, "there is a lack of sequence, a defiance of law, that is a constant irritant to a normal mind. [. . .] The pattern is torturing" (25). By moonlight, the outside pattern resembles bars (26). At such points the colonial mansion becomes a prison, and its tenant, a prisoner behind bars. The Katzenbachs provide all kinds of delightful illustrations and imaginative verbal descriptions of American wallpaper in the eighteenth and nineteenth centuries that students will find instructive. Here the instructor may want to refer to Heather Kirk Thomas's essay "'A Kind of "Debased Romanesque" with Delirium Tremens': Late-Victorian Wall Coverings and Charlotte Perkins Gilman's 'The Yellow Wall-Paper,'" which explores Gilman's familiarity with late-nineteenth-century aesthetics of wall covering. This essay is useful to the students because of the connection that Thomas makes between Gilman's story and the wallpaper designs by the British designer William Morris, whose wife and daughter both happened to be named Jane, though the daughter was always called Jenny (Thomas 190). Thomas reads the story as Gilman's attack on egregious decorating excesses from a feminist viewpoint and concludes that "Gilman's wallpaper 'codes' function in the story to critique her era's increasing exercise of the decorative arts in domestic spaces spatially to define, and consequently further to confine, women's lives" (201). Because of Morris's "androgynous Craftsman styles," Thomas argues, Gilman views such wallpapers as reinforcing the "medieval aura of female entrapment" (195).

Thomas is not the only critic who reads the wallpaper as detrimental to mental and physical health. Tom Lutz in his book *American Nervousness, 1903* holds similar views. Chapter 7 of Lutz's book, "Women and Economics in the Writings of Charlotte Perkins Gilman and Edith Wharton," is especially illuminating to the reader of "The Yellow Wall-Paper." Gilman and Wharton both experienced neurasthenic illness and both wrote about it; both knew Dr. S. Weir Mitchell and received treatment from him; and both showed interest in and knowledge of interior decorations. Lutz links the wallpaper to neurasthenia, suggesting that Gilman not only knew the discourse of the disease but also knew "how to manipulate it rhetorically" (229). He asserts, "Not only is the narrator's abnormal response to the wallpaper a normal process according to medical opinion, but she is poisoning herself in her attempt to tear the wallpaper from the walls" (230). The poisonous wallpaper contributes to neurasthenia that inevitably deprives the influenced woman of her mental health.

It seems appropriate to conclude this discussion with an enlightening quote from Katzenbach and Katzenbach: "No one doubts that the influences and effects created by wallpaper are very real. Its stripes can imprison or release, its textures impoverish or enrich, its flowers and foliage can smother or delight, its narratives fatigue or fascinate, and its colors depress or elate" (125). Gilman's "The Yellow Wall-Paper" delineates the former of these influences and effects symbolically and eloquently.

A Psychological Approach
to Teaching "The Yellow Wall-Paper"

Judith Harris

Long before writing "The Yellow Wall-Paper," Gilman had studied the edges between fantasy and reality, the borderlines between sanity and insanity. In her autobiography, *The Living of Charlotte Perkins Gilman*, she recollects that, as a child, she was such an avid daydreamer that her mother had to impose on her fantasy world, insisting she put such idle pleasures away: "My dream world was no secret. I was but too ready to share it, but there were no sympathetic listeners. It was my life, but lived entirely alone" (23). Gilman's mother seized her "inner fortress" (23) of happiness by simply detecting its existence behind closed doors. Eventually, Gilman chose to comply with her mother's wishes, severing herself from the fantasy that pushed hard to be let back in. Years later, and after her nervous breakdown, Gilman equated her mother's intrusion into her dream world to Freud's objectives in analysis. She accused Freud and his disciples of being "mind-meddlers" who violated the human spirit, which she equated with her creativity (*Living* 314).

Gilman's lifelong animosity toward psychoanalysis can only be understood through recognition of her dramatic struggle with mental illness and the obstacles she had to confront personally and professionally. In teaching Gilman's "The Yellow Wall-Paper," I have adopted a psychoanalytic approach to help students interrogate the Victorian norms represented by Freudian psychoanalysis. When students are better acquainted with Freud, they gain not only a historical and scientific context for defining the "female malady" but also an understanding of Gilman's moral outrage at being treated as a pawn of early psychiatric study. Hence I encourage students to use the fiction of "The Yellow Wall-Paper" as a critical tool for scrutinizing Freud and his ethics and to use knowledge of Freud as a critical methodology for interpreting the story. This pedagogical approach is particularly effective when conjoined with a supplementary reading of Freud's "Fragment of an Analysis of a Case of Hysteria ('Dora')," which is itself a compelling precedent for the Gilman story.

Although "The Yellow Wall-Paper" predates Freud's analyses, the story is startlingly modern in its depiction of mental illness. Anticipating Freudian discoveries, the story situates the narrator-patient in a childhood space where she is compelled to confront what Freud called "the half-tamed demons released by the work of analysis" (Freud and Breuer 47). Dr. S. Weir Mitchell, who treated Gilman for a severe and continuous nervous breakdown, himself noted that "the cause of breakdowns and nervous disasters and consequential emotional disturbances and their bitter fruit are often to be sought in the remote past. [The doctor] may dislike the quest, but he cannot avoid it" (qtd. in Berman, *Talking Cure* 49). Mitchell's rest cure was a method of enforced inactivity, which included isolation, bed rest, and the injunction to "live as domestic a life as possible [. . .]

and never [to] touch pen, brush, or pencil" (Gilman, *Living* 96). Mitchell's remedy forced the female patient to revert to an infantile state and to relinquish her will to male authority.

Indeed, Victorian women of social standing were often forced to comply with patriarchal expectations and rules, although their natures may have told them otherwise. When I ask students to tell me about the narrator, they comment on how she has reached her breaking point, that she has been denied an expressive and creative outlet for her emotions and is self-destructively bound up by secrecy and repression. Traditional psychotherapy involves a patient's disclosing secrets to get to the root of guilt-ridden thoughts and defensive behaviors. To cure his patients, Freud sought to purge them of the secrets that were making them ill. Bertha Pappenheim (Anna O) referred to Freud's "talking cure" as a kind of "chimney sweeping"—a clearing away of one's regrettable past (qtd. in Berman, *Talking Cure* 2).

Gilman's "The Yellow Wall-Paper" is on one level a defiant response to Mitchell's rest cure and what it meant for women of her social background and education. But the narrative is on another level Gilman's defiant response to the psychiatric violations of her personal boundaries, in her roles as a woman and as a writer. Years after her unsuccessful treatment, Gilman indicted Freud for offenses ranging from the violation of the human spirit to an unnatural emphasis on sex (Berman, *Talking Cure* 36). Gilman's debilitated narrator in "The Yellow Wall-Paper," already on the verge of helpless resignation, asks, "And what can one do?" (10). The condition itself was so enervating, so lacerating, that the hysterical patient had no option but to rely on the care of those people whom she feared or distrusted.

An introduction to Freudian theory provides students with a background against which they can better evaluate the narrator's condition in "The Yellow Wall-Paper." Students are naturally concerned with self-depictions by woman writers that serve as a critique of the constraining conditions in which women find themselves. Through a psychoanalytic approach, which includes reading Freud's case study of Dora, this concern is heightened as they expand their knowledge of the story to a knowledge of a female patient in the midst of a mental crisis and precisely what that might entail in accordance with Freudian theory and treatment.

Both Dora and Gilman were diagnosed as hysterics: Dora by Freud in 1895, Gilman by Mitchell in 1887. *Hysterical*, in the nineteenth century, was a term given to women's emotional disturbances, anxiety, or excitability. Thought to originate in the uterus, it became a metaphor for everything men found mysterious and unmanageable in the opposite sex (Herman 10). Freud credited Jean-Martin Charcot for being the first to take hysterical phenomena seriously, restoring "dignity" to patients whose bizarre symptoms were, more often than not, treated as curiosities (Herman 11). But Freud understood that taxonomy wasn't sufficient for understanding the actual causes of hysteria, especially in its severest forms. Freud then resolved that to understand what was at the bottom of his patients' troubles, he would have to listen to them. As Freud listened, he became convinced that hysteria was caused by psychological trauma and that emotional reactions to psychological trauma produced an altered state of consciousness which, in turn, induced women's hysterical symptoms.

By the mid 1890s, these investigations led Freud further to the startling hypothesis that hysteria could be attributed to painful memories of premature sexual experiences. He disclosed his troublesome conclusions in *The Aetiology of Hysteria* (1886): "I therefore put forward the thesis that at the bottom of every case of hysteria there are one or more occurrences of premature sexual experience, experiences which belong to the earliest years of childhood, but which can be reproduced through the work of psychoanalysis despite the intervening decades" (qtd. in Herman 13). But after publishing *The Aetiology of Hysteria*, Freud apparently changed his mind and stated that those scenes of seduction had never taken place and were fabricated. This conclusion led him to his famous oedipal theory, in which he proposed that all children entertain sexual fantasies about their parents. Hence a patient's confession about a sexual encounter with a parent, or a parental figure, might be as much wishful fantasy as actual event.

Freud's conflict concerning his patients' credibility reached its height in the Dora case. Eighteen-year-old Dora sought treatment from Freud in October 1900 but abruptly terminated her analysis only eleven weeks later. Unwilling or unable to exploit his patient's transference as a productive means of furthering her progress, Freud failed to win Dora's trust and cooperation. Her hostility toward Freud undermined his attempts to cure her.

Dora's symptoms included a cough and hoarseness, severe abdominal pain, morbidity and depression. To discover the etiology of Dora's hysteria, Freud had to work swiftly toward extracting the cause of her repression. Although Freud initiated the attack against the girl's defensive repression, he found that he had to fend off Dora's retaliatory attacks at the same time that he absorbed them. Instinctually, Dora refused to surrender her secrets to the psychoanalyst, and her profound opposition to therapy is well documented throughout the study.

From its origins in treating hysteria, psychoanalysis consisted mainly of encouraging the patient to recall the past in order to isolate traumatic events of childhood. In the clinical view, trauma is always related to neurosis. Freud then isolated trauma as part of the larger pattern of repression and defense anxiety, postulating that the nature of symptoms could be seen as compromises or "somatic compliances" ("Dora" 193) within the psyche, allowing the scenic aspects of the trauma to be forgotten, while the wounding in or of the body remained. The discourse of the symptom is also the discourse of the illness, for as the traumatic incident is converted into somas, a physical (but not unrelated) sign of the body, it is also trying to protest against the original threat that caused the symptom to be split off in the first place. In hysterical patients, especially, the symptom serves as a means of ridding trauma from memory by acting it out covertly. Hence students may well theorize that the woman in the wallpaper functions as a sign projected outward from within the core of the narrator's psyche, a sign that is repetitive and reenacts the narrator's wish to break out of a pattern of domestic life in which she feels encased or imprisoned.

Freud, consistent with his earlier contention that the course taken by illness always connects back to traumatic sexual experiences ("Dora" 193), speculated that Dora's throat irritation and cough derived from an unconscious fantasy involving oral sex. Freud attributed Dora's later anxieties to her repression, in which anxiety is awakened as a signal of an earlier situation: hence the weight given to infancy and the past. He observed that mental events, especially dreams, can be seen as a chain successive in time and development. In the long thread of mental connections that spins itself out between a symptom of the disease and "a pathogenic ideal," a dream is yet another link or stitch in the larger design, or pattern, of the signifying unconscious. The dreamer, by permitting the mind to wander freely in connection with various parts of the dream, is guided to the meaning of the dream, "to the wish at its center" ("Dora" 176).

Students are intrigued to learn that patients undergoing psychoanalysis are encouraged to free associate (and be guided by dream imagery), not unlike the way the narrator free associates in "The Yellow Wall-Paper." What results is a stream of consciousness, a meandering design of interlinking, but seemingly unrelated, thoughts or memories. In "The Yellow Wall-Paper," the narrator lets her mind wander aimlessly over the wallpaper pattern, just as Freud encouraged Dora to do. However, the narrator becomes noticeably irritated and frustrated by its lack of consistency, its artistic "sins" of style: "It is dull enough to confuse the eye in following, pronounced enough to constantly irritate and provoke study, and when you follow the lame uncertain curves [. . .] they suddenly commit suicide [. . .] destroy themselves in unheard of contradictions" (13).

Forced into seclusion, in which she can do nothing but think aloud, the narrator attempts to follow the meandering pattern of the wallpaper, ultimately submitting to a monstrous self-projection. Like any patient in analysis, the narrator is vulnerable to the blockages, inconsistencies, and "talking" suicides incurred when something crucial to expression refuses to give itself up to consciousness. Although a patient may resist full disclosure in the analytic session, Freud insisted in the Dora case that he could decode a patient's secrets: "He who has eyes to see and ears to hear may convince himself that no mortal can keep a secret." Thus Freud concluded that the "task of making conscious the most hidden recesses of the mind is one which is quite possible to accomplish" ("Dora" 215).

Indeed, Freud was convinced Dora intended to "play secrets" with him, that she withheld the narratives that, once exposed, would best help to cure her, and that she was on the verge of having her secret violently "torn" from her by "the doctor" ("Dora" 189). The word "torn"—Freud's word—will become increasingly significant as we begin to analyze the narrator's compulsion to strip back the floral pattern in "The Yellow Wall-Paper" in order to release the entrapped secret phantasm. Her husband, John, also demands that his wife relinquish her imaginative fantasizing by suspending all creative writing. If she is no longer able to hide her inner thoughts in writing, he is at liberty to examine them. Stressing the physical dimension of Dora's psyche as a kind of interior space, a space within the body, that could be entered like a room or a house and in which the analyst is at liberty to look about, Freud wrote, "If the trauma theory is not to be abandoned we must go back to her childhood and look about *there* for any influences or impressions which might have had an effect analogous to that of a trauma" ("Dora" 183; my emphasis).

Once they have been introduced to the basic precepts of Freudian theory, students are able to see that Freud pursued his trauma theory in a manner that was voyeuristic and detective-like. After he covers Dora's childhood through the analytic process, he is free to look about there for parental influences or impressions that might have contributed to traumatic effects. Students begin to realize that this resurfaced childhood space, as Freud described it, is exemplified in Gilman's story by the nursery, a room covered by layers of yellow wallpaper. As Gilman's narrator surveys her surroundings, she describes it as "a big, airy room, the whole floor nearly, with windows that look all ways, and air and sunshine galore. It was nursery first and then playroom and gymnasium, I should judge; for the windows are barred for little children, and there are rings and things in the walls" (12).

The narrator's syntax reveals that she is increasingly susceptible to paranoiac distortions. She reports that "the windows look all ways," implying that while they may look out to the exterior world, they also stare, guilelessly, in on her. Moreover, when one thinks of how this narrator suffers from a chronic sense of being espied by "absurd, unblinking eyes" (16)—her description of the botanical shapes of the wallpaper—it seems more than coincidental that Freud emphasizes the importance of sight as an accessory to analysis. We may assume that Freud's histrionic patients ventilated intolerable emotions in the analytic session, rendering them "in the mildest cases in tears" (Freud and Breuer 43). However, an analyst would have to remain detached to observe them. It is no surprise, then, that Gilman's frustrated narrator views herself as a kind of infantile, even savage, spectacle where even the walls are endowed with the power to scrutinize her.

Additionally, we learn that the nursery "floor is gouged and splintered, the plaster itself is dug out, here and there, and this great heavy bed. [. . .] looks like it has been through the wars" (17). Ravaged by the marks (the signs) of children, the nursery (like the psyche) is both aged and yellowed. It is then not unexpected that we find much of Gilman's discourse emanating from a psychiatric patient's reclining position, "follow[ing] that pattern about by the hour" (19), just as Dora painfully labors (as a mother gives birth) to remember trauma in order to please the expectant father Freud.

In the story, the narrator spins out her anxieties and fears, hour by hour, punctuated by condescending visits by her husband (as doctor): "I lie here on this great immovable bed—it is nailed down, I believe—and follow that pattern about by the hour" (19). Students are encouraged to discover how language in such a situation becomes a mechanism of repetition, a proliferating circuitous discourse. They come to realize that, caught in a web of her own exacting but dispiriting complaints, the narrator's free-associative speech forms an effluent, orbicular pattern like the wallpaper itself. The key to successful analysis is the doctor's (and the student-reader's) ability to decipher the meaning of the patient's unconscious, by determining what these repetitions mean.

Once students are able to identify repetitious patterns, I ask them to consider the similarities between the narrator's insistent talk of the wallpaper—which she continues to focus on— and the patient's insistent talk deriving from the unconscious. In the analytic session, the analyst does not resolve the open-endedness of the patient's associations. Rather, the repetitions and elisions in a patient's monologue are goals in themselves; they are, in a sense, devices for the analyst. As a pattern is gradually established, the analyst works toward discerning its operative elements. The wallpaper pattern, too, like the associations produced in the pattern of a patient's talk in analysis, is always one sequence ahead of itself. Each identical, successive, image in the wallpaper motif must refer backward to the previous image (which it has already preempted), giving the impression of simultaneous progression and regression. In psychoanalysis, too, the patient speaks now and into the future but only with the aim of revealing the far past.

John's disposition, like the analyst's, causes him to be "practical in the extreme" (9) and to restrict his wife to a room ordinarily reserved for dependent children. Barred windows confine the narrator as well as protect her from herself. Living within a daily schedule prepared by John, the narrator finds herself high above the rose-covered gardens and velvet meadows. Suspending her connection with the external world, she displaces her attention to a fantasy replica of the outside world, the wallpaper.

John enforces all measures of restraint against his wife's fantasizing in the hope of bringing her back under his control, yet he only aggravates her nervous condition. He even seems to suspect that his wife's mental state has deteriorated to a delusional state and that her hallucinations are actually aiding her in denying deeper, negative feelings about John and the baby that would otherwise affect her real life. As the narrator confides, "[John] says that my imaginative power and habit of story-making [. . .] is sure to lead to all manner of excited fancies and that I ought to use my will and good sense to check the tendency" (15–16).

As a child, Gilman sought refuge in fantasy where she was free to act out and, at the same time, to control her anxieties. Such impulses, although in an inverted, demonic form, may well be at work in "The Yellow Wall-Paper," where the narrator is also misunderstood by more than one severe parental figure in her household. When Gilman's mother insists that she forfeit her "guarded" secrets (qtd. in Berman, *Talking Cure* 35), she is, quite literally, intruding on her daughter's mind, just as, in Gilman's later view, psychiatrists meddle with their patients' minds, which Gilman considered unethical, if not immoral.

Students are reminded that in conventional psychotherapy, a patient would be encouraged to explore all types of fantasies, good and bad. But Gilman's narrator was repeatedly denied an outlet for her "excited fancies" (15). In fact, the story begins with the narrator's being stultified, as John uses his dominant roles as husband and doctor to keep her imagination in check. Redolent with Freudian discoveries about the unconscious, the story's depiction of the otherwise suppressed monological center of the text—the narrator—is released only by free association, or stream of consciousness. As the hallucinatory woman asserts herself, emotions become more strenuously vocalized. This emergence is a ripe, but often agonizing, moment in analysis. If the mind is like the womb, as Freud conjectured, then the birthing of one's past self results in an infantile but often monstrous form.

The scene of "The Yellow Wall-Paper" is a place of secrecy and a place of labor and delivery. The narrator, who has recently given birth, is only too aware of being enclosed in a space as repellent as the relic of the empty womb:

> The color is repellent, almost revolting; a smouldering unclean yellow, strangely faded by the slow-turning sunlight.
> It is a dull yet lurid orange in some places, a sickly sulfur tint in others.
> No wonder the children hated it! I should hate it myself if I had to live in this room long. (13)

John's rest cure secures his patient in the nursery, as a patient in therapy is regressed to infancy, for the purposes of her incubation and restraint. But in such a subservient position, the patient is always subject to John's (or the analyst's) attacks. It is not insignificant that infants and children in the midst of tantrums have occupied this space, which is the territory of the postpartum womb: "How those children did tear about here! [. . .] I have locked the door and thrown the key down into the front path" (34).

As the narrator grows more agitated, John insists that she lie down for "an hour" after meals. Ironically, only the aberrant pattern of the wallpaper keeps her quiet, again "by the hour" (26). In such a passive state, the patient is also susceptible to analytic suggestion. Whether it is Freud's voyeurism or Mitchell's injunctions against female willlessness, the male analyst counters a patient's resistance by demanding that she give something up. The patient, if convinced that such a relinquishing is necessary for recovery, often submits to the desire of the analyst. But if a patient resists, progress in therapy is halted. In "The Yellow Wall-Paper," John alone holds the master key to the nursery. If we substitute Freud for John, then it follows that the analyst must, as Gilman charged, violate the inner space of the patient (as Freud violated Dora's psychic space) to coax the secret out.

But in this story, and in the Dora case as well, the secret is indistinguishable from the symptom, and both are locked within the same conflated space—the psychic womb. Nineteenth-century physicians, anxious to explain women's symptoms, had already conflated the mind of the hysterical patient with the womb, by blaming women's psychological maladies on malfunctioning reproductive organs. Uncannily, Gilman, while discussing the wallpaper, refers to the nursery's hymenium, or spore-bearing fungus, that is growing just beneath it: "All those strangled heads and bulbous eyes and waddling fungus growths just shriek with derision!" (34). I point out to students that violation of the psyche-womb suggests, by analogy, the tearing of the hymen, a kind of protective wall or barrier that has been overexposed to light and insemination and must be peeled away: "Then I peeled off all the paper I could reach" (34). The phantasm—ugly, terrified, and outwardly suppressed—starkly represents the difficulty of bringing repressed material, or trauma, to necessary catharsis.

As students become more and more aware of the psychoanalytic background behind Gilman's writing, they begin to see that, for the narrator, John's strict rationalism breaks down and that the divisions between reality and fantasy are not so clear. I ask students to consider how women writers use their imaginations, although, no doubt, they may be judged intemperate or insane, for defying convention and formality. As class discussion progresses, I assign a paper in which students are directed to put in writing what the yellow wallpaper symbolizes for them. I ask them to analyze the narrator's projection and how much that projection has to do with self-denial and self-mutilation. Implicit in any psychoanalytic analysis of the narrator's phantasm is the ideological assumption that women have great difficulty reconciling their roles as authors with being submissive subjects in literature. (Since feminist critics center on the absence of women in literary texts and on the stereotypes male writers have traditionally used to depict women, students might find William Veeder's essay "Who Is Jane? The Intricate Feminism of Charlotte Perkins Gilman" a useful tool for exploring this dichotomy.) How can women, like Gilman, write about female experience without appropriating male bias? How will they balance their presumed domestic roles as silent observers and as submissive daughters like Dora with their roles as active, articulate originators of their own texts? Which keys are necessary to open locked Pandora's boxes?

Appropriately, the narrator describes the woman in the wallpaper as a wordless, sulky creature, a woman who epitomizes this archaic pattern of infantile dependency and rage underlying the vileness of the paper. That the figure goes awry, stalking about in anger or uproar, confirms what Freud suspected was at the bottom of hysterical symptoms: some kind of trauma tied to childhood or infancy. Only by excising the ancient injury is recovery possible. Hence the wallpaper woman is described as ancient and crawling, suggesting how the past, particularly when revisited in the psychoanalytic self-encounter, is old, ancient.

While psychotherapy should assuage suffering, Gilman considered it more of an exorcism than therapy. Her narrator, equally skeptical, fears the possibility of future treatment: "John says if I don't pick up faster he shall send me to Weir Mitchell in the fall" (18). Through a psychological and historical approach, students see how "The Yellow Wall-Paper" is, in many ways, a case study. Ultimately, students come to judge Gilman's mistrust of "mind-meddlers" (*Living* 314) as an appropriate reaction to the patriarchal biases of early psychoanalytic practice.

Using Role-Playing in Teaching
"The Yellow Wall-Paper"

Carol Farley Kessler and Priscilla Ferguson Clement

In a course introducing first- and second-year college students to women's studies, "The Yellow Wall-Paper," by Charlotte Perkins Gilman, raises questions whose answers cut across disciplines: the short story serves admirably to demonstrate that gender roles can be explained adequately only with reference to several disciplines and that social problems have complex, multifaceted origins and ramifications. The story also illustrates the extent to which individual freedoms and identity, such as those of the female narrator, exist or not within a given sociocultural context. In a timely article Karen Kilcup corroborates our satisfying experience in teaching "The Yellow Wall-Paper" through dramatization (4–5). She suggests that using shorter rather than longer works can permit more-detailed consideration of textual interpretation and recommends imagining cross-genre approaches to teaching, thus as here treating a short story as if it were a play. Additionally, she notes, this is "one of the best ways to involve students in understanding the subtle character portraits that appear in many shorter texts" (4). Dramatizing "The Yellow Wall-Paper" could certainly work effectively in literature courses as well—the context for Kilcup's comments; however, it is especially illuminating in women's studies classes, since instructors frequently aim to enlarge students' understanding of human experience by helping them hear frequently silenced voices. How better to instruct students than through their enacting these voices?

In January 1990, we decided to co-teach Women's Studies 001: Introduction to Women's Studies at the Delaware County Campus of the Pennsylvania State University, located in Media, a southwestern Philadelphia suburb. At the time, introductory courses in women's studies were just beginning to be offered at Penn State campuses other than University Park. We thought that both we and our students would benefit from our differing perspectives—Priscilla Clement, a historian of nineteenth-century American women with a focus on childhood, family, and poverty, and Carol Kessler, a cultural critic of nineteenth-century American women's fiction, especially utopian writing. We labeled ourselves the course coordinators, selected textbooks, and launched our joint venture. Before each class, we met to refine the day's activities: in general Clement oversaw presentations of materials in the social sciences, and Kessler in the humanities. Thus Kessler was primarily responsible for planning the classes involving Gilman's story. Neither can be sure which one originally suggested the role-play idea: each credits the other.

The course was designed to introduce the study of historical, literary, and health issues concerning United States women of varying social, racial, and class identities, from a predominantly contemporary disciplinary and cross-disciplinary perspective. It offered general education distribution credits in diversity to classes for the most part composed of women but also regularly including a handful of men. The course goals were listed as follows:

> to introduce a variety of disciplinary approaches to the study of gender, examining how we become female and male in the United States, the scientific basis of gender identity, and the ways gender-related roles, images, and assumptions have been reflected in literature, law, politics, the economy, and art
>
> to develop skills of critical thinking and analysis as we assess the ideas and information that scholars have developed on the subject
>
> to examine the impact of contemporary feminism, exploring options and problems confronting both sexes as individuals and as members of the larger society

The three required titles were Virginia Sapiro's text *Women in American Society: An Introduction to Women's Studies*, Edith Blicksilver's anthology of fiction and essays *The Ethnic American Woman: Problems, Protests, Lifestyle*, and the Boston Women's Health Book Collective's *Our Bodies, Ourselves for the New Century*. (Clement suggests that instructors could as well use many other current introductory titles, such as the Hunter College Women's Studies Collective's text *Women's Realities, Women's Choice* or Sheila Ruth's collection of articles *Issues in Feminism*: most introductory women's studies texts or anthologies contain discussions of gender-role socialization and maintenance.)

Sapiro provided the basic course structure, and readings from Blicksilver's predominantly literary anthology exemplified Sapiro's chapter topics, while assignments in *Our Bodies* replaced comparable chapters in Sapiro by providing greater depth on those topics. Students kept journals of reading notes in which they reacted to the content of readings and their classroom discussion: these were submitted biweekly to be checked for completeness, but not graded. Such journals provided opportunities for students to both reflect and comment on course material; they also let us see how students were processing the course materials. In addition, we showed five videos and invited six guest speakers to expose students to a variety of perspectives. Three exams, a final group presentation, and a final individual essay were required. Such was the course context within which we taught "The Yellow Wall-Paper."

Our discussion of "The Yellow Wall-Paper" was prefaced by assignments for four fifty-minute classes covering three topics: the definition of women's studies, the status of women in the United States (Sapiro, ch. 1), and theories of gender-role differentiation (Sapiro, ch. 2). In conjunction with these topics, students read Maxine Hong Kingston's "No Name Woman" (Blicksilver 18–26) for the fourth class and "The Yellow Wall-Paper" for the fifth class session. (Instructors today might also assign Kessler's reference article "Charlotte Perkins Gilman," which provides a readable, midlength biographical overview of Gilman's life and work.)

At the beginning of the third class—because we wanted to devote most of the fourth class to the Kingston story—Kessler provided a brief introduction as preparation for students' reading of "The Yellow Wall-Paper." (With seventy-five-minute periods, the background could, of course, be provided during the fourth class.) She offered a capsule biography of Gilman (who was still called Charlotte Perkins Stetson in 1892, when she published the story), background on late-nineteenth-century medical and psychological attitudes toward women, and a set of guiding questions for consideration during reading. For instructors wanting a single source as background for teaching "The Yellow Wall-Paper," Elaine Hedges's "Out at Last" provides a reliable critical overview.

Kessler began by stressing Gilman's family circumstances—the Beecher family legacy, her parents' failed marriage, her relationships to parents and brother, her multiple childhood residences and subsequent disjointed education, and her girlhood friendships (see Kessler, *Gilman* 13–25; Gilman, *Diaries*; Hare-Mustin and Broderick; Hare-Mustin and Maracek). She then moved on to Gilman's marital dynamic—her approaching adulthood, her ambivalence about and then capitulation to marriage with Charles Walter Stetson, her apparent postpartum depression after her daughter Katharine's birth, the impact on her of the institution of mothering, Stetson's constricted view of wifehood, and her own awakening sense of the importance of what she would term "women's world service" (Gilman, *Living*; Hill, *Endure*; Lane; Rich, *Of Woman*). With respect to medical and psychological attitudes toward women, Kessler explained nineteenth-century diagnoses of hysteria (DeLamotte; Herndl, *Invalid Women*; Smith-Rosenberg, "Hysterical Woman"), neurasthenia (Sicherman; Wood), and their treatment, especially as practiced by S. Weir Mitchell in his rest cure (Bassuk; Berman, "Unrestful Cure"; "Backgrounds" section, Golden, *Imagination* 45–119; Poirier; Wood); she also considered two twentieth-century perspectives concerning a "trauma of eventlessness" and "insanity of place" (Seidenberg; Goffman, respectively). Today this background might well include consideration of racist overtones in Gilman's use of "yellow" (see esp. Lanser; Knight, "Gilman"; Lane; Kessler, *Gilman*), since sexist and racist attitudes frequently intertwine. When students began to read "The Yellow Wall-Paper," Kessler asked them to notice the interfaces among family, parenting, and gender and between health and gender. They were to consider what the story reveals about the power of a husband over his wife and what it reveals about the success of medical "treatment." They were also to consider how they understood the story's ending: positive escape? negative loss of self? some other interpretation? Finally, they were to note whether they saw any connection to the evolutionary theory of gender differentiation that Gilman professed in her 1898 *Women and Economics*, as presented in their text (Sapiro 49–50).

During the fourth class, students discussed a 1924 Chinese instance of women's oppression, Kingston's "No Name Woman," excerpted from *The Woman Warrior: Memoirs of a Girlhood among Ghosts* (1975). We wanted students ultimately to generalize oppression of women across cultures and so assigned two autobiographically based selections from different times and places. Themes stressed in our discussion of Kingston prepared the class for discussing Gilman's 1892 tale of oppression in the United States. (Clement suggests at least two more autobiographical selections paralleling themes of Gilman's story, namely, the Puerto Rican Judith Ortiz Cofer's 1993 "The Story of My Body" and the Japanese American Mitsuye Yamada's 1983 "Invisibility Is an Unnatural Disaster." In each of these tales, women explain how they are not seen for who they truly are; either could be taught with Gilman as well as Kingston. In contexts with a focus on Gilman, Kessler has assigned Gilman's short stories "Through This" [1893], "Making a Change" [1911], and "Dr. Clair's Place" [1915] to complement "The Yellow Wall-Paper"; the earliest tale reveals a moment-by-moment view of maternal frazzled focus, while the latter two offer solutions, such as a mother-in-law's live-in child care or medical treatment geared to women's needs.)[1] During the class devoted to Kingston, we asked students to consider how important the silencing of one person by another or by a group might be and what fears could lead people to shun a woman, as villagers had the narrator's aunt. We also asked why people make rules and insist that others obey them. The class then considered connections between explanations for women's social status (Sapiro, ch. 2)—biological and religious theories; liberal and modern views; and Marxist, economic, and materialist views—and illustrations of each within "No Name Woman."

At the end of the fourth class, we set up a role-playing activity that, we told students, would help them understand male and female gender-role expectations for the 1890s. They were to make connections and find relations between concerns of "The Yellow Wall-Paper" and concepts being learned from the course textbook (Sapiro, ch. 1 and esp. ch. 2). Most of the class would play a medical board of specialists in women's illnesses, convened to evaluate the case. The roles of John and Jane (for interpretations of Jane, see Hedges, Afterword; Knight, "Reincarnation"; and Veeder) were offered to two of our stronger students, against their gender, to call further attention to the demands of gender constructions. These two students were each to review their assigned characters throughout the story and be prepared to answer questions from the specialists. The rest of the class, going around the circle that they sat in, then counted off into pairs to become experts on assigned diary entries of the story: depending on class size, approximately one pair was assigned to each of the twelve diary entries. Members of the pairs were to study the assigned pages and be ready to ask questions of Jane about her case and of John about his treatment of it—the lefthand member asked questions of John, the husband and physician; and the righthand member, of Jane, the wife and patient-narrator. Thus every student had a designated role to play: all of the story was assigned in segments to specialist pairs for close analysis and the development of questions for Jane and John so as to elicit the circumstances of the case. With the instructors circulating among pairs to offer clarifications or leading questions, students made their preparations. At the beginning of the next class, students performed the activity. It consisted of three parts: first, the question-ing of Jane and John by all the expert pairs; second, the experts' suggestions on the basis of their consultation; and third, a debriefing.

Students asked their questions in turn around the circle, with each member of the pair alternating questions for Jane and for John. For instance, one expert asked John why he laughs at Jane, and the other asked Jane how she feels about this laughter (9). In his reply, John commented on the superiority of his role as husband and of his knowledge of female complaints as a physician; Jane observed that she feels belittled, discounted by such a trivializing act. The ques-tions began to increase in complexity: one expert asked John to define what he means by "a slight hysterical tendency" (10), and the partner asked Jane to explain why "tak[ing] pains to control [her]self" leads to her being "very tired" (11). These questions elicited from John and Jane more extended responses concerning nineteenth-century gender roles and perceptions thereof. Yet another pair asked John why he considers a nursery an appropriate location for a woman with his wife's symptoms and Jane to explain what feelings the yellow wallpaper evokes in her (12–13). Both questions again elicited gender differ-ences as perceived by John and some misogynistic comments on his perception of her symptoms, while Jane enumerated her several sensory reactions to the paper as well as her physical actions regarding it, which prompted an initial decoding of the titular wallpaper and its multiple significances in the story. Once the experts concluded their questioning and following a brief recess for them to prepare their conclusions, student experts again spoke in turn around the circle offering their advice on the case. Their summation clarified the sig-nificance of each diary entry and its contribution to the story's concluding epiphany. Finally, we debriefed: students explained how they felt about por-traying Jane or John or about acting as pairs of consulting experts.

We spent the last third of this fifth class by asking for examples of structural-functionalist and evolutionary explanations of women's status, as illustrated by the stories we had discussed thus far. As Sapiro explains (46–52), evolutionary theories of gender differentiation, such as those of Charles Darwin (1809–82) or Herbert Spencer (1820–1903), were among the first structural-functionalist theories. Although feminists accepted an evolutionary explanation of human adaptation over time, they did not accept male superiority as an outcome of such adaptation. Neither the theologian Antoinette Brown Blackwell (1825–1921) nor the social worker Jane Addams (1860–1935) nor the sociologist Gil-man accepted female inferiority as a necessary outcome of human evolution. Blackwell's *The Sexes throughout Nature* (1875; Rossi 356–77) is among the ear-liest studies to reveal scientific bias in research: Blackwell saw no reason to con-clude that men naturally dominate women. In *Newer Ideals of Peace* (1907), Addams argued that by acting politically, women would raise the standard of government, then dominated by men (Rossi 604-12). Gilman believed that male domination—what she labeled "androcentrism"—and female subordination led to social dysfunction (*Women*, see esp. chs. 8, 10, 11; Rossi 572– 98). We discuss with our students how "The Yellow Wall-Paper" exhibits her gynocentric perspective and her belief in the learned nature of gender roles, her own as well as Blackwell's and Addams's disbelief in male dominance as an inevitable evolutionary outcome. Sapiro considers twentieth-century versions of these theories as well; for instance, Peggy Reeves Sanday, in her *Female Power and Male Dominance: On the Origins of Sexual Inequality*, has found that "aggressive subjugation of women must be understood as a part of a people's response to stress" (184), a finding that intrigues, given the social stresses of the postbellum United States. We concluded the class by asking students to write two sentences, one each for "No Name Woman" and "The Yellow Wall-Paper," explaining how each story could exemplify one theory of gender differentiation.

End-of-course evaluations indicated that this role-playing successfully aided students in better understanding the complexities of "The Yellow Wall-Paper": the activity required students to put themselves in the places of people from another era with different experiences. In pairs they endeavored to figure out the pertinent questions to ask of John, the husband and physician, and Jane, his wife and patient, in order to elicit the facts of the patient's case and her physician's treatment, as well as to imagine the experiences those characters undergo. The exercise also provided a concrete context enabling students more easily to appreciate theoretical explanations of the gender differentiation underlying women's oppressed social status.

NOTE

[1]Gilman's three stories are in Knight's Penguin edition of *Herland*.

Teaching "The Yellow Wall-Paper" through French Feminist Literary Criticism

Janet Gabler-Hover

Many students who enter an upper-division undergraduate course in women's literature have already encountered "The Yellow Wall-Paper." They have read the text on the high school or college level as a paradigm for feminism. Usually "The Yellow Wall-Paper" is taught in feminist terms as a pioneering document of feminist resistance. Because of this understandable but limited approach, students observe, somewhat dismissively, that they have read and reread this tale. Likely, such students have been taught to recognize its place in feminist history as Charlotte Perkins Gilman's protest against the infamous infantilizing rest cure administered by Dr. S. Weir Mitchell. However, the text can be deanesthetized and made more exciting and provocative if students read it as problematically feminist, grappling with the endorsement of feminist assumptions relatively unfamiliar to them.

As we know, enthusiastic critics of "The Yellow Wall-Paper" often read the narrator's language—and its extension in the wallpaper—as a metaphor for feminist resistance. In fact, Gilman's story itself anticipates the assumption of several French feminist critics who argue that since language is either masculine or feminine, turning language feminine, or into *l'écriture féminine, is* social action. On invitation, most students respond viscerally to the relative success of the heroine in "The Yellow Wall-Paper" on the basis of their sometimes limited knowledge of the power and nature of language, especially, in this tale, the power of the narrator's unique style of private, nonlinear language as a vehicle of social change for women. Of course, students must also examine and be allowed to judge for themselves whether or not there actually is such a thing as masculine or feminine language. Class discussions can challenge students to become creatively confused and self-reflexive about their critical assumptions. Let me stress that the validity of French theoretical criticism, although ultimately very much on the minds of the students in the course, is never actually the point. Its validity can and should be passionately debated, but the purpose of the debate is to provide students the opportunity to struggle with profound ethical questions that have direct impact on their lives. It should never be about what the teacher thinks—the teacher's thoughts may even fluctuate in response to the relative passion and cogent arguments of vehement students who are on one side or the other of a feminist question in a given semester. What is needed is an environment in which the students can examine their own feminism and discover that they are implicated by feminism whether or not they are aware of it. This awareness in the instance of "The Yellow Wall-Paper" can be experienced through the provocative lens of French feminism and, of course, pragmatic resistance to it. Questions central to French essentialist criticism arise organically out of "The Yellow Wall-Paper" and provide the most relevant theoretical heuristic for a discourse on the nature of the story's feminism.

It will probably help to realize that Hélène Cixous's "The Laugh of the Medusa," which can serve as the illuminating text, is itself a rhetorical strategy based perhaps not so much on her conviction that there is an essentialized feminine language as on her desire to finesse the nullification of female identity by the post-Freudian psycholinguistics of Jacques Lacan. And so what we have is a series of critical hypotheses that critics and students alike seriously engage in, trying them on for size and examining their strengths and weaknesses from the fascinating perspective of how they allow the reader to experience "The Yellow Wall-Paper" problematically.

Especially for the few students who are unfamiliar with the text, it is important to review the historical and protofeminist context of "The Yellow Wall-Paper." The pedagogical challenge is to render accessible fairly sophisticated readings of the relative success of the narrator's textual actions. These include her projected identification with a woman in the wallpaper, her tearing down of the wallpaper to let that woman loose, and her subsequent creeping along the walls of the room in which her husband imprisoned her. A major camp of critics began more sophisticated readings of "The Yellow Wall-Paper" that are explicated well by French theoretical criticism. Elaine Hedges's 1973 Feminist Press edition of "The Yellow Wall-Paper" marked the beginning of a series of laudatory readings of the narrator's final actions as a kind of feminist discourse—in many ways resonant with *l'écriture féminine*—resistant to the confinement of woman's role within the patriarchy (see Hedges, Afterword; Kolodny; Gilbert and Gubar, *Madwoman*; Kennard; Treichler, "Escaping"; Feldstein). But an equally vehement camp of detractors argues the feminist failure of the story's conclusion, reading regression in the narrator's final actions, a dangerous retreat from the sphere of social action (Kasmer; Haney-Peritz; Neely; Ford).

I want students to understand the feminist assumptions behind this debate, first so that they do not become swamped in critics' adversarial arguments without an awareness of what is at stake. Students may not immediately see the connection between Cixous's "The Laugh of the Medusa" and Elaine Hedges's feminist reading, but this is part of the inevitable process of a Socratic approach to philosophical, and in this case specifically feminist, questions. Students must apply themselves to make the connection between theoretical abstractions and concrete explication. But in a more visceral sense again, students are also usually enchanted with Cixous's flowing rhetoric—both male and female students feel empowered—but they are then disorientated and feel slightly defrauded when "The Laugh of the Medusa" meets the conclusion of "The Yellow Wall-Paper."

I like to think that any theoretical approach provides students with a metaphorical entry into a literary text while enriching and deepening the interpretive possibilities. An ambitious theoretical text creates a provocative critical confusion among upper-division undergraduate students, who may feel uncertain about their grasp of its complexities. As I have implied, to launch our discussion of the feminism in "The Yellow Wall-Paper," I use Cixous's "The Laugh of the Medusa," one of the most exciting theoretical texts for students and feminist critics alike. Because of Cixous's exuberant exhortation of an almost pre-Edenically (pre-male) rich woman's language—*l'écriture féminine*—that defies the sterile repressions of a patriarchally linear discourse, her essay is highly adaptive to "The Yellow Wall-Paper," and I assign the two works simultaneously. Students are sometimes confused by the high degree of abstract language, and while they do not usually understand Cixous's attack on patriarchal psycholinguistics, they do sense her celebration of a transformative language tied to near-mystical forces such as "flying colors, leaves, and rivers plunging into the sea" (889).

It is generally necessary to give a concrete form to the students' somewhat fuzzy comprehension of Cixous's *l'écriture féminine* so that they can glean from it how French feminism posits language as social action. My first step in class—after biographical and historical particulars of "The Yellow Wall-Paper" have been competently summarized—is to reorient my students from their focus on plot to the more formal linguistic features of the tale that stir up the feminist controversy. When I point more specifically to the yellow wallpaper as a form of *l'écriture féminine* and ask them to match up Cixous's descriptions to Gilman's textual details, one of the first things they see is the parallel between the lawlessness of the narrator's wallpaper and that of Cixous's woman's writing. In one class, a student suggested that in Cixous, language is supposed "to break up, to destroy" (875) and in Gilman, it is "committing every artistic sin [. . . ,] plung[ing] off at outrageous angles, destroy[ing . . .] in unheard of contradictions" (13). This observation leads to other comparisons: with a pattern to take hold of, students begin to look at finding parallels as a type of treasure hunt. In Gilman the wallpaper is "not arranged on any laws of radiation, or alternation, or repetition, or symmetry, or anything else that I ever heard of [. . . with] bloated curves and flourishes" (20). In Cixous *l'écriture féminine* comes in "waves, these floods, these outbursts" and "her speech, even when 'theoretical' or political, is never simple or linear or 'objectified,'" because "woman unthinks the unifying, regulating history that homogenizes and channels forces, herding contradictions into a single battlefield" (876, 881, 882). In the wallpaper "there is a lack of sequence, a defiance of law, that is a constant irritant to a normal mind" (25). In Cixous "at times it is in the fissure caused by an earthquake, through that radical mutation of things brought on by a material upheaval when every structure is for a moment thrown off balance and an ephemeral wildness sweeps order away" (879).

Patriarchal language is implicitly defined in Cixous as the opposite: linear, sequential, logical, emotionally repressive, and controlling. I summarize these features that the students connect easily to the narrator's husband's language in "The Yellow Wall-Paper," although students can accede to the linearity of the husband's language without a conscious grappling with Cixous's gender essentialism. Because I want students to think about all the premises behind the feminist theory we are discussing, I point out that Cixous is "essentializing" woman's language—that is, she is suggesting that women are naturally more creative and tied to unconscious forces than men. I indicate the debate in feminism about whether gender differences are precultural or socially constructed and why social constructivists find danger in a biological essentialism on which arguments for the inherent inferiority of women (and other minorities) have long been based. Students are sometimes uncertain about how they feel in the face of their endorsement of Cixous's essay, but that's ok; I want to engage them in the paradoxical ambiguities of many feminist questions.

Students need more than an intuitive grasp of Cixous's ambitions in "The Laugh of the Medusa" to gain access to the larger stakes involved in the question of whether or not to endorse her essentialist definition of feminist language as ultimately empowering. Cixous's essay is an all-out frontal assault against the post-Freudian structuralist Jacques Lacan's theoretical distinction between a world of symbolic, explicitly male-empowered language and a regressive (and impotent) imaginary world gendered female by Lacan (see, e.g., "Signification of the Phallus" and "Seminar on the 'Purloined Letter'"). Indeed, the name Jacques Lacan and the psycholinguistic terms *symbolic* and *imaginary* permeate the feminist scholarship on "The Yellow Wall-Paper"— from that of Lisa Kasmer to that of Janice Haney-Peritz to that of Richard Feldstein. Students need an awareness of these terms to tackle both Cixous's abstractions and the specific critical readings of the text. Cixous, then, is not simply provocative but leads directly to a more precise understanding of the battling feminisms involved in specific critical disagreements about the ending of the tale.

Cixous attacks Lacan's theory of the symbolic on the grounds that it is misogynist—she calls it a "phallogocentric sublation" (885) and a "*Penisneid*" (890). Students understand at the outset that the narrator's language in "The Yellow Wall-Paper" is definitely not symbolic, as defined by Lacan, because it remains private from the others in the tale and highly imaginative. As French feminists describe it, Lacan's symbolic order "is a patriarchal order, ruled by the Law of the Father" (Moi 11). To illustrate for the students the crucial distinction between Lacan's imaginary and symbolic, which, by the way, Cixous does not so much dismantle as quite differently evaluate the uses for and deployment of, I write "imaginary" on one side of the board and "symbolic" on the other.

Under the heading of "symbolic," I point out Cixous's obvious antagonism toward Lacan's symbolic, where she writes that "Lacan preserves it [the old Freudian realm] in the sanctuary of the phallus [. . .] 'sheltered' from *castration's lack!* [Men's] 'symbolic' exists, it holds power—we, the sowers of disorder, know it only too well" (884). So "lack" goes under "symbolic"—lack of what, we ask, and we examine that word "castration." The Freudian theory that men fear being castrated by women with penis envy is the referent, I explain, for "lack." Lacan transfers the sexual anxiety Freud hypothesized men have about losing their penis to the social anxiety men have about losing their pen, although the pen is already a symbolic substitution for the penis. The symbolic social language both compensates and substitutes for the male's anxiously feared lost phallus. Language both points to and substitutes for the male's fear of phallic loss: the language act is man's transition to the world of social discourse and action. The unconscious then becomes man's villain; it returns man to a regressive mode of unconscious castration fear that would immobilize him. I explain that for Lacan, women represent lack; it is their lack of a phallus that precipitates the male's fear of losing his own. And for Lacan, the women's realm is that impotent nonsocial sphere of the regressive imaginary where women do not actually even exist because they do not have a phallus.

For critics such as Luce Irigary and Cixous who wish to rescue language for women, the female must try to "disrupt" the symbolic level of language that defines womanhood as "lack" by "let[ting] unconscious forces slip through the symbolic repression, put[ing] her in a position of revolt against this regime" (Moi 11). Important to note here is that French feminists do not lay claim to the symbolic for women; they simply recuperate the unconscious imaginary as the more authentic mode of living and exhort it as a revolutionary mode that would defeat the inauthenticity of the symbolic. This is where the imaginary enters in. If, on the board under "symbolic," I have written "Lacan," "woman as lack = no language," "language = substitution for the phallus," "male language = consciousness," "rational," and "repressive," the first word I write under "imaginary" is "unconscious." What becomes clear from Cixous and *l'écriture féminine* is that while the unconscious is the villain—disabling male power through its message of the fear of castration—it is "home" for women who "return from afar, from always; from 'without,' from the heath where witches are kept alive; from below, from beyond 'culture': from their childhood which men have been trying desperately to make them forget" (877). Cixous argues that the unconscious is the origin of female sexual drives fearfully denied on the level of the patriarchal symbolic. "Women," claims Cixous, "must write through their bodies" (886) to counteract patriarchal obliteration of the desiring female body. To point out how timely the statement is that women must learn to embody themselves in language, one need only refer to such ambitious works as Judith Butler's *Bodies That Matter* or Michael Bennett and Vanessa D. Dickerson's *Recovering the Black Female Body*. For Butler, certainly, as for Cixous, the goal is the recuperation of an obviously erotic "forelanguage" "closest to [. . . the] unconscious," "closest to [. . . sexual] drives" (Cixous 889).

However, the conclusion of "The Yellow Wall-Paper" raises the serious question of how a relatively privatized ebullient language gets translated into social action. Students and critics alike often lament the conclusion of "The Yellow Wall-Paper," even while acknowledging that the eerie image of the heroine ambiguously creeping around the walls of her prison house, apparently mad, can still be read as *l'écriture féminine*. As Karen Ford acerbically notes, "Suicide [or her apparent disintegration at story's end] is not a viable alternative to a fulfilling life" (313). "Fulfilling life" suggests the social (symbolic?) dimension of feminism. It raises the question of what constitutes women's empowerment in a feminist text and also of what is possible: what do we expect a feminist text to do? For critics like Ford, Haney-Peritz, and Kasmer rhapsodic language does not translate into a social discourse that promotes ameliorative action for women in the political world. To embellish this point, I bring in other problematic feminist resolutions by fin de siècle writers such as Kate Chopin and Edith Wharton.

Do I want to resolve this dilemma of less than optimal female resistance in classic nineteenth-century American women's texts? No. I simply want to raise the level of understanding of what can be read positively or negatively in "The Yellow Wall-Paper" in terms of different feminist agendas—and to raise the bar, also, for the entertainment of critical theory in the discussion of much-rehearsed texts. It is fitting that I conclude this paper with the dialectical opposite of a valuation of the heroine's language as power in "The Yellow Wall-Paper" and that my readers know that this perspective is often the one ultimately endorsed by many of my students, although the spectre of *l'écriture féminine* still haunts them. One problem for feminist detractors of *l'écriture féminine* is the seemingly private, onanistic nature of this language; after all, the narrator is *creeping* at the end of "The Yellow Wall-Paper"; her resistance, even if construed as resistance, seems untranslatable in the social world of action.

That argument is condensed in the last three pages of Kasmer's "Charlotte Perkins Gilman's 'The Yellow Wallpaper': A Symptomatic Reading": I summarize these pages in a handout so that students can follow along with the salient points. I keep it to three pages (focusing on pages 11–13) so that students can easily grasp Kasmer's theory. Kasmer expresses both hope and then dismay at how the narrator uses the yellow wallpaper to effect a *conscious* liberation (emphasis added). I quote to the students Kasmer's reference to the wallpaper as something that gives the narrator a message: "Through studying the wallpaper and experiencing this new pattern of thinking, the narrator surmounts her stifling condition." The narrator is able to "deconstruct the false text of contentment she has created so far in her journal" by seeing how the wallpaper analogically represents her own condition of being "unrepresentable" in the patriarchal world of John's discourse (11).

It is important to stress Kasmer's use of the word "symbolic." Ideally, for Kasmer, the narrator is supposed to "grasp this symbolic representation of her true feeling" (11) by rejecting the wallpaper as a real representation of herself. Kasmer laments the narrator's seeing the wallpaper as her "reality," because it "shifts [the narrator] from the symbolic realm to what Lacan calls the imaginary" (12).

Since the class has just considered the imaginary as a celebrated realm of feminine expression that liberates woman's identity, Kasmer's criticism of the imaginary and praise of Lacan's symbolic is a puzzler they must think through in terms of the legitimate grounds for feminist action. They wonder why the narrator's shift to Lacan's symbolic level is so good since Cixous indicts Lacan's symbolic as already owned by the patriarchy. Cixous told us that for Lacan, language is the bridge toward shared social discourse among *men only*, who are the only gender in the particular, inevitable position of lamenting the loss of their phallus (which defines them) through the utterance of language.

Kasmer wants that same level of consciousness that leads to social discourse for the narrator in "The Yellow Wall-Paper." I also quote her comment that by "tearing down the paper, [the narrator] destroys her only access to *symbol*, through which she can *consciously* understand her own thoughts" (12; my emphasis). By this time, students are aware of Cixous's attack on Lacan and the conscious symbolic, so that when Kasmer criticizes the narrator's tearing down the paper, students tend to question Kasmer's use of (implicitly) the Lacanian symbolic as an ideal model for female action. To act in the world, in a Lacanian sense, women would have to repress their unconscious desires—the language of their resistance: *l'écriture féminine*. Or would they? What would a reading look like that "outed" women's sexuality in a warring social context that pits the Lacanian symbolic against a more emotionally rich form of the symbolic?

Kasmer begs the question of how a woman can enter the symbolic realm of the oppressor when the very logic of that realm serves to oppress her. The class ponders what women do to succeed in a man's world and what, if anything, of their feminine (imaginary) creativity and fluidity is given up. (Of course, this same question could be equally applied to men.) This is the question we, as a class, are finally led to in our contentious debate about both the repression and celebration of feminine drives. If, as Cixous suggests, the imaginary realm (the unconscious) is so rich in what it gives women—women's sexual drives, their rich wellspring of imagination—it is nevertheless largely inaccessible on the level of discourse; the wallpaper must be translated out of its primary form of desire into a substitutive lack. Students supply anecdotes about powerful women they know who seem to have become at least the socially constructed definition of men in their repressive stoicism and negating modes of judgment. If men must give up the imaginary (phallus) to gain its pale linguistic complement in the world of social discourse, must women follow a similar logic in order to be social? This is a question our discussion on "The Yellow Wall-Paper" problematically engages.

Teaching *Herland* in Context

Melanie V. Dawson

Students often perceive Gilman's 1915 utopian novel, *Herland*, as fantastic and unrealistic, particularly in the light of the novel's portrayal of parthenogenesis, Gilman's fictional response to the problem of continuing an all-female society and a means of desexualizing motherhood. Radically inventive though some of Gilman's fictive elements of her utopian world may appear, *Herland* is also deeply invested in the social quandaries of Gilman's day. Read as a novel of its time, *Herland* reflects on the author's serious attempts to question and redefine women's roles in twentieth-century America. In the context of controversies over women's roles, as they were being reconsidered during the early decades of the twentieth century and in the fin de siècle years that preceded them, Gilman's novel poses solutions to women's and families' daily dilemmas, dramatizing and narratively expanding on the day-to-day possibilities available to women.

One benefit of invoking the context of Gilman's novel for students stems from the fact that Gilman's text can be a particularly divisive classroom reading, since it yields discussions that clearly align students for or against Gilman's project. What alarms me when I hear students begin to label Gilman's "agenda," often deployed as a particularly dismissive term, is an accompanying tendency to categorize (and thereby reject) Gilman's work in the effort to label it feminist or reactionary. While scholars see the work as inventive, parodic (particularly of adventure stories, as Susan Gubar has noted ["*She* in *Herland*"]) as well as ironic, students may need to be convinced that the text is more than a purely ideological vehicle—a positioning that is something of a struggle in the teaching of many utopian fictions, given their tendency to detail the mechanisms of a new society rather than flesh out individual conflicts between characters.

There are many ways to bring a discussion of the novel's context into the classroom, from accompanying literary and historical texts to be read in concert with Gilman's to background debates and popular images of women from the period (many of which can be found in advertisements from the time and which students tend to be particularly adept at locating and interpreting as a prelude to class discussion). I often ask students to participate in contextualizing projects, some of which may take them to sources from the period, among them periodicals. If these sources are not available, there are a number of studies about turn-of-the-century advertising, including those by T. J. Jackson Lears, Richard Ohmann, and Ellen Garvey, that allow students to locate period images or ad slogans. By looking at images of active young women, for example, we can see that Gilman shared with others in her culture an interest in strong, physically able female bodies, as studies by scholars such as Harvey Green suggest. In *Herland* she depicts a nation of young Amazonian women garbed in tunics and breeches, whose demeanors and abilities are so profound that Van announces, early in the novel, "Nobody will ever believe how they looked" (3). In the popular culture and advertising practices of the 1890s through the 1910s, images of physically robust and active "New Women" abound. From bicyclists (who appear in the advertising pages of the major period magazines such as *Scribner's, Century,* and *McClure's*) to advocates of Delsarte exercise and therapeutic movement (often pictured in etiquette and elocution books) to golfers (in sporting journals such as *Outing Magazine*) to towering, confident, athletic Gibson girls, women in advertisements tend to exert a vigor and vitality that students may find unexpected. Images of women whose confidence combines with an outdoorsmanship suggest an interest in redefining both recreation and body image, although it is clear from many such illustrations that women's femininity was to remain uncompromised by physical activity; it is equally true that, at least in the larger culture, concerns with fashion accompanied the nascence of women's athletic pursuits. Gilman, however, eschewed fashion trends, considering them unnecessarily distracting.

Popular images of active, athletic women also suggest shifting attitudes toward women's place in a developing twentieth-century America. Many depictions of sporting women, for example, portray women in the athletic costumes deemed appropriate to freedom of movement. Rather predictably, women bicyclists often appear in bloomers rather than long skirts. Some images of therapeutic movement and ads for home gymnasium equipment portray women in Grecian costumes, which suggest a freedom from corsets. These images also suggest an aesthetic apologia for exercise itself, particularly in regard to the "natural" Greek woman, with a waistline that would have far exceeded the wasp waist that was popular during the late nineteenth and early twentieth centuries and that was debated among dress reform advocates, particularly B. O. Flower, editor of the reformist magazine the *Arena* (Smith and Dawson 273). Gilman's short-haired, swift Herlanders were created during the decades when dress reform advocates frequently cited the rearrangement of the internal organs necessitated by corsets, the undergarments that created cinched waist styles and that severely impeded the flexibility and lung capacity of the women who donned them. The reformers' most scathing remarks about women's dress also focused on the weight of multiple layers of under and outer garments, which, when trimmed in laces and gathered, pleated, or bustled, could weigh up to twenty pounds.

The realities of reform movements may have a profound impact on the teaching of Gilman because of students' emphasis on the supposed restrictions experienced by turn-of-the-century women. With some consternation, I have heard students assert that women of the early 1900s could not own property (when women could and did) or were denied educations (when in fact women's and coeducational colleges were becoming prominent) or bore dozens of children (when the average family size was rapidly decreasing to an average of 3.56 births by 1900) (Kett 113). When fictions such as Gilman's have the potential to appeal strongly to some students in a class, what can result is a championing of the author's radicalism, along with an exaggeration of oppressive historical situations, which can make an author such as Gilman incomprehensible except as transparently reactionary.

A historicizing of Gilman's involvement in the contestations of her time promises to prevent the exaggerated and reductive histories of oppression that would allow those students to treat Gilman as either far ahead of her time or, alternatively, as wildly out of touch. Instead, stressing Gilman's imaginative responses to very real social quandaries allows for a serious investigation of existing debates about women's gradually evolving social roles, a historicizing which suggests that Gilman, instead of reacting against her time, was deeply invested in accelerating the already ongoing emergence of new roles and goals for women. While women in the 1910s did not possess the right to vote, for example, they were taking an active interest in physical culture. While many chose to marry, thereby attaining social position and material security, many others explored the possibilities of single life and extradomestic employment.

One reason I stress the importance of positioning Gilman as comprehensible in the context of her society lies in students' highly critical attitude toward Gilman's biography, which is discussed in many introductory and prefatory essays, some with the intention of stressing Gilman's radicalism. With the knowledge that Gilman suffered from an illness that remains somewhat controversial and that Gilman not only divorced her husband but also gave up their child for him to raise with his second wife, students inclined to resist Gilman may point to what they see as the apparent hypocrisy that such a woman would elevate motherhood in *Herland*. My attention to the overlap between the novel's most minute details and the ongoing social revisions experienced by early-twentieth-century Americans can challenge the monolithic narratives to which students may cling in their efforts to essentialize the positions of potentially controversial authors. In contrast to the blatant textual politics for which student readers may search, Gilman's attention to the smallest details of dress and movement, for example, illustrates the depth of the text's nuanced arguments about the need for change in every dimension of women's life and experiences.

While arguments about dress reform may suggest obvious parallels in the text, Gilman's position on eugenics may not. As part of *Herland*'s argument for improved family planning and a greater social control, the citizens actively "breed out" undesirable characteristics, among them criminality and the "lowest types" in women, having appealed to these women to renounce motherhood for the social good (83). Even in the planning of forests and with the population of animals, similar impulses to control the physique and characteristics of the society can be seen—interests that were prevalent in the early twentieth century and that were directed toward fears of immigration, resistance to ethnic populations, and an interest in preserving what was broadly termed an Anglo-Saxon heritage. As various scholars have pointed out, Gilman's beliefs were both insular and protectionist, leading her to champion policies that would isolate white Americans from what she saw as an unwelcome infiltration from other races, ethnicities, and nations. This interest in highly controlled populations, moreover, reflects on the impulses that contributed to the nationalism that helped fuel the First and Second World Wars, thereby linking Gilman (albeit problematically) to debates that range beyond the feminism that students may have anticipated. (For investigations of Gilman's stance on racial and ethnic views, see Doskow; Kessler, *Gilman*; Rudd and Gough; and Williams.)

Similarly, the novel's attention to health, fitness, and vitality, like Gilman's interest in vegetarianism, intersects with a broad range of health reform movements, including those pursued by John Harvey Kellogg, cereal maker and heath sanitarium owner. Gilman's interest in such movements, however unfamiliar they may initially be to students, leads back to the novel's emphasis on the subtle gendering of daily life. *Herland*, then, suggests the myriad ways in which changes in the smallest of details had the vast potential to affect wives, mothers, sisters, and daughters. Something as seemingly innocuous as a vegetarian diet (for Herlanders eat mostly nuts and fruits) has the potential to free women from the arduous domestic work of meal preparation. In fact, we see no private kitchens in Herland or women defined as cooks or housekeepers. Because individual dwellings are small and modestly furnished and because meals are prepared elsewhere, homes are easily maintained, thereby requiring no domestic work to speak of. Indeed, there is little personal responsibility attached to living quarters, since the work of the foresters, in particular, requires them to move frequently, thereby countering ideas of domestic pride as well as private ownership itself.

In the light of these debates, students can see that Gilman's portrayal of simplified daily living also builds on late-nineteenth- and early-twentieth-century debates over home design and maintenance. As families shrank in size, the possibilities of work outside the home began to appeal to a range of women, who had the opportunity to become store clerks, office workers, and teachers. As a consequence, smaller, less formal homes became more prevalent by the late nineteenth century; in contrast to the large, ornate rooms typical of large Victorian homes, houses with fewer bedrooms and formal spaces became the trend. Narratively, Gilman accelerates what were, by all accounts, changing attitudes toward domestic space, portraying Herlanders as invested in public, communal spaces rather than private, consumeristic ones. In addition, the Herlanders take great pleasure in public beauty, which they deem more satisfying and more egalitarian than private sumptuousness, and invest their labors in forestry, landscape beautification, and civic architecture rather than individual decors, much as Edward Bellamy's citizens do in his utopian novel *Looking Backward*.

On the basis of this type of domestic history, students recognize that Gilman's portrayal of space is linked to more than women's domestic labors. It also teaches us much about early-twentieth-century attitudes toward domestic servitude, consumer spending, familial comforts, and, especially, class relations. In Herland, there is no servant class, nor is there an inequity between wages for men and women. Rather, the hierarchies that do exist are nonmaterial, being rooted in ability. The elders, as Gilman presents them, are the most honored members of society because of their knowledge and experience rather than their accoutrements or social positions. There are not even "best" mothers, for children are seen as products of the community rather than of an individual child rearing.

Related to the issue of communal contentment is, of course, the issue of family size, which serves as another issue through which students can see Gilman's connection to the broader cultural debates. As a perceptible increase in the middle-class standard of living became associated with smaller families, there was an accompanying interest in birth control—a conversation for which Margaret Sanger, the creator of an organization that evolved into Planned Parenthood, became the public spokeswoman. Sanger's crusade to bring affordable birth control to the masses, a controversial movement of the 1910s, points to a debate over the perceived benefits of controlling reproduction. Whereas Sanger advocated birth control, originally termed "voluntary motherhood," in the interest of women's health and in the management of family resources, Gilman portrays birth control as an issue of practical, civic responsibility. The citizens of Herland, whose primary interest lies in the good of the community, find that they can control parthenogenesis by suppressing the desire for a child, should the needs of the society point to the benefits of lowering the population.

While Sanger's efforts to publicize birth control met with religious as well as male resistance to women's control over reproductive issues, Gilman enters that debate by presenting birth control as a mother's choice—and as a sign of women's commitment to quality of life. Notably, Herlanders do not have to negotiate with either partners or religious institutions (for, indeed, their religion appears as a logical rather than faith-based belief). By eliminating the possibilities of what Gilman had earlier termed "sex distinction" in *Women and*

Economics (40), she creates a unique fictional nation that is populated and governed entirely by a single, genderless sex.

Female governance of civic societies was not an uncommon concern during the turn of the nineteenth century and just beyond—at least on the noncommercial level. With the rise of women's clubs (particularly the Women's Club Movement, which was national in scope), reading groups for women, and growing opportunities for young women to attend colleges and universities (many of which had begun accepting female students in the 1870s and a few of which were solely for women), there was a pronounced interest in the ways affiliated women could enact social change (see Stevenson). Initially met with widespread skepticism, these institutions were generally treated as social clubs rather than serious scholarly arenas. The boom in fiction about college girls, from the late nineteenth century and early decades of the twentieth, sought to familiarize readers with the intricacies of the college experience among women, focusing on the complex social relations and high intellectual standards of the schools (see Marchalonis).

While stressing grace as well as strength, an attractive fearlessness as well as logic, *Herland* exhibits a similar struggle to situate women in control of a specific and specialized social sphere. Gilman's women, much like the college girls of the period's writing, are nonthreatening (they are not violent, self-interested, or vindictive) and, at the same time, appear rightfully empowered (and hence able to govern justly). When the male explorers suppose that they will find women who vainly compete for male attention (as Terry's attempts to entice the women with scarves and jewelry suggest), the novel instead presents a society of women who remain uncompromised by individual interests and whose commitment to their social system reflects the strength of their social institutions, particularly their education and government.

Through classroom discussions of the various movements focused on women's societies, domestic space, birth control, and physical health, students realize that Gilman's interest in portraying social reforms was shared and, indeed, preceded by a number of fin de siècle and early-twentieth-century authors, whose texts also investigated women's means of reinventing their lives. One such text to teach as a complement to Gilman's novel is Mary Wilkins Freeman's 1891 short story "The Revolt of 'Mother.'" Connecting the difficulties of reenvisioning women's roles as involving issues of domestic space and familial authority, the story charts a wife's frustration with her home (and her control over that domestic space) and culminates in her attempt to colonize the family's new barn, which, in the absence of her spouse, is remade into a dwelling. Sarah Penn, the protagonist, is long-suffering in her domestic labors; as she remakes her life by appropriating new spaces, Sarah is compared to a pioneering Puritan forefather who breaks new ground, even while the text details the consternation and amazement of all on-lookers. Similarly, Gilman's uncle Edward Everett Hale's short story "Susan's Escort" (1890) records the frustrated efforts of a single young woman who attempts to make the most of the cultural offerings in Boston, despite the absence of a male escort. Like Freeman, Hale records the obstacles facing an adventurous woman—here, the culture-loving Susan: the Boston streets can be lonely at night, and their inhabitants (particularly the drunken ones) are daunting to women who venture out alone. Susan's response to her plight is to create an escort from an old umbrella and some men's clothing. For a time, this fanciful solution is ideal; unlike a real escort, Susan's creation amiably attends without complaint all the offerings that interest Susan. As representative short stories of the turn of the century, Freeman's and Hale's chart the moments when women attempt to control their worlds, but they also record the tensions encountered by women reaching for unexpected and creative solutions to existing dilemmas. We can interpret the narrativizing of such solutions as an effort to highlight the silly everyday restrictions with which women lived and the absurd situations necessitating responses that would otherwise appear extreme (as with Freeman's Sarah) or ridiculous (as with Hale's Susan).

As these stories reveal, the tensions of rewriting women's traditional domestic roles permeate the fictions of the late nineteenth and early twentieth centuries, with narratives carefully charting both provocations and solutions. The fissures between one type of long-suffering feminine characterization and a solution-oriented, self-actualized one are particularly visible as Foucauldian fault lines, which are frequently expressed in a single work, where the expectations of characters (or even authors) are revised substantively over the course of the text. In the above fictions, for example, both "Mother" and Susan remake their lives, shocking the people who know them. A slightly different revision is visible in the collaborative novel *The Whole Family* (1907–08), to which figures such as William Dean Howells, Henry James, Mary E. Wilkins Freeman, and Elizabeth Stuart Phelps contributed; the first two chapters make a compelling companion to Gilman's novel. Originally proposed and outlined by Howells, who wrote the initial chapter, the novel was to stand as a realistic romance, detailing the ways that the engagement of a young woman affected her extended family. It was Howells who set out a fairly staid, if somewhat predictable, cast of characters, which included the young couple, parents, and an "old maid" aunt, who was to become the figure at the center of controversies surrounding the novel. Freeman, who was to take on the novel's second chapter, narrated from the stance of the aunt, radically rewrote Howells's vision by reconceptualizing the retiring spinster sketched by Howells and substituting a slim, fashionable, self-actualized, athletic, vibrantly attractive sexual woman, who outshone the newly engaged niece. More extreme yet was Freeman's contention that the aunt had previously engaged in a dalliance with the younger man who was the niece's fiancé and that he was still infatuated with the aunt. Portraying a female character whose relative youth, vitality, and canny judgments challenged old-time patriarchal relations, Freeman's work was roundly criticized by Howells, along with Mark Twain (a potential contributor when he read Freeman's chapter). Literary history rarely marks the dissonances between traditional women's roles and the challenges to them as completely as this project does, with its multiple and competing visions of what counted as a realistic vision of society; the project as a whole, however, demonstrates one example of the tensions involved in remaking roles for turn-of-the-century American women.

As the women characters in turn-of-the-century literature negotiate the minutiae of their lives; deal with controlling husbands or anxious suitors; overcome limited access to cultural opportunities; and handle unrealistic expectations of domestic contentment, they highlight the myriad nagging difficulties of women who attempt to take charge of their destinies in new and often startling ways. Gilman, by contrast, rids her fictive world of the limitations facing other women characters of the same era, whose husbands, lovers, and family members insist on their maintaining "womanly" roles and whose innovations are positioned as "abnormal," uncomfortable, or merely cause for amusement. Tellingly, Freeman rewrote traditional characterizations of women in her section of the novel. Comparing the two works, students come to see that Gilman's novel also reveals the mechanisms of cultural revision, primarily concerning the expectations voiced by her narrators, who gradually comprehend the degree to which Herland's women have reinvented formulations of modern womanhood. Hence Terry, Jeff, and, most of all, Van are forced to reassess their conceptions of womanhood—moving from the expectation of discovering (or, indeed, creating) domestic caretakers to the recognition that the women of Herland cannot even comprehend the nuances of the term *domestic*. Thus the conceptual revisions, along with the humor of the text, indicate the ways in which the male explorers need to adjust to a progressive society, rather than detail the ways that women readjust their roles within existing social frameworks. While Freeman's "Mother" and "old maid aunt" and Hale's Susan are the source of the humor in those texts, Gilman's wit is directed toward the fallible men, thereby showcasing the absolute logic of the women's behaviors.

Gilman places the necessity for revising cultural expectations on the society rather than the individual. Having anticipated a nation governed by feminine vanity, "given over to [. . .] 'frills and furbelows,'" "pettiness," "jealousy," and "hysteria," the men discover what Van terms "daring social inventiveness," "broad sisterly affection," "fair-minded intelligence," and a "calmness of temper"—qualities so unexpected that Terry deems them "deuced unnatural" (82). Nor is there "modesty," "patience," or "submissiveness," or "that natural yielding" that Terry associates with womanliness (99). In fact, there is no "womanly" behavior or any accompanying comprehension that there are social or maternal "duties" associated with being a woman (98).

By attending to the ways that gendered expectations affect a range of social relations, Gilman rewrites the conventions of fiction. As I discuss with my students, she broadens what is realistic or possible in the interest—as she termed it in *The Man-Made World*—of composing a "broader, truer fiction" (122). Contending that "[f]iction, under our androcentric culture, has not given any true picture of woman's life, very little of human life, and a disproportionate section of man's life," Gilman sought to render her utopian novel broader and truer by incorporating period debates, arranging them around the contested issues of women's lives, and challenging readers through the text's many and often subtle details about the necessity for social change (122). Teaching *Herland* in context allows students to see the novel and its writer not as radical anomalies but as very much invested in ongoing cultural debates.

This Land Is *Herland*, This Land Is Our Land? Teaching *Herland* in a Course on Community and Identity in American Literature

Wendy Ripley

"How boring to live in Gilman's imagined world. Everyone dresses the same, looks the same—there's no individuality. And besides," she continued, "I like men." These words, spoken by a student at the beginning of our class discussion of *Herland*, reflect a common initial response to the text. But when I ask for a show of hands of who is not wearing something from the Gap, Nike, or Old Navy and prompt students to see the results, they start to wonder. Do they really have as much choice in deciding who they are as they had thought? Taught in the context of an undergraduate American literature survey course, the book is one of a series of texts that challenge students to explore the role communities have in shaping, influencing, and creating American identities. In particular, the course traces how American cultural ideas about race, gender, and class are constructed and enforced. Teaching *Herland* gets students thinking about their experiences with communities, and after a close reading and extensive discussion of the book, I ask students to create their own ideal communities.

I often teach *Herland* in the context of ten other texts that examine the role of community and identity in American culture. To help students develop critical skills for examining their culture, we start by critiquing worlds that are not their own—those found in the utopian novel. Students first read Edward Bellamy's *Looking Backward* and compare how their experience at the beginning of the twenty-first century aligns with Bellamy's predictions. At the outset, I also present an overview of utopian writing in America.

The class turns next to personal and popular conceptions of utopias. Students contemplate their individual ideas of a perfect world and draw pictures of their visions. We look at film clips of ideas of utopias, such as the Emerald City in *The Wizard of Oz*, and, for contrast, utopian worlds gone wrong, such as the dystopian works *The Handmaid's Tale*, *The Matrix*, or *Gattaca*. One student brought to class a videocassette of *Pink Floyd: The Wall* to illustrate students challenging the idea of a perfect world created by teachers. We also discuss current utopian ideas, such as simplicity movements, communes, home schooling, and militia groups. Students especially enjoy a visit to and tour of a nearby commune whose purpose is to create a more perfect world, separate from society. Here buildings are named after famous utopian worlds—including the main community building, which is called the Emerald City.

In the first week of class, we investigate the actual communities in which we live, work, and study. Students perform community inventories, taking stock of the communities they belong to and evaluating how decisions were made to join certain groups. We examine any differences in our attitudes toward groups we choose and those to which we are assigned. Then, we wonder, how do these communities function in our lives? How do they define our individual success? Students this semester were surprised to learn that they feel more strongly obligated and affected by communities they had no choice in joining (e.g., families, race, nationality, gender) and that these involuntary groups have the most power in shaping their identities. But one student wrote, "I thought I had more control over the person I become, but I'm amazed to see how much influence the groups I have joined by chance have on my ideas of success."

As preparation for reading *Herland*, I provide students with prereading questions to facilitate a more active reading of the text. The questions require students to perform a variety of tasks, including the following: to look up the term *utopian fiction* in a literary handbook and keep track of which conventions of this genre Gilman uses and which ones she subverts; to think about who Gilman's audience is and why Vandyck is chosen to tell the story of this all-female utopia; and to compare Gilman's constructed land with the one they have just read about: Bellamy's futuristic Boston. In addition, before students read, they write descriptive paragraphs on two or three words they choose from a list, all of which are associated with social roles. The list includes the terms *marriage, home, love, sex, motherhood, wife, husband, friendship, feminine, masculine,* and *parent.* After reading the text, they compare their ideas about these labels with what Gilman presents in her novel.

Equipped with historical literacy and lexical context, along with questions that guide both critical thinking and literary exploration, students come to class eager to talk about what they have read. Led by two students who have the freedom to guide the in-class conversation, the discussion of *Herland*, of course, varies. Inevitably, however, the perception of Herland's culture as controlling, static, and unnatural surfaces. Ideas about gender are an easy place for students to connect with Gilman, and they often begin discussion with insightful and frank observations and disagreements with one another about how their roles as sexual beings are defined. Sometimes they realize how much they have been, in one student's language, "programmed" to meet the expectations of gender set out by their communities. They remember being told by family members to "act more like a lady" or "take it like a man." They enjoy seeing these expectations through the eyes of Gilman's three visitors and are amused by comments such as Jeffrey's "If their hair was only long [. . .] they would look so much more feminine" (32). Or Terry's statement "Women like to be run after" (19). It is fairly easy for students to nod in agreement with Gilman when she exposes the arbitrariness of the physical limitations placed on women, with stereotypes such as women cannot work as hard or that women must dress in certain ways. What is more difficult for students to unravel is what constitutes true feminine and masculine nature.

Much of this discussion about "nature" has a starting point in students' being disturbed by what they see as an absence of sexuality in Herland's women. They are troubled by Van's statement that "[t]here was no sex-feeling to appeal to, or practically none. Two thousand years' disuse had left very little of the instinct" (92–93). They label unnatural Van's and Jeff's resignation to a sexless marriage and Van's admission that "these women were not provocative" (127). As young adults very much occupied with exploring and defining their sexual selves, a lack of sexuality is not part of their utopian vision. In a typical class, several male students defend Terry's expectations in his relationship with Alima. One student usually argues that even though Terry is presented as impatient, roguish, and chauvinistic, he is the most authentic character in the book, acting out his true nature, rather than surrendering it as Jeff does or compromising it as does Van. Inevitably, however, students do recognize that masculinity and femininity in our culture are linked to sexuality, though this link is distinctly severed in their Herland definition. They realize that "male-man," "female-woman" can be understood as biologically sexual markers or as formalized gender roles and expectations and that these roles are heavily constructed by cultural communities.

Though often hesitant at first, students begin to reveal their own assumptions about what girls and boys are really like. When one student admitted that he thought women were, in fact, more emotional by nature than men and that like the interlopers, he expected a woman-only land to be marked by hysteria and confusion, another class member quietly inquired whether he had ever seen men at a football game. Gradually the class came to the conclusion that definitions of emotion have been restricted to only certain kinds of feelings, such as sensitivity or sadness, and then assigned to women. In contrast, emotions such as anger, aggressiveness, and enthusiasm are not typically considered emotions at all, but a natural part of being a man. One student cited as evidence for this division of masculine and feminine traits Van's conclusion that "those 'feminine charms' we are so fond of are not feminine at all, but mere reflected masculinity—developed to please us because they had to please us" (60). This is not to suggest that all students agreed with this position. Throughout the discussion of the text there continued to be vigorous debate about the extent to which gender roles are determined by biology or culture.

Another point of resistance to Gilman's community is what students read as a lack of freedom and choice. Their objections range from fashion and clothing choices ("What if a woman wanted to wear her hair long or put on something tight and clingy?") to career choices to parenthood choices, the fact that not all women in Herland can decide for themselves to have children. This perceived lack of choices is perhaps where students most keenly discern a threat to what they think of as the essence of their individuality. They argue that what they choose to wear; how they color, cut, and comb their hair; the design and application of their make-up; and their jewelry choices are all an expression of who they are. In addition, they think they should have the right to try any career, even if they don't have the aptitude or nature for it, and that they have the right to fail at any occupation, including parenthood, if they choose.

But when pushed to examine the similarity of what they all are wearing, including hairstyles, they start to wonder. Sure, in theory they could shave their heads and wear anything they want, but they tend to look remarkably alike despite so much choice. Similarly, when thinking about their academic majors, they admit that they could take art or drama or environmental studies (and some students are enrolled in such programs), but a majority of the class stated that their prelaw, business, or premed major is in large part shaped by pressure and influence from family members who expect them to be successful. In addition, their professional choices are influenced by a culture that sets up a hierarchy of careers, where being a medical doctor is more important than being a trash collector. Their idea of some work being more prestigious and important than others is, in fact, one of the difficult issues the class struggled with in Bellamy's utopia, where everyone, in every profession, is paid the same. It is hard for students to accept this leveling of the professions from their cultural context, which so clearly establishes only one ladder of success.

Perhaps because I teach in a college where only one-third of the students consider themselves Caucasian and where there are students from forty-seven countries outside the United States, discussion may contain more objections than usual to Gilman's emphasis on specifically Aryan women. The students are challenged by not seeing themselves reflected or represented in her utopia. In addition, they criticize Gilman for simplifying the idea of world harmony, arguing that it is too easy to conceive of people getting along beautifully together if there are no racial or cultural differences. "How easy to have a perfect world when everyone in it is exactly like you," one student observed in her written response to the text. Students also point to this ethnic homogeneity as adding to a static and dull world. They often agree with Terry when he says, "Life is a struggle, has to be [. . .]. If there is no struggle, there is no life—that's all" (100). Part of what makes life interesting and helps define individuality, they argue, is being in conflict with communities who have contrasting ideas, cultures, and customs.

The concept of a variety of cultures attempting to coexist surfaces in the discussion of the consequences to people who are different from the mainstream or who decide to deviate from the rules of social conduct. We compare these rules with the rules, and the consequences of breaking them, in *Herland*. Students often cite high school as a subcommunity where social rules are rigidly enforced. In this world, students who challenge rules established by adults are usually separated in detention, special classes, or, in extreme cases, expelled from school. Also, if teenagers do not follow the accepted social rules, they are rarely admitted into peer groups or invited to social events. Society at large works this way as well, students decide. It is difficult for a person to get a job in business without wearing the uniform of a suit. And the citizen who breaks a major rule can be imprisoned. They see the same principles at work in Herland, from which Terry is expelled for not respecting Alima's marital boundaries. Exporting offenders such as Terry, students note, seems an easy and unrealistic way to deal with crime, however. In all discussions, to continually emphasize accurate comparisons between Herland and their land, I urge students to work toward basing their ideas about their world on cultural evidence and their ideas about the text on textual evidence.

After reading Bellamy and Gilman, students write their own utopian fiction. This assignment gives them a chance both to address issues they think are missing in either text and to engage in a conversation about community and identity with these authors while creating their own perfect worlds. They read these pieces to the class to continue the discussion of the influence of the group on the individual. Even though many students object to the agrarian setting of Herland, arguing that they would be bored "stuck way out in the country without a city nearby," many of their own visions of a perfect world follow this utopian convention. These fantasy worlds are often set on tropical islands with roaring waterfalls and perfectly ripening fruit. Some are fiercely private utopias set in the mountains with only close friends and family nearby. Many students focus on specific aspects of social change such as educational reform and social welfare. And a few students write dystopias, stating that they find the uncertainty and imperfection of these worlds more appealing than the unchanging happily-ever-after of an invented paradise.

The power of *Herland* in this class comes not just through reading the book itself but also through reading it in the context of the authors that precede and follow it. Gilman's text becomes a touchstone, informing our reading about community and identity throughout the semester. Her observations and analysis help students realize, through subsequent texts in the class, how the decisions of others can affect a person's life in crucial ways—for example, decide whether a person is "American" enough (as in Abraham Cahan's *Yekl* or Willa Cather's *My Antonia*) or whether a person can move into the middle class instead of being held back by invisible social forces (as with the Holbrood family in Tillie Olsen's *Yonnondio*) or whether a person is black or white rather than biracial (as in Nella Larsen's novels). Through reading and interacting with *Herland*, students ultimately gain a much clearer awareness of the constructions of their own land and their place in it.

Confronting Issues of Race, Class, and Ethnicity in *Herland*

Lisa Ganobcsik-Williams

Charlotte Perkins Gilman was widely recognized as a feminist and social theorist during her lifetime and, more recently, in 1994, was honored by being inducted into the National Women's Hall of Fame ("Gilman Inducted"). As feminist scholars have begun to read an increasingly broad range of Gilman's writings, however, we find ourselves facing ethical problems posed by her treatment of race and ethnicity. The difficulties are even more pointed when we attempt to teach, for at the same time that we celebrate Gilman's contribution to feminist utopian thought, we have a responsibility to address the racist and ethnocentric tendency in her work. We can expect that students, perhaps encountering her 1915 novel *Herland* as part of an undergraduate literature or women's studies course, will be sensitive to and even turned off by Gilman's problematic views on race and ethnicity that are clearly manifested in the narrative. In my experience in teaching the novel, students object in particular to the need for Herlanders to have descended from "Aryan stock" in order to be capable of creating a perfect society and to the notion that this society's success rests on the homogeneity and common lineage of its population (55, 76). Students also question the Herlanders' use of selective breeding, with its classifications of "fit" and "unfit," and detect elements of prescriptivism and conformity in the Herland brand of "education for citizenship" (69–71, 76–84, 106–08). In a post-Holocaust world, such descriptions are rightly suspect. It would be unfortunate, however, for students, scholars, and teachers to dismiss Gilman's achievements because of her prejudices. On the other hand, glossing over the difficulties in her writings also does a disservice to the complexity and insight of Gilman's thought.

It is inadequate to argue that Gilman's beliefs were simply symptomatic of the racism and ethnocentrism that pervaded early-twentieth-century American public discourse. Not only does this suggest that Gilman could not think outside the prevailing assumptions of her time, but it falsely implies that there was a lack of debate on racial and cultural issues during this period. A more productive approach is to encourage students to explore Gilman's cultural biases alongside her vision for improving society. Gilman's wide-ranging worldview, which she called humanism, sought to accelerate the progress of all races and nations. As I demonstrate, however, Gilman's use of social scientific concepts and language to express this vision allowed her to evaluate other races and cultures by drawing on criteria specific to her own position as a white American.

One way to stimulate students to consider Gilman's biases in relation to her human vision is to teach *Herland* in conjunction with the 1916 sequel, *With Her in Ourland*. Although students should read *With Her in Ourland* in its entirety, teachers may wish to focus discussions of Gilman's biases on passages from chapters 2 and 3, which detail Van and Ellador's tour of European and Asian countries; chapters 4 and 6, which deal with the treatment of people of nonwhite races and immigrants by and within the United States; and chapter 10, which confronts issues of race and religion in the United States. I suggest teaching the novels in tandem because *With Her in Ourland* provides, as part of its own narrative, a retrospective metacommentary on the first novel and demonstrates that Gilman herself recognized potential limitations in the homogeneity of the social vision that *Herland* outlines.

With Her in Ourland moves Gilman's model of a feminist democracy from Herland to test its applicability in what she portrays as the wider world of the early twentieth century. In *With Her in Ourland*, Van returns to the "Real World" with his Herland wife, Ellador (271), who is eager to gauge to what extent the principles of community welfare with which she is familiar have been integrated into societies made up of both women and men (271). What she discovers as the pair travel around the United States and the world is the degree to which these societies are also racially and ethnically diverse, and much of the book becomes a discussion between Ellador and Van about the complexities this cultural diversity adds to social relations and the formation of public policies. Reading *Herland* in conjunction with its sequel illuminates for students Gilman's broader vision: the progress of the human race as a whole toward participatory, egalitarian forms of governing society. In doing so, *With Her in Ourland* demonstrates Gilman's recognition that to be effective in public policy making, feminism, as the driving factor in this humanist vision, must attempt to take into account other factors such as ethnicity and race.

Despite these laudable aims, *With Her in Ourland* is a difficult book to teach. As well as being didactic, it is dense, because Gilman uses it to raise all her various criticisms of American society, including domestic oppression, religious patriarchy, and monopoly capitalism. Gilman confronts with candor topics including American slavery and imperialism, as well as the genocide practiced by the United States government against Native Americans (303, 307, 322). Though Gilman makes an effort to provide a balanced treatment of race and ethnicity when discussing these issues, she tends to employ language that Ellador speculates readers of the period may find "too abusive" and that is certain to offend most readers today (377).

I recommend teaching *With Her in Ourland* with attention to the use of social scientific concepts and vocabulary. I point out to students that, as a relative of a prominent nineteenth-century family of preachers and social reformers, the Beechers, Gilman was convinced from an early age that it was her duty—and her right—to help humanity "improve" (Gilman, *Living* 70). She saw that the way to make herself credible as an intellectual was not through preaching in the traditional way, however, but through adopting the language and ways of reasoning that would serve as currency in her era.

Like many reformers at the beginning of the twentieth century, Gilman was drawn to the conceptual framework of social science. I suggest giving students two short pieces of background reading—"Revisiting the Optimism of the Progressive Era," in Polly Wynn Allen's book on Gilman, and Lois N. Magner's article "Darwinism and the Woman Question: The Evolving Views of Charlotte Perkins Gilman"—to help them understand, in ways that apply to Gilman, the intersections of science and social science at the end of the nineteenth and beginning of the twentieth century. As Allen explains, the theory of evolution made popular by Charles Darwin in the mid-nineteenth century inspired many social thinkers of Gilman's day with a sense of optimism that, both biologically and socially, humanity was and had always been evolving in a progressive direction (26). Gilman assumed, as many of her contemporaries did, that evolution necessarily meant progress, and she agreed with the social Darwinist Herbert Spencer's theory that evolution progresses "according to natural laws of organization from unstable and homogeneous forms to complex, differentiated, and heterogeneous forms" (Magner 122). Gilman modeled her concept of social evolution on biological theories to argue that women could speed up their own progress toward attaining the civic and social rights that many (white American) men already enjoyed, including the right to pursue education and a career and the right to participate in public decision making. As Magner notes, Gilman was an interpreter and popularizer of scientific ideas "in an era when evolutionary theory was applied to virtually every facet of the human condition" (116).

It is important to recognize, too, that Gilman was a reformer who was trying to effect social and political change. By utilizing scientific language and concepts, Gilman aimed to make her writing "specific enough" to convince her audience, whom she perceived to be not the "average reader" but "the reform devotee" ("Summary" 287). *Herland* and *With Her in Ourland* were originally printed in the *Forerunner*, the journal that Gilman wrote, edited, and published monthly from 1909 through 1916. The *Forerunner* served as a public forum for Gilman's writing that was uncritiqued and uncensored by editors and that allowed her "the serene freedom of expression indispensable to right work" (287). The *Forerunner's* audience consisted of women and men who considered themselves enlightened in some way, whether through feminism, socialism, or general progressivism. To help think about Gilman's audience for *Herland* and *With Her in Ourland*, and thus the reasons for the types of appeals she launches, students may wish to examine her statement of purpose when inaugurating the *Forerunner* ("As to Purposes") and the article entitled "A Summary of Purpose" that appears in its penultimate issue. In particular they should consider Gilman's own observation about audience, set out in the 1916 *Forerunner* edition in which *With Her in Ourland* was serialized: "The variety, the breadth, the depth of social alteration suggested in *The Forerunner* inevitably narrow the circle of readers. Those agreeing on some counts *violently disagree* on others . . ." ("Summary" 287; my emphasis). This remark demonstrates that Gilman was aware of her readership and anticipated that her ideas would provoke controversy.

The following passage from *Herland* serves as an example of one troubling issue the novel raises for students. In speaking of the Herlanders' origins, Van notes:

> [T]here is no doubt in my mind that these people were of Aryan stock, and were once in contact with the best civilization of the old world. They were "white," but somewhat darker than our northern races because of their constant exposure to sun and air.   (55)

To better understand why Gilman specifies the Herlanders' racial and cultural origins, my students and I attempt to formulate a close reading of Gilman's logic for ranking racial and ethnic groups on the basis of their supposed readiness to participate as citizens. The following paragraphs outline one possible way to carry out this reading and, in doing so, substantiate how *With Her in Ourland* can help to explain—or at least to explore in more depth—implications about race and ethnicity that are raised but not discussed in *Herland*. This reading can also be used to show how Gilman's choice of scientific discourse enabled her to categorize racial and national development.

Van follows up the comment about Aryan civilization in *Herland* by comparing the Herlanders' highly developed minds with those of Plato, Aristotle, and the collective mentality of ancient Greece (86). On the strength of Van's two comments, readers are led to believe that the early civilization from which the Herlanders emerged was a classical one. *With Her in Ourland* emphasizes more specifically how classical civilizations grew and influenced the rest of the world and provides clues, based on Gilman's social evolutionary theory, about why an experimental system of government, such as Herland's, could best be developed by white women (292).

"Being women," Ellador tells Van in *With Her in Ourland*, "we had all the constructive and organizing tendencies of motherhood to urge us on and, having no men, we missed all that greediness and quarreling your history is so sadly full of" (383). The government that women have created in Herland, Ellador points out, is an example of a perfectly run political democracy. Ellador's definition of democracy, which she derives from her experience as a Herland citizen, is "[j]ust people co-operating to govern themselves [. . . to] manage their common interests" (326–27). As implied throughout *Herland* and theorized in *With Her in Ourland*, men historically have been less socially evolved than women in the capabilities needed for running a democracy, because of their natural instincts for "greed and sheer love of adventure and fighting" (272). Conversely, women have evolved as being well suited to carrying out democratic principles, because their mothering instincts make it natural for them to think in terms of the welfare of others.

This analysis of gendered predispositions, while providing an opportunity for students to discuss the problematic nature of Gilman's gender essentialism, makes clear why Gilman thought women were more suited than men were to creating or reformulating public-policy-making systems. Gilman's reasoning on the suitability of various racial and ethnic groups for civic participation is more complicated and less palatable. Because most students see Gilman's racial and ethnic biases as obvious and offensive, however, they generally are more prepared to engage in classroom debate about them than they are about Gilman's reasoning on gender.

In *With Her in Ourland*, Ellador claims that all races and nations are in the process of evolving toward improved principles of social organization, but each is at a different stage of development (323). Ellador learns that although Mediterranean and Asian societies were the most intellectually and technologically advanced peoples for thousands of years, Asian women have been held back from developing as a result of gender oppression (291–92, 297–99). This reasoning, as theorized in *With Her in Ourland*, may "justify" why the women of Herland necessarily would have descended from classical (white) Mediterranean rather than Asian or other supposedly less feministically developed societies.

At this point, students are often interested in taking our analysis of gender, race, and ethnicity further, to scrutinize Gilman's conclusion in *With Her in Ourland*. Gilman implies that one outcome of Ellador and Van's visit to the world and subsequent return to Herland is that Herlander "missionaries" will soon join with a contingency of advanced, socially conscious American women to initiate "a glorious time" of "cleaning up the world!" (381, 386). My students and I begin our examination by looking again at Gilman's social evolutionary stratifications. By the time of his and Ellador's trip to China and other Asian countries during World War I, Van notes, the Asian nations have become "static" under the weight of tradition (296). The progress of European nations has also been checked because of a regressive combative ethos that has broken out into war (314). In the United States, Ellador explains, the white race dominates the black race because when blacks were enslaved, they were already at a low stage of intellectual and social development, and whites arrested this development through slavery (356–59). White Americans are generally superior in reasoning capabilities than most immigrants, too, Ellador surmises, because immigrants tend to arrive seeking asylum from the most undeveloped areas of other nations: "the poor and oppressed were not necessarily good stuff for a democracy" (321).

Given this view of Asian and European societies and despite the allegedly insufficient intellectual development of America's racial and cultural others, Ellador argues that the United States is the best place for a model of true democracy, incorporating both female and male citizens, to evolve: "This is the top of the tree [. . .] this is the last young nation, beginning over again in a New World—a New World! [. . .] Oh, surely, surely, surely this should be the Crown of the World!" (314). Since women have been excluded from participating in the nation's political inception and growth, however, American democracy has not worked as well as it should. Masculine models of government historically have been founded on patriarchal power hierarchies: "Kings and Fathers, Bosses, Rulers, Masters, Overlords—it is all such poor preparation for a democracy" (331). An authentic democracy, Ellador contends, "means the people socially conscious and doing it themselves—doing it *themselves*! Not just electing a Ruler and subordinates and submitting to them—transferring the divine right of kings to the divine right of alderman or senators" (325).

Ellador argues that within the United States, groups of progressive, thinking women exist, women who are part of the Women's Club movement, church groups, and other forums (317). Ellador's recommendation is that these women, whose minds have been broadened beyond their individual families to care for community issues, need to enter the nation's political sphere. Thus a contingency of (white) American women are ready for citizenship because many of them have already begun to evolve as cooperative rather than combative or individualistic beings. As we have seen, however, in *With Her in Ourland* the framework of conscious evolution that so successfully empowered the Herland women and that Ellador says has the potential to empower white American women proves at the same time to be a convenient way for Gilman to justify postponing the integration of people from other marginalized positions, such as African Americans and immigrants, into the American sphere of public debate.

Despite her convictions about race and ethnic stratification that surface in *Herland* and *With Her in Ourland*, students should realize that Gilman's conception of social evolutionary progress was essentially optimistic. Even within a vision tainted by the prejudiced view that other races and nationalities are generally at lower stages of development than white Americans, Gilman consistently saw education and the development of social consciousness as keys to progress. This optimistic way of looking at human nature differed profoundly from the view of Herbert Spencer, who believed in a negative vision of the fittest individuals struggling against the elements and against one another to survive. As Magner notes, whereas Gilman was convinced that the entire social organism had potential to evolve, "within Spencer's system the individual units of the social organism owed nothing to each other or to the whole" (122).

What I try to get students to think about as we analyze specific passages in *Herland* and *With Her in Ourland* is that, through her writing, Gilman was trying to gain cultural authority: as a woman she wanted to fashion for herself the role of public intellectual, and this objective, she believed, required her to adopt the increasingly respected discourse of social science. I encourage students to discuss the ways in which so-called scientific concepts—such as the preoccupation with natural laws, social progress, and race stratification, as well as with categorizing peoples and behaviors and ranking the progress of races and nations—are manifested in both novels. Gilman's use of rational dialogue and the valorization of logic and reason over emotional appeals are also features I ask students to consider.

Focusing on social scientific discourse teaches students to see Gilman as a systematic thinker, and this is important because even in her imaginative writing, Gilman is primarily a social theorist and reform activist. Analyzing Gilman's use of social science also reveals the extent to which the threads of her social thought are inextricably linked, for the same discourse that empowers her utopian feminism and her humanist vision expresses her racist and ethnocentric views. By following the strands of her social scientific thinking in two novels, we can see both aspects of Gilman, while also recognizing that she occasionally modified or reformulated her ideas in ways in which we would expect from a complex and powerful intellectual.

By examining the persuasive techniques of *Herland* and *With Her in Ourland*, students can move beyond recognizing Gilman's prejudices and explore questions that are as relevant today as they were in Gilman's time: How can lay people intervene in the discourses through which public policy is made? How can one gain access to public and academic cultures of expertise? And perhaps most important, how can those interested in influencing social policy or changing the world promote agendas that are at once ethical *and* inclusive?

The Intellectual Context of *Herland*:
The Social Theories of Lester Ward

Gary Scharnhorst

Whatever else may be said of her, Charlotte Perkins Gilman was emphatically not a social Darwinist in the normal sense of that phrase. Those who paraded under the social Darwinian banner—that is, those who applied Darwin's biological theories of natural selection to models of social organization—argued by analogy that just as the fittest of each species in nature struggles for existence by adapting to its natural environment, the fittest human competitors best adapt to social conditions and accumulate wealth or honor and prestige. In varying degrees, they embraced the dogma of determinism implicit in this conservative brand of social philosophy. To illustrate these ideas, I often share with my students the following allegorical poem by Stephen Crane:

> The trees in the garden rained flowers.
> Children ran there joyously.
> They gathered the flowers
> Each to himself.
> Now there were some
> Who gathered great heaps—
> Having opportunity and skill—
> Until, behold, only chance blossoms
> Remained for the feeble.
> Then a little spindling tutor
> Ran importantly to the father, crying:
> "Pray, come hither!
> See this unjust thing in your garden!"
> But when the father had surveyed,
> He admonished the tutor:
> "Not so, small sage!
> This thing is just.
> For, look you,
> Are not they who possess the flowers
> Stronger, bolder, shrewder
> Than they who have none?
> Why should the strong—
> The beautiful strong—
> Why should they not have the flowers?"
> Upon reflection, the tutor bowed to the ground,
> "My Lord," he said,
> "The stars are displaced
> By this towering wisdom."   (1337–38)

Following Darwin's lead, moreover, social Darwinists often presumed that males of each species, including homo sapiens, exercise the prerogative of sexual selection. As Darwin had claimed, "Man is more powerful in body and mind than woman," so "it is not surprising that he should have gained the power of selection. Women are everywhere conscious of the value of their beauty; and when they have the means, they take more delight in decorating themselves with all sorts of ornaments than do men. They borrow the plumes of male birds, with which nature decked this sex in order to charm the females" (*Descent* 2: 355). Lester Frank Ward (1841–1913) subsequently quoted these lines in his 1903 book *Pure Sociology: A Treatise on the Origin and Spontaneous Development of Society* (361–62).

Gilman repeatedly repudiated the androcentric theory of masculine superiority during her career. Instead, she adopted an alternative gynaecocentric theory of social evolution—what she once hailed as "the greatest single contribution to the world's thought since Evolution" (*Living* 187)—largely inspired by Ward that may be termed reform Darwinism. In Ward's view, human beings alone among all species are exempt from ruthless struggle for existence because they have evolved a consciousness or a social intelligence—what Ward called telic forces or psychic factors of civilization—that enables them to live by ethical laws and to affect or direct the course of evolution by acting in concert, intervening in nature, and ameliorating conditions through social planning or the agency of government. To illustrate this complex of ideas, I often distribute to my classes copies of Gilman's early satirical poem "The Survival of the Fittest" (1891), first published by Edward Bellamy in the Boston *New Nation*, his utopian weekly paper, and reprinted in the socialist paper *The Appeal to Reason* in 1902:

> In northern zones the ranging bear
> Protects himself with fat and hair.
> Where snow is deep, and ice is stark,
> And half the year is cold and dark,
> He still survives a clime like that
> By growing fur, by growing fat.
> These traits, O Bear, which thou transmittest,
> Prove the survival of the fittest!
>
> To polar regions, waste and wan,
> Comes the encroaching race of man;
> A puny, feeble little lubber,
> He had no fur, he had no blubber.
> The scornful bear sat down at ease
> To see the stranger starve and freeze;
> But, lo! the stranger slew the bear,
> And ate his fat, and wore his hair!

These deeds, O Man, which thou committest,
Prove the survival of the fittest!

In modern times the millionaire
Protects himself as did the bear.
Where Poverty and Hunger are,
He counts his bullion by the car.
Where thousands suffer, still he thrives,
And after death his will survives.
The wealth, O Croesus, thou transmittest
Proves the survival of the fittest!

But, lo! some people, odd and funny,
Some men without a cent of money,
The simple common Human Race,
Chose to improve their dwelling-place.
They had no use for millionaires;
They calmly said the world was theirs;
They were so wise, so strong, so many—
The millionaire? There was n't any!
These deeds, O Man, which thou committest,
Prove the survival of the fittest!
                    (*In This Our World* [3rd ed.] 78–79)

According to Ward's revision of Darwin, moreover, the female is the original "race-type" and the male the "sex-type"; that is, women are the transmitters of those traits, both inherited and acquired, that guarantee progress, and men merely assist in the process of fertilization. To prove the point, Ward speculates about the possibilities of "asexual reproduction" or "virgin birth" or partheno-genesis, noting that the "unfertilized eggs" of plant life reproduce females of the species, which are in turn "capable at maturity of repeating the process" (*Pure Sociology* 306–07; see also "Our Better Halves" 272). As Terry remarks in *Herland*, such a phenomenon was known in "some rather high forms of insect life" (47).

In any event, Ward insists, to women should belong the prerogative of sexual selection. While men throughout recorded history may have exploited their superior strength to oppress women and to reproduce indiscriminately, Ward argues, women in prehistoric times selected their mates. As he explains in *Pure Sociology*:

The only selection that took place down to the close of the protosocial stage was female selection. The females alone were sufficiently free from the violence of passion to compare, deliberate, and discriminate. [. . .] While the voice of nature speaking to the male in the form of an intense

appetitive interest, says to him: fecundate! it gives to the female a different command, and says: discriminate! The order to the male is: cross the
strains! that to the female is: choose the best!   (360, 325)

Among Ward's other ideas: the importance of education as a tool of social
change and the superiority of sociocracy, the cooperative commonwealth or
planned community, to the man-made world built through cutthroat competition. According to Henry Steele Commager, Ward may fairly be regarded as
the architect of the modern welfare state (xxii). In the end, it is unnecessary to
accept Ward's entire argument—after all, he is virtually unknown today—to
recognize at the very least that it builds on a base of scientific evidence. That
is, Ward was no less (and perhaps no more) scientific than Herbert Spencer
and other social Darwinians in their reading of Darwin.

Gilman trumpeted Ward's ideas throughout her career. She first read his
essay "Our Better Halves" (1888)—one of a handful of secondary sources she
cited in *Women and Economics* (1898)—in about 1890, and they soon began
a private correspondence that lasted until Ward's death. As early as 1894 she
referred to him as "a great man, a clear, strong, daring thinker" ("Editorial
Notes"). They met personally for the first time at a women's suffrage conference in Washington, DC, in January 1896 (*Living* 187), and in 1900 she wrote
him, "[I have] advanced nothing that conflicts with your teaching, have I?"
(Letter to Ward, 28 Nov. 1900). Three years later, she referred to *Pure Sociology* as a "remarkable book" that marshaled "an immense amount of indis-
putable fact" to prove the female "the original and permanent thing in
creation" and the male "subsidiary" (Scharnhorst, *Gilman* [Twayne] 79). In
1897 she urged her cousin (and future husband) Houghton Gilman to read
"Our Better Halves" (Hill, *Journey* 70), and in 1910, in the pages of her
monthly magazine the *Forerunner*, she urged "every woman who knows how,
to read" chapter 14 of *Pure Sociology* ("The Phylogenetic Forces"), and
detailed his feminist theories ("Comment" Oct. 1910). I echo her recommen-
dations: when teaching *Herland*, I ask undergraduates to read "Our Better
Halves" and graduate students to read both it and "The Phylogenetic Forces."
That is, students of Gilman's writings would do well to heed her advice even
today. She wrote Ward in 1904 that she considered his gynaecocentric theory
"the most important contribution to the 'woman question' ever made" (Letter
to Ward, 20 Jan. 1904) and in 1906 that she had "been preaching your doc-
trine, with specific reference to you and 'Pure Sociology,' ever since it was
known to me" (Letter to Ward, 15 Mar. 1906). In 1911 Gilman dedicated her
book *The Man-Made World* to him, and on Ward's death in 1913 she declared
in the *Forerunner* that he had "enlarged, illuminated and co-ordinated human
thought. There is no greater service. He has taught us to understand and
relate the facts of social life; he has pointed out to us our line of march, our
best steps upward" ("Comment" June 1913). As late as 1933, two years before
her death, Gilman proclaimed him one of "our two greatest Americans" (the

other was Walt Whitman), and in her posthumously published autobiography she described him as "quite the greatest man I have ever known" (Ruedy 9; *Living* 187).

In brief, *Herland* may be fairly regarded as Gilman's gloss on Ward's theories. As Mary Jo Deegan has noted in passing, "Ward's discussions of 'gynaecocracy' and 'parthenogenesis,' his systems model approach," and his "theory of societal revolution were applied in Gilman's Herland/Ourland saga" (Introduction 32). To be sure, Gilman may have read Ward selectively (see Findlay 263; Gilbert and Gubar, "Fecundate!" 200–01); still, I am less interested in whether she fully appreciated all the nuances of Ward's thought than in the way she interpreted his writings. Much of the humor of the narrative, in fact, derives from the role reversals or ironic contrasts between Herland and Ourland that Gilman based on Ward's theories. When the three male invaders first arrive in Herland, for example, they spy Celis, Alima, and Ellador "close to the great trunk" or clinging to the "main trunk" of a tree (16), much as Ward had argued in "Our Better Halves" that "[w]oman is the unchanging trunk of the great genealogic tree; while man, with all his vaunted superiority, is but a branch" (275). Much as Gilman's characters speculate about the "Amazonian nature" of a country built along the lines of "some kind of matriarchate" (Herland 7, 15), Ward had referred in chapter 14 of *Pure Sociology* to the "*amazonism*" or "the matriarchate" of "at least a score of races" (338, 339). Of course, in the views of both Gilman and Ward, such a country would be more advanced than Ourland.

The sociologist-narrator of *Herland*, Vandyke Jennings, initially articulates orthodox social Darwinian dogma, moreover. "We tried to put in a good word for competition," he reports, "and they were keenly interested. [. . .] We rather spread ourselves, telling of the advantages of competition: how it developed fine qualities" (61–62). Van explains to the Herlanders

> that the laws of nature require a struggle for existence, and that in the struggle the fittest survive, and the unfit perish. In our economic struggle, I continued, there was always plenty of opportunity for the fittest to reach the top, which they did, in great numbers, particularly in our country.   (63)

In the course of the novel, however, Van is gradually converted to a Wardian perspective, embracing reform Darwinism and feminism, as he is reborn in Herland. There telic or psychic forces propel evolution, what Van calls "conscious improvement" (78). Early in the history of the Herlanders "they recognized the need for improvement" and "devoted their combined intelligence to that problem—how to make the best kind of people" (61). Van is struck by "the most astonishing thing" when he "dug into the records"—their "conscious effort to make [their institutions] better" (77). The Herlanders have transcended the base struggle for existence and established a version of Ward's sociocracy founded on cooperation. How have they solved the problem of overpopulation? "Not by a 'struggle for existence' which would result in an everlasting writhing mass of underbred people trying to get ahead of one another" (69). Instead, they "sat down in council" and settled on population targets. The children who are borne to Herlanders are raised communally by "co-mothers" and educated "for citizenship" (108), and Van allows that after he studied the "vigorous, joyous, eager little creatures, and their voracious appetite for life, it shook [his] previous ideas so thoroughly that they have never been re-established" (104).

Above all, the women of Herland practice sexual selection, three of them choosing their mates from the masculine interlopers Van, Jeff, and Terry. At first, the women do not seem attractive to the men. "They were not, in the girl sense, beautiful" (21), according to Van; they "were strikingly deficient in what we call 'femininity'" (60). Their functional or "mighty sensible" clothing (28) and their cropped hair (32) reduce their sex appeal. In fact, Gilman directly satirizes Darwin's suggestion that women adorn themselves with plumed hats to attract the attention of men—an idea Ward had originally ridiculed in *Pure Sociology*.

> Terry asked them if they used feathers for their hats, and they seemed amused by the idea. He made a few sketches of our women's hats, with plumes and quills [. . .]. [T]hey said they only wore hats for shade when working in the sun. (51)

In traditional gender-role reversals that Ward's ideas invite, men who are accustomed to selecting mates themselves become sexual objects, if not objects of sexual desire. At first the hypermasculine, oversexed Terry insists, "Women like to be run after" (19). Midway through the novel, however, Van, Jeff, and Terry begin to groom themselves to attract the attention of women. Van remembers

> how careful we were about our clothes, and our amateur barbering. Terry, in particular, was fussy to a degree about the cut of his beard [. . .]. We began to rather prize those beards of ours; they were almost our sole distinction among those tall and sturdy women, with the cropped hair and sexless costume. Being offered a wide selection of garments, we had chosen according to our personal taste, and were surprised to find, on meeting large audiences, that we were the most highly decorated, especially Terry. (85)

The parthenogenetic Herlanders conclude at length to "experiment" (94) with "cross-fertilization" (78), to take an evolutionary leap forward. What they call "the strange new hope and joy of dual parentage" (127) Ward had called in *Pure Sociology* the "effect of securing variation and through variation the production of better and higher types of organic structure" (309). Ellador, Celis, and Alima court Van, Jeff, and Terry, respectively. That is, the women in Herland exercise the prerogative of sexual selection. Because they have not been acculturated to the courtly love tradition, however, these courtships are troubled. "They were not choosing a lover; they hadn't the faintest idea of love—sex-love, that is," Van admits. "We thought—at least Terry did—that we could have our pick of them. They thought—very cautiously and far-sightedly—of picking us, if it seemed wise" (89). "There was no sex-feeling to appeal to, or practically none" (92–93).

The women are unfamiliar, of course, with the roles the men assign them as traditional lovers. "While Jeff's ultra-devotion rather puzzled Celis, really put off their day of happiness, while Terry and Alima quarreled and parted, re-met and re-parted," Van notes, "Ellador and I grew to be close friends" (90). Intercourse seems to them suited only for the purposes of procreation. "For that had they agreed to marry us," according to Van (137). That is, as Susan Gubar notes, Gilman "drain[s] away the erotic" or retreats from sexuality in the novel to emphasize maternity (198). In the end, each of the couples negotiates the terms of their relationship: Jeff and Celis reach a sexual agreement that apparently allows for procreation only. Terry attempts to rape Alima when she denies him sex, and she not only repulses him but also wants him killed. He is soon expelled from Herland. ("The female animal or the human female in the gynæcocratic state would perish before she would surrender her virtue," Ward had written in *Pure Sociology* [345]). Van and Ellador presumably have a more "normal" relationship. They enjoy the "customs of marital indulgence" (135), though Ellador remains sexually aloof as the novel ends. "So we won't try again, dear, till it is safe—will we?" (138), she pleads. The Herland women "could not, with all their effort, get the point of view of the male creature whose desires quite ignore parentage and seek only for what we euphoniously term 'the joys of love'" (136).

Students gain a better understanding of the ideological underpinnings of *Herland* if they are first introduced to the theories of Lester Ward. In all, Gilman elaborated in *Herland* many of the reform Darwinian ideas she originally gleaned from Ward's writings, especially "Our Better Halves" and *Pure Sociology*. In particular, she illustrated in the novel Ward's idiosyncratic notion that the female of the human species ought to exercise the prerogative of sexual selection. She structured her novel to correspond point by point with many of the other details of Ward's gynaecocentric theory. So in the end, as Van insists to Ellador near the close of *With Her in Ourland*, the sequel to *Herland*, "there is no getting around Lester Ward" (172).

Charlotte Perkins Gilman's
Herland and the Gender of Science

Lisa A. Long

The first four chapters of Charlotte Perkins Gilman's noted feminist utopia, *Herland*, are relatively action-packed. Gilman charts the daring escapades of three young American men as they ingeniously make their way into the uncharted territory of Herland; she follows their imprisonment and thrilling escape from incarceration in a mountain-top fortification; and she offers enticing glimpses of the seemingly inscrutable female inhabitants of Herland. But at the beginning of chapter 5, Gilman's narrative mouthpiece, Van, informs us, "It is no use for me to try and piece out this account with adventures. If the people who read it are not interested in these amazing women and their history, they will not be interested at all" (51). At this point the novel shifts narrative gears. Thwarting many readers' expectations, Gilman turns what could have been a science fiction romp into a sociological treatise, methodically charting the social practices and rituals of the Herlanders. A useful strategy for leading disappointed students through the last two-thirds of the novel involves asking them to view each chapter as a condensed field report on a particular cultural characteristic: kinship structures, child-rearing practices, national duties, educational theories, religious beliefs, and reproductive practices. Gilman scholars have already charted Gilman's engagement with the sociological debates of her day; it is no coincidence that Van is a sociologist and that his perspective mediates our experience of Herland. Directing students to attend to the novel's disciplinary flexibility can help them appreciate the cultural work Gilman accomplishes in the latter sections of the text.

While such a strategy helps students work their way through the novel, it does not suffice as a means of making sense of the novel's many theoretical entanglements. In my experience, Gilman read her audience well. Many do, indeed, find "these amazing women and their history" fascinating enough, delighting in Gilman's clever and detailed denaturalization of cherished Western notions of motherhood, Christianity, private property, heterosexuality, and sexual desire itself. But others are discomfited by what they label Gilman's "sexism," that is, her cavalier treatment of the bumbling male characters and her idealization of a world without men. I teach *Herland* precisely to elicit such responses, for the novel dramatizes the concept of the cultural construction of gender clearly and powerfully—better than I could ever hope to explain it through lectures. This objective permeates the novel, from the simplest observations on the way that Americans are "so convinced that the long hair 'belongs' to a woman" (32) to more complex explanations of signification and gender difference, such as "When we say men, man, manly, manhood, and all the other masculine derivatives, we have in the background of our minds a huge vague crowded picture of the world and all its activities. [. . .] And when we say *women*, we think *female*—the sex" (135). The novel's utility in my gender and women's studies courses is self-evident.

Those who read *Herland* in my survey of twentieth-century literature also come to terms with what some view as a poorly written text. We can fruitfully use *Herland* to discuss a modernist ethos apart from the high modern aesthetic to which literature from this period is often reduced. The stylistic sparsity of Ernest Hemingway and the linguistic playfulness of Gertrude Stein, though complex, are conventional and privileged areas of literary interest and are, then, easier for students to discern and accept as legitimate topics of analysis. Gilman's modernism is characterized by the generic and disciplinary freedom to which she blithely alludes at the beginning of chapter 5: her stylistic cuts between science fiction, action adventure, and romance novel and her participation in the disciplinary conversations of sociologists, anthropologists, psychologists, educators, and eugenicists. The novel negotiates early-twentieth-century readers' appetites for the thick, scientific descriptions that Americans increasingly relied on to found their realities and an exploration of the fragmentary nature of modern consciousness, indicated by Van's initial admission that "this is written from memory" and by the fact that even if it hadn't been, his "descriptions aren't any good" (3).

However, neither the novel's stylistic adroitness nor its sociological bent wholly account for the powerful responses *Herland* elicits from undergraduates—both positive and negative. I believe it is significant that my students' passions ran highest when I taught the novel as part of an interdisciplinary writing seminar, Science and Technology in America. Whether or not they enjoyed the text, students were uniformly perplexed by my decision to include this novel in a class on science and technological development. I was equally perplexed by their responses, for I believe that the scientific milieu in which Gilman was immersed dictates the action of this novel. What I detail here—that which most vexes my students—is not only the way that Gilman shifts generic terrain or engages in scientific discourses but also the way that she probes the very core of scientific praxis itself. Ever since science came to be perceived as twentieth-century America's secular religion of choice, scientific method has become a sacred protocol, a seemingly reliable means of improving our lives, predicting our futures, and ensuring the possibility of verifiable truths. As such, the masculinist assumptions on which Western science is founded must be maintained, and a book that is clearly feminist, that is, ideological, illogical, passionate—in short, so stereotypically female—cannot be scientific. Gilman foregounds the gendered dimensions of all scientific pursuits—the "social" inherent to all "science." In her late-life autobiography, Gilman labeled herself a "social inventor, trying to advance human happiness by the introduction of better psychic machinery" (*Living* 182). As this quote demonstrates, Gilman insists on the fundamental connection between sociology, psychology, and technology—a fertile conjunction that emerges clearly in *Herland*. And it is Gilman's muddying of social and natural sciences and her reengendering of objectivity, I argue, that both stimulates and challenges students. She envisions a world where passionless women take on the scientific pursuits performed so ineptly by hypersexualized, violent men. In *Herland*, women's reproductive capabilities are firmly linked to successful scientific method, repetition or reproducibility being one of its primary tenets. Thus in my courses I focus our discussions on the trope of reproduction, examining it in the novel and in contemporaneous texts as both a biological imperative and as the troubling foundation of the scientific method on which our culture relies.

One reason students are perplexed by *Herland* is that unlike much science fiction, it is not futuristic. Gilman's male explorers stumble on a womanland where almost every technological achievement either mirrors the developments of the Western world at that time or seems within the realm of possibility. Motorcars, finely engineered roads, sanitation systems, functional architecture, highly developed agricultural practices, communication devices—sans "dirt," "smoke," and "noise"—mark Herland as a cleaned-up version of industrial America in 1915 (21). Instead, Gilman offers a vision of society in which human bodies and minds become the focus of cultivation and subsequent technological development. In this way, the novel more properly exploits the fictions of science, rather than adheres to the conventions of science fiction. Herland is like a parallel universe, a world apart that has followed an uncannily remarkable, alternative evolutionary track (much like Darwin's Galapagos islands, which Gilman had read of eagerly in her youth). Evolutionary time has been consciously sped up in Herland. Indeed, human bodies became so efficient that they anticipated and superseded technological advances. When men became extinct in their geographically isolated land, Herland women developed the ability to reproduce parthenogenetically; they will their pregnancies to occur. Thus I employ the term *reproductive technology* to refer not only to Herland's most miraculous development—mental rather than biological conception—but also to the ethos that motivates all technology: "to make the best kind of people" (Herland 61).

Significant, however, are the visible technological differences between Herland and American society: not only the Herlanders' symbolic and miraculous mastery of reproductive technologies but also the American explorers' possession of the biplane, the technology that makes the discovery of Herland possible. For both groups, the biplane is a potent symbol of civilization—a "proof of the higher development of Some Where Else" for the Herlanders—and a means for the explorers to display their superiority (65). In facilitating travel over difficult landscapes and allowing westerners to more accurately map out the surface of the earth, planes inaugurated a whole new worldview, not only for the explorers possessed of such technology but also for those made visible to the Western world by it. In Herland, "everybody heard it—saw it—for miles and miles, word flashed all over the country" (88). Thus the mere existence of the plane in the skies above causes a fissure in their world and eventually disrupts their evolution. We know at the end of the novel that Jeff and Celis are reestablishing a bisexual race.

The plane is an integral symbol of colonialism, which Gilman ties to reproduction through the tropes of heterosexual violation. Our narrator, Van, explains that he is reluctant to reveal the location of Herland to his readers, as they may "take it upon themselves to push in" (3). For their part, the Herlanders remained contented and inviolate until the booming buzz of the biplane "tore the air above them" (88). This violation is later literalized when the hypermasculine Terry attempts to rape his Herland wife, Alima. Despite their technological acumen, Gilman reveals that the male explorers alone know "the stuff that savage dreams are made of" (4). The Herlanders sew up the plane in a resilient material, providing a condom-like protection from further penetration into their land. However, the plane had already ventured far enough into the feminized body of Herland, sidestepping the women's scarlet rag, working its way up the steep, narrow waterway, and ejecting the three explorers into the womblike country. This mechanized sexuality allows the men to pass on their violence, knowledge of the outside world, and, ultimately, genetic materials to this and other previously undefiled societies.

Gilman allies fighting, whether through colonial exploits or war, with male modes of reproduction and the failure of such endeavors. The action of the novel is generated by the violent bisexual culture of early Herland. "They were decimated by war, driven up from their coastline till finally the reduced population, with many of the men killed in battle, occupied this hinterland," Gilman explains (56). Thus patriarchal culture does not strengthen the race but rather degenerates it, resulting inevitably in race suicide. Although two boys are born to the surviving women, they are weak and die immediately. But the violent element that had disappeared with Herland's male progenitors reappears with the Americans. Terry sings this rhyme as he prepares for his Herland marriage:

> I've taken my fun where I found it.
> I've rogued and I've ranged in my time, and
> The things that I learned from the yellow and black
> They 'ave helped me a 'eap with the white.   (129)

He alludes to the rape of African and Asian women and then aligns colonial rape with Western heterosexuality. The Herland women easily defuse Terry's efforts to act out his philosophies. Once captives, the men are subjected to a version of Dr. S. Weir Mitchell's rest cure: stripped and divested of any weapons, infantilized, fed, and put to bed. In response, they become petulant, irritable, irrational—in acting out their dominating, violent masculine roles, they ultimately lose possession of themselves.

Gilman devotees are quite familiar, of course, with the famous Philadelphia nerve specialist, Dr. Mitchell, and his cures. Gilman and Mitchell, violently opposed in their views on women and the medical establishment, are enduringly linked in modern literary and cultural studies. Mitchell's rest cure treatment for Gilman's persistent depressions inspired her most famous fiction,

"The Yellow Wall-Paper." And despite his literary achievements and wide-ranging medical research, Mitchell appears in literary history primarily as the inventor and implementer of Gilman's cure. Although Mitchell and Gilman had many differences of opinion, they were both deeply interested in the emergence of a postbellum medical science based on notions of objectivity, standardized methodology, and the demand for repeatable results. Mitchell's fatally flawed fictional doctors of the late nineteenth and early twentieth centuries—notably Dr. Ezra Wendell of *In War Time* (1884)—struggle precisely with these expectations. While Mitchell's fictional doctors are rendered professionally and psychologically impotent by their inability to reproduce knowledge and, then, replicate consistently healthy human bodies, Herland women's bodies link them to scientific and reproductive success. Significantly, Gilman writes, in Herland "[p]hysiology, hygiene, sanitation, physical culture—all that line of work had been perfected long since. Sickness was almost wholly unknown among them, so much so that [medicine is] a lost art" (72). Note that despite the aggressive scientification of medicine during the latter half of the nineteenth century, Gilman situates medicine as an art, not a science. Disease is linked both with the male gender and with the inability to control reproduction of any sort. When confronted with Herland women's lack of nervousness or fear and their calm potency, Van likens them to a "vigilance committee of women doctors"—perhaps an indictment of the masculine bias of Mitchell's profession (22).

After discussing these matters with my students, I inform them that in focusing on reproductive technologies—envisioning a world where female bodies have evolved to make such necessities obsolete—Gilman weighs in on the contemporary birth control debate spearheaded during this time by Margaret Sanger. "New women" in this text are not just women who demand reproductive knowledge. They are, literally, a new race: women who reproduce without men and who are, then, eminently in control of their sexuality (or lack thereof) and their bodies. Sanger agreed with Gilman that by controlling motherhood, women had the power to "remake the world" (1). Women's individual reproductive choices and collective efforts to limit birth rates were not shameful or illegal in Herland but matters of national import, the central motivating concern of their society. Such attitudes starkly contrasted with those held by the vast majority of health professionals and family planners in 1915 America, where Mitchell's heirs continued to promulgate eugenical theories of maternal culpability. Indeed, Gilman's fictional narrator comments on the "physiological limitations of the sex [women]" (11), while Mitchell's late-century medical work was instrumental in attaching degenerate behaviors to women's wombs. Thus Mitchell's fiction and medical texts (such as the influential *Fat and Blood* [1877], in which he systematically and misogynistically details the diagnosis and treatment of female neurasthenia) are equally useful in teaching *Herland* as they have been in elucidating "The Yellow Wall-Paper." While in the latter story Gilman dramatizes women's illnesses and Mitchell's dangerous "cure," in

Herland she directly reverses those theories, revealing what she viewed as the perverse drives at the heart of what Adrienne Rich has termed the heterosexual romance ("Heterosexuality"). Herland women's lack of sexual desire—of "sex-feeling," as Van calls it (92)—allows Gilman to manipulate contemporary medical views. It is not women's supposedly unstable wombs but the aggressive colonial-sexual-scientific appetites that men enact on and through women's bodies that must be cured. As Gilman notes, "there were no adventures" in Herland, "because there was nothing to fight" (51). Competition for sexual partners and genetic materials is the fight at the heart of Darwin's and Spencer's theories of survival of the fittest. Herland women's wombs are no longer subject to penetration from outside sources, no longer the site of such battles. Thus the Herlanders' ability to purify their minds and heal their bodies is linked to the exclusion of heterosexual reproduction and patriarchal cultures, which are figured as contaminating forces. The end of the birth control debate in Herland, and the end of medicine more broadly, is the end of competition, individuality, desire, sickness—in short, of a diverse and unpredictable human nature.

As important as the universal standard of perfect physical health in Herland is the careful cultivation of mental health. In the early 1900s, clinicians and physicians began to manufacture means of measuring physical and mental norms: standardized eye tests, weight and height charts, and IQ tests, for example. Herland succeeds in cultivating emotional and intellectual norms. "They had the evenest tempers, the most perfect patience and good nature," Van raves (48). Gilman wrote in her autobiography that "adhesion, cohesion, torsion, the law of the screw, and the lever, the pendulum, and that crowning miracle, the law of the hydraulic press [. . .] all] had parallels in psychology" (*Living* 29). In imagining a world where human emotion, desire, and cognition are completely standardized through the implementation of such mechanical models—the press of willpower—Gilman creates a technological future that reliably and efficiently reproduces a unified, homogeneous population. Herlanders progress toward a fixed, ever-closer end: ironically, complete conservation and stasis. Gilman argues for the inherent progressiveness of scientific method, a progressiveness, as Sandra Harding notes, that "resides in the separation of its logic and its facts from its social origins, social uses, and social meanings" (40–41). Thus Gilman subscribes to the notion of an enduring, logical, and verifiable natural and moral universe outside and apart from the subjectivity of human consciousness, at the same time that she deftly reveals the way that sexist social institutions such as marriage, motherhood, capitalism, and sexual desire are naturalized by those very truths. This inherent tension in the novel leads to her assertion that Herland children are "perfectly cultivated [. . .] yet they did not *seem* 'cultivated' at all—it had [. . .] become a natural condition" (73). Gilman offers up highly developed psychic and physical machinery as the natural result of human evolution.

Gilman resolves this tension in part through her creation of "new women" scientists who have consciously bred out the passion, desire, and individualism that make the practice of objective medical science suspect. Evelyn Fox Keller reminds us that the proportion of women trained in science and technology was at an all-time high by 1920. Indeed, Herland is clearly a reflection (and perhaps parody) of a scientific community and the stereotypes of male scientists and technologists emerging at the time—a community distinguished by members who were seemingly objective and dispassionate, who eschewed individual attachments for the larger good, and yet who were intensely curious and absorbed in the pursuit of their fields of study. The Nobel Prize–winning genetic engineer Barbara McClintock's account of her life as a young "plant breeder" in the 1910s bears remarkable resemblance to the path of many Herlanders. Finding her long hair and skirts hindering her work with corn plants, McClintock cut off her hair and started wearing knickers. Also like Herland women, McClintock finds "there was not that strong necessity for a personal attachment to anybody" in particular (Keller 34). As McClintock began her undergraduate studies, her mother worried that she would become "a strange person, a person that didn't belong to society" (Keller 27). Gilman imagines a home for such women, a world apart, where a "corps of inventors" are bred selectively to correct the flaws of society (Herland 77). Van describes their educational games: "It was like two people playing solitaire to see who would get it first; more like a race or a—a competitive examination, than a real game with some fight in it" (34). Such a description mirrors the international endeavors of the modern laboratory rather than the egotism of the American marketplace. As Herlanders claim, ideally "the finished product [of scientific pursuits] is not a private one" but knowledge to be shared among all for the better good (77).

In a society that was (and still is) entrenched in masculinized notions of scientific inquiry and men's facility for mechanics, Gilman claims a space for women. Yet Gilman's novel also demonstrates the limits and dangers of scientific method when the "finished products" are presumably better, healthier human beings. It is only through the extermination of men that Gilman can imagine the emergence of such seemingly flawless creatures, just as Mitchell and fellow doctors such as George Beard denied the ability of women to contribute significantly to an ever-changing, technological world. In addition, the convergence of Gilman's Lamarckian belief in the evolution of human beings through education, her faith in scientific and technological progress, and her application of mechanical models to human societies and bodies lead her inevitably to the pseudoscience of eugenics. As in many eugenical texts, human beings become commodified; here, "since they were restricted in quantity [. . .] they set to work to improve that population in quality" (Herland 72). As "Conscious Makers of People," Herland's finest product and eventual export is their carefully engineered progeny (69). Gilman is careful to note that after two thousand years of careful cultivation the people were a "pure breed" of "Aryan stock," with "'white'" skin, made somewhat darker by their constant exposure to the elements (55). Thus the eugenical efforts of Herland are not only gendered, they are also immediately racialized; Herlanders are always distinguished from the dark-skinned and supposedly dim-witted savages who populate the forests below Herland (and who, despite Herland's apparent avoidance of modern social ills, live on the edges of the river that is polluted by the Herlanders' textile industry). This primitive, inferior Africanist presence fills the role played by white women in Mitchell's most sexist medical texts. Just as troubling is the Herlanders' willingness to "breed out, when possible, the lowest types" by prohibiting fertile but "unfit" women from reproducing themselves (83). Class discussions often center on the ethics of governmental intervention in women's reproductive affairs.

In her autobiography Gilman refers to a favorite story, one of a noted English engineer who claims that when he dies he should be judged not by his questionable moral conduct but "by the bridges [he had] built" (*Living* 42). In this ethos technological achievement becomes the measure of a human being's worth. Adherence to so-called scientific principles is a morality in and of itself, Gilman suggests, that supersedes the prejudices and injustices apparent even in utopian Herland. Like most men and women of science, Gilman wanted to believe in the perfectability of human beings and in the promises of scientific method: "we are the only creatures that can assist our evolution," she insists, "according to the laws of nature, adding the conscious direction, the telic force, proper to our kind" (*Living* 42). In some sense, then, students have every right to be provoked by this novel and to embrace or deny its claims to science, though not necessarily for the reasons they might think. Gilman's text imagines a community built wholly on the most advanced scientific theories of her day, and in this way she teaches us that utopia and dystopia, the mechanics of human homogeneity, and the imperative of discursive license are integral to all fictions of science. Whether readers are angered like Terry, enthralled like Jeff, or enlightened like Van, *Herland* elicits responses to a scientific worldview that still structures our lives, for good or ill.

Teaching "The Yellow Wall-Paper" in an Introductory Literature Course

David Faulkner

> Josephine was kneeling before the closed door with her lips to the keyhole, imploring for admission. "Louise, open the door! I beg; open the door—you will make yourself ill. What are you doing, Louise? For heaven's sake open the door."
>
> "Go away. I am not making myself ill."
>
> Kate Chopin, "The Story of an Hour"

Faced with the necessity of responding to a compelling yet uncannily threatening text, a fledgling interpreter bemoans her inadequacy:

> I don't know why I should write this.
> I don't want to.
> I don't feel able.   (Gilman, "Yellow Wall-Paper" 21)

What teacher can fail to hear in this moment the inchoate lament of diffident students in an introductory literature course, students who are feeling vaguely coerced into writing about something they may suspect they are unable to grasp, as they strive anxiously to discern the dreaded "hidden meanings" that pedagogical authority supposedly requires them to produce? Indeed, "The Yellow Wall-Paper" famously adumbrates the relation between writing and (patriarchal) authority. Moreover, the story unfolds in a kind of classroom—a nursery and gymnasium combined—staging a scene of instruction. This recognition should give any teacher pause. But what is Gilman's narrator learning to do or to become? What kind of activity is taking place in that classroom? The sketchy analogy I have outlined so far, between the narrator's situation and literary pedagogy, grows more complex when we consider that, unlike the husband, John, in the story, the English professor as the provisional figure of cultural authority does not prohibit, but rather seeks to enable, written expression. I explore how an approach to "The Yellow Wall-Paper" can productively engage the paradox of trying to teach young people to write about what silences them.

I would speculate that most undergraduate readers of "The Yellow Wall-Paper" first encounter it in introductory courses: general education requirement-fulfilling classes at the sophomore level, populated by nonliterature majors. Over the past dozen years, I have found that it is precisely such neophyte students who gravitate toward "The Yellow Wall-Paper," in both oral and written discussion, beyond all other works. The tale's Gothic atmosphere appeals to undergraduate tastes; even an unsophisticated close reading allows the inexperienced interpreter to make some headway. Beyond these "teachable" aspects of the story, however, I suspect that what draws so many students to "The Yellow Wall-Paper" is that they glimpse in it an oblique reflection of their predicament, a veiled allegory of the experience of being "introduced to literature," a semiconscious transference of their interpretive activities onto those of Gilman's narrator. In my own teaching, I have begun trying to turn these remarkable parallels to explicit pedagogical use, exploiting my students' natural identification with the heroine to help dismantle their resistances, to break the silence that plagues the classroom.

I attempt to do so not only by addressing the issues I have raised here but also by setting "The Yellow Wall-Paper" amid a cluster of closely related works. For the story attracts both introductory-level students and introductory-level textbooks of literature. Surely it is now one of the most widely anthologized, widely taught works of short fiction in the American academy. Moreover, such anthologies tend to contain a whole series of fictions that offer parallels to what I have called the allegorical aspects of "The Yellow Wall-Paper," stories like Kate Chopin's "The Story of an Hour," William Faulkner's "A Rose for Emily," or D. H. Lawrence's "The Rocking-Horse Winner." Such fictions revolve around a recurrent structure of fantasy linked, I believe, to the problems my students face. In each, as in Gilman's tale, a protagonist learns to read—or perhaps merely to compulsively contemplate and reenact—his or her interpellation in the social text. Here is the basic theme: behind a closed door—usually a locked bedroom door—something mysterious, tantalizing, yet deeply disturbing is occurring or has occurred. This activity is associated with pleasure and exaltation, with power and self-gratification. At the same time, it is suffused with dread and secrecy, guilt and shame. While intensely private, this practice also betrays a kind of open secret of the culture, hidden in plain sight, whose existence is both widely acknowledged and officially suppressed. To engage in it can be, in a sense, to subvert the values of the dominant order, even to strike a covert or symbolic blow against an oppressive status quo (to flirt with perversity or parricide and thus to court retribution). The paradoxes continue: even as this activity entails the making and remaking of identity, it often takes the form of regressive, obsessive behavior. Such behavior makes manifest the repetition compulsion that psychoanalytic theory links to the death instinct and to the response to traumatic shock, devastating loss, or wrenching psychological conflict.

Surely this description covers much of "The Yellow Wall-Paper." However, it also fits any of a dozen famous fictions that swell most of the textbooks I know: not only those I have already mentioned but also Edgar Allan Poe's "The Tell-Tale Heart," Margaret Atwood's "Death by Landscape," Susan Glaspell's *Trifles*, Henrik Ibsen's *A Doll House*, Arthur Miller's *Death of a Salesman*, perhaps more obliquely Sophocles's *Oedipus the King* and Shakespeare's *Hamlet* or Franz Kafka's "The Metamorphosis," John Steinbeck's "The Chrysanthemums," Joyce Carol Oates's "Where Are You Going, Where Have You Been?," Sherwood Anderson's "I Want to Know Why," Nathaniel Hawthorne's "The Minister's Black Veil," or even Joseph Conrad's *Heart of Darkness*. On my syllabus, the list often includes Willa Cather's *A Lost Lady* and Charles Dickens's *A Tale of Two Cities*. Chestnuts like these continue to be reproduced in common anthologies and courses like mine not merely out of pedagogical convenience or literary value alone. I am suggesting that such narratives are somehow *about* the "introduction to literature" or at least that the highly charged private activities at stake in them can be related productively to both the students' putative work of "close reading" and their anxieties about performing it.

In the typical phantasmagoria I have been sketching, those characters (such as the husband, John) who are drawn to approach this locked, forbidding door from the outside do so with a gripping mixture of fear and fascination, suspecting the truth and yet not wanting to know, even actively denying what they do know. The exposure of the secret behind that door, the violation of a quasi-sacred taboo, often forms the dramatic climax of the narrative. I eventually urge my students, after they have read a number of such texts, to consider such repetitive fantasies in the light of what psychoanalytic theory names the "primal scene." The anxieties, sexual and otherwise, that surround this remembered or fantasized glimpse of parental coitus also characterize the frisson of uneasiness with which beginning students sometimes approach the task of interpretation. These students come to such courses without much training in analytical writing skills. They usually lack a critical vocabulary or a sense of literary-historical tradition; perhaps they lack practice, perhaps merely confidence as interpreters of literature. They are sometimes just afraid, more so than they can bring themselves to acknowledge: afraid of reading, afraid of writing, afraid of "criticism," afraid of speaking in class, afraid of controversy, afraid of passion, afraid of ambiguity, afraid of failure. They share with Gilman's narrator a fear of having to uncover what so-called hidden meanings the wallpaper may hold, just as they share her husband's paralyzing anxiety about having to make sense out of what is happening on the other side of that door. Such students frequently either angrily dismiss analysis as an unproductive, self-indulgent, vaguely illegitimate activity or bewail their incapacity in the search for the obscure, taboo knowledge of "hidden meanings." I wish to avoid condescension or unwarranted generalizations; still, for many inexperienced readers, the literary text resembles a locked room, an ominous threshold behind which lies an anxiety-producing initiation into adult mysteries, whose existence is somehow acknowledged and disavowed in the same breath. In my classroom practice, therefore, I introduce Freud's basic discussion of the "primal scene" in *The Interpretation of Dreams* to allow students to speculate about its application not only to literary texts but also to the powerful text of fearful curiosity that the very act of interpretation potentially evokes in them.

Indeed, I have begun to acknowledge their anxieties directly at the outset. At the first meeting of this past semester, for instance, I handed out photocopies of an undeniably challenging poem, "The Emperor of Ice-Cream," by Wallace Stevens. Just before doing so, without specifying further, I informed the group that I would be asking them to "write something" in response. (At this point, they usually glance at one another uneasily and squirm in their seats.) I then strolled around the room, reciting the poem from memory as they read. Meanwhile, I quickly distributed an anonymous (age and gender only), nonjudgmental, fifteen-minute survey in which I asked them not to interpret the poem but rather to reflect on the prospect of doing so. I asked them to pinpoint what passed through their minds before, during, and after their reading. I asked them to name and briefly develop their feelings about literature and the act of interpretation. I asked them to describe any fund of knowledge they could draw on to help contextualize this idiosyncratic poem: did they know anything about literary history or poetic tradition (e.g., modernism or the funeral elegy) or about theories of mind, language, or culture or about the debates that structure the academic discipline of literary study? Finally, I asked them to explain the similarities and differences, if any, between the way that they might approach such a poem and the way that they supposed I (or someone like me) might approach it.

The remarkable thing is that, when I take such polls, the answers almost invariably mirror the response of Gilman's narrator to the oddly textualized pattern of the yellow wallpaper, to her own reading and writing practices, and to her husband's authority. A few characteristic examples follow, taken directly from students' anonymous responses. To the first query, about how students feel about interpretation, the bulk of the answers revolve around terms like "nervous," "full of dread," "intrigued and anxious," "naive and ignorant"; respondents self-protectively claim a "blank" mind, a feeling of "confusion," boredom, and discomfort projected outward onto the language of poetry. Sometimes the response is positive but also defensive—and here the unconscious echoes of oedipal anxiety seem to me unmistakable: "I feel as if I am trying to figure out a riddle that I do not have the answer to. I have always been taught that there is a hidden meaning in poetry and that I have to try and find out what it is. I hate that! I take poetry to heart and what it means to me is all that matters. I think that is the whole point of poetry. Whatever you get out of it is what it 'means.'" A more extreme but not unrepresentative view involves an ambiguous dialectic of labor and pleasure that also characterizes the rhetoric of Gilman's narrator: "I approach literary texts with resentment and as a burden. I just find it tedious and much more like work than enjoyment or leisure time."

Surely many teachers encounter these passive-aggressive attitudes daily. I elicit such reactions deliberately, to validate those attitudes, and I tell my students so up front. More precisely, I try to get students themselves to validate their own reflexes by seeing them inscribed in "The Yellow Wall-Paper," which I assign once in the first week of the course and again several weeks later. I hand out questions for journal writing that ask participants to connect their responses to my survey with the narrator's anxieties. For instance, her sense of something "queer" or "strange" about the house and the wallpaper (9, 11) resonates with my students' uneasiness in a decentralized, discussion-based classroom focused on ambiguous texts. (Indeed, many openly admit that classes like mine resemble little else in their educational experience, which at my institution still consists mainly of large lecture courses, scannable multiple-guess examinations, and virtually no writing.) Moreover, I urge them to hear, in passages like the following, echoes of their prejudices about the paradoxical language of poetry: "It [the wallpaper pattern] is dull enough to confuse the eye in following, pronounced enough to constantly irritate and provoke study, and when you follow the lame uncertain curves for a little distance they suddenly commit suicide—plunge off at outrageous angles, destroy themselves in unheard-of contradictions" (13). Even my students' angrier responses about the supposed frustrations of an interminable "literary" reading seem anticipated by the narrator: "On a pattern like this, by daylight, there is a lack of sequence, a defiance of law, that is a constant irritant to a normal mind.[. . .] You think you have mastered it, but just as you get well underway in following, it turns a back somersault and there you are. It slaps you in the face, knocks you down, and tramples upon you. It is like a bad dream" (25). Consciously or not, their attitudes toward interpretation betray a suspicion that something literally abnormal or uncanny lurks in the literary text; at the very least, they seem to harbor unexamined assumptions that oppose the sanity of a supposedly transparent or "shallow" text to the derangements of a "deep" or opaque one.

Once I have suggested the implicit analogies, my students often proceed further. For instance, like them, Gilman's narrator stands in an uncertain relation to cultural tradition and authority. Part of her diffidence springs from her want of detailed knowledge concerning the heritage of the "ancestral [hall]" (9) she temporarily occupies but does not herself possess. (Furthermore, I never can resist the coincidence between her "three months' rental" [15] and the length of a college semester.) While her predicament is sometimes read as emblematic of the anomalous position of the woman writer athwart a male-dominated literary tradition, I would argue that it also evokes the crisis of authority amid which so many of my students embark on the academic study of literature. Their responses to my surveys bear out this impression. Most of them, neither surprisingly nor necessarily to their discredit, profess a fundamental ignorance of literary history—even a suspicious distaste for it—which ushers in an uncanny feeling of being thrown abruptly among unfamiliar signs and monuments. Young American readers, lacking a sense of cultural history, may feel especially inadequate in this respect, just as the narrator vaguely connects the "colonial mansion," the "hereditary estate" (9) with "English places that you read about" (11). My students, as "mere ordinary people" (9) rather than figures of authority in their own minds, judge themselves incapable of fathoming the issues at the bottom of "some legal trouble [. . .] something about the heirs and coheirs" (11). Small wonder, then, that passionate academic battles over literary value or the canon can seem, to such apprentice readers, either impossibly remote or utterly pointless. Moreover, my students admit to the narrator's ambivalent sense of inferiority to John's interpretive authority. The narrator both acknowledges his superior diagnostic skill as a physician (connecting it with his cultural authority as a husband under patriarchy) *and* privately resists it with her own relativistic what-it-means-to-me-personally impulse (10). I see this attitude nearly every day in class as well as in writing. The surveys I administer speak it loud and clear. I certainly can understand my students' ambivalence about the institutional authority they imagine me to wield; I shudder when I recall my own mixture of arrogance and cravenness toward my instructors when I was nineteen.

To try to remedy this reticence and inexperience, as well as to foster richer analytical discussion, I follow our first pass at "The Yellow Wall-Paper" with fictions like those I invoke above and then reassign Gilman afterward, about halfway through the course. My theory in doing so is that such an evolving archive of cross-references may enhance my students' grasp of any individual work, since a thicker context of literary history or secondary criticism is unattainable at the introductory level. My admittedly quixotic hope is that the cumulative effect of these stories will induce my students to reflect more fully on their obscurely motivated acts of reading and writing. Let me, therefore, sketch the kind of emphasis I place in class on a few representative examples of works structurally and thematically adjacent to "The Yellow Wall-Paper." In Chopin's "The Story of an Hour," just before the moment I have quoted as an epigraph, Louise Mallard experiences an intensely pleasurable yet oddly menacing epiphany behind the locked door of her boudoir. The overdetermined moment seems loaded with overtones of orgasm and trauma at once: "Now her bosom rose and fell tumultuously. She was beginning to recognize this thing that was approaching to possess her, and she was struggling to beat it back with her will—as powerless as her two white slender hands would have been. When she abandoned herself a little whispered word escaped her slightly parted lips. She said it over and over under her breath: 'Free, free, free!' [. . .] Her pulses beat fast, and the coursing blood warmed and relaxed every inch of her body" (72). Given Josephine's anxious reaction outside the keyhole, I often ask my students whether they think we should conclude that Louise has been masturbating. They tend to groan and complain that literary interpretation—or maybe just a filthy-minded English professor—"reads too much into" a straightforward, face-value text. Their unacknowledged implication, of course, is that some kind of reading exists that is *not* "reading into" or else that the right amount of reading can be so finely quantified or calibrated. In this cliché, the very act of interpretation, which they may dismiss as "reading too much into" a text, emerges as itself a kind of excessive, self-indulgent, unproductive behavior—as a perverse, even a perverted or vaguely onanistic, set of practices, rather like the feared yet desired activities occurring behind that door. One male respondent to my original survey unintentionally betrayed these paradoxical anxieties: "I do not have any interest in poetry. I dread having to read them. For some reason I feel they are a waste of time. I feel that the message that they send could be written in a single sentence. I think that poets are just trying to be creative with a single idea."

However, my students' eye-rolling begins to diminish somewhat once we reach D. H. Lawrence's "The Rocking-Horse Winner." Secreted in his top-floor bedroom, the pubescent Paul rocks obsessively on his hobby horse, seeking to fulfill his fantasies of omnipotence and to gratify his mother's insatiable consumer desires. This behavior arouses his mother's fascinated dread, which builds toward a climactic breaking-point:

> She stood, with arrested muscles, outside his door, listening. There was a strange, heavy, and yet not loud noise. Her heart stood still. [. . .] She felt that she knew the noise. She knew what it was.
>
> Yet she could not place it. She couldn't say what it was. And on and on it went, like a madness. [. . . F]rozen with anxiety and fear, she turned the door-handle. [. . . I]n the space near the window, she heard and saw something plunging to and fro. She gazed in fear and amazement. [. . .]
>
> "Paul!" she cried. "Whatever are you doing?"   (329)

("You will make yourself ill," I often add aloud.) In my experience, both Chopin's and Lawrence's tales, along with several others, provide rich raw material for comparative discussions that include "The Yellow Wall-Paper."

While the behavior my students witness in story after story often veers toward neurosis, deviance, or outright crime—as in "A Rose for Emily," "The Tell-Tale Heart," or *Trifles*—sometimes it is explicitly connected to forbidden, subversive acts of *writing* as a crucial form of cultural labor. "The Yellow Wall-Paper" famously mobilizes such metaphors, but introductory-literary examples can be further multiplied: in *A Doll House*, Nora secretly copies legal documents, without her husband's knowledge, to repay the loan she originally obtained through another "illegitimate" act of authorship, namely forging her father's signature. Such work is exhausting and shameful, yet also gratifying and empowering for her. In *A Tale of Two Cities*, Dr. Manette's twinned identities as shoemaker and historian-autobiographer both exhibit the obsessive symptoms of prison neurosis that Dickens so lavishly anatomizes: mindless repetition, self-division, regression, masochism, and emasculation. In the same novel, Madame Defarge's compulsive knitting takes the form of a coded, secret writing that only she knows how to read, an interpretation of history aimed at overthrowing tyrannical authority. Even so, her psychopathological makeup ultimately springs from the same traumatized root as that of the political prisoner in Dickens, whose neurotic will to write is never stronger than at the moment the key has turned in the lock of his prison cell.

By the time we have reached the version of the fantasy in which the mysterious, obsessive, seemingly perverse activity behind the door has become writing itself, my students have often begun to make connections across the group of fictions on the syllabus even without my urging. These connections sometimes form the basis of insightful essays that proceed by comparison and contrast; Gilman resurfaces repeatedly in class discussion, especially when we tackle *A Tale of Two Cities* about two-thirds of the way through the term. The final twist that her tale retrospectively provides is the recognition that its narrator's secret activity is not only writing but also symbolically a kind of *reading*. Her secret journal records an interpretation of the wallpaper's pattern in which she reads her own oppression; it narrates an allegorical act of protofeminist criticism in which, by literally tearing the paper off the wall, the critic liberates the suppressed feminine identity so long entrapped by the prison bars of a patriarchal pattern. My students usually have little trouble catching hints like these. I do, however, have to keep prompting them to consider how each successive work might offer a kind of running commentary on their own practices, attitudes, or libidinal investments as readers and writers.

For I believe that "The Yellow Wall-Paper" does offer such a commentary, as well as a means of helping students begin, against their grain, to work through their half-acknowledged but stubborn resistance to what they call "reading into." I have already suggested how, in identifying readily with the narrator's diagnosis of her predicament, they indignantly reject her husband's culturally sanctioned condescension and his self-ignorant coerciveness. They perceive, with justifiable self-congratulation, the irony of the fact that what John prescribes to cure his wife is precisely what drives her mad. Yet I challenge them to consider equally the possibility that, on some level, they may be allied with John as well, that they may tacitly endorse many of his assumptions and anxieties. I point out how John's character embodies an antianalytic ideology of transparency, an appeal to a putatively common-sense practice of reading—a "just enough" reading, committed to actively suppressing that which would "read too much into" a text or experience. Gilman's narrator certainly pegs him as such: "John is practical in the extreme. He has no patience with faith, an intense horror of superstition, and he scoffs openly at any talk of things not to be felt and seen and put down in figures" (9). Indeed, his dismissal of his wife's "silly fancies" (22) consorts easily with his patriarchal privilege, his occupational authority, and his blithe investment in the status quo. Crucially, however, John's pragmatism serves ultimately to render invisible the functioning of power, which operates through the narrator's internalized willingness to collaborate in policing herself: "He says [. . .] I ought to use my will and good sense to check the tendency. So I try" (15–16). Many of my students have unwittingly revealed such veiled allegiances in their own minds when they pit a hardheaded economic and educational realism (probably associated with a perception of their parents' expectations) against the effete, demoralizing seductions of aesthetic contemplation. "All this discussion is interesting enough," an especially thoughtful sophomore once said to me privately, "but what *good* will it do me?"—thereby implying that it just might do him ill. Another student typically confessed on my survey, "It's a good thing I don't need this kind of thing for my major"; another wrote, "I read things for information [. . .] were as [*sic*] someone like you reads for enjoyment." Still another went so far as to justify his stubborn refusal to accept the value of interpretive speculation by linking it to a cultural conservatism, a distrust of subversive "liberalism," inherited from his father and grandfather. In class and in journal questions, I try to recast responses like these into the terms the story provides, urging my students to hear and reject John's voice speaking through their own, just as they reject his constricting definition of his wife's interests and needs. When I turn the tables on my students in this way, I aim not to mock, scold, or outflank them but rather to teach them: to use a story that undergraduates enjoy and find empowering to open up the possibility that they, like Gilman's narrator, may learn to check their own tendencies to silence themselves. She asserts rightly, in a sense, that "[t]here are things in that paper nobody knows but me, or ever will" (22). If they can follow through on their perception of the pathogenic nature of John's "sane" regime of reading, then my students may be able to stop fearing that they're not smart enough or grown-up enough to read literature perceptively and discuss it convincingly. If they can relinquish the lingering dread and denial that overwhelms John as he contemplates that locked bedroom door, they may begin to realize, as Gilman's narrator does, that they may merely be "introduced" to ghostly and previously unknowable aspects of themselves. Indeed, "literature" is one name for that which does not know all that it knows.

I have no unambiguous triumphs, stunning breakthroughs, or collective epiphanies to record. My classroom isn't always less silent now than before. I do sense, though (perhaps wishfully), that by the end of the semester many of my students have become at least measurably less anxious or dismissive. At the beginning of the term, when they allege they're silent because they're afraid of "saying something wrong," I wonder whether they're not, rather, afraid that "saying something" is in itself "wrong," in the sense either that interpretive critique is dimly connected with autoerotic or pathological behavior or that the search for "hidden meanings" encroaches on some unspeakably primal taboo. In fact, I think that this widespread hidden meaning assumption actually arises from the pervasive distrust of "reading into"; a suspicion of hermeneutics engenders a hermeneutics of suspicion. In other words, if you're not supposed to look for it, something must be concealed there. Moreover, I suspect that one reflexive yet influential justification for requiring courses called Introduction to Literature in the first place—the ameliorative or therapeutic role of the humanities in a liberal education—is deeply implicated in that same appeal to occult significance. But in "The Yellow Wall-Paper," the narrator's hermeneutic activities, in themselves, neither heal her nor make her ill. I push my students away from the idea that the academic study of literature is either the search for hidden meanings or the cure for what ails them. And I try not to present literary analysis as an initiation into adult mysteries, however much we may end up facing troubling questions of sexuality. Rather, I strive to introduce reading and writing about literature in something like Gilman's narrator's terms: simply as a box of tools with which we can perform a particular kind of work. It is a form of labor not exclusive of pleasure, for which anyone is fitted and within which the authority to speak is the writer's own to create. Let me give the penultimate word to one of my anonymous students, who wrote this before she had ever heard of Charlotte Perkins Gilman: "to me, the poem was confusing, but I am not going to let it bother me. I will just absorb the words and try to make some form of sense out of them [. . .] without going crazy." What I have always loved most, and found most valiant, about "The Yellow Wall-Paper" is that, against all odds, its heroine teaches herself to read.

Teaching the Politics of Difference and "The Yellow Wall-Paper" in Women's Literature Classes

Mary C. Carruth

On the first day of my women's literature survey classes, I try to model for my students the self-reflexivity that I consider one of the hallmarks of feminist methodology. Using my course syllabus as an example, I demonstrate to the students how the body of knowledge taught at universities is a historically contingent and politically inflected construction, not a permanent, transmittable truth. Many students who enroll in a women's literature class are already aware of the biases of an androcentric literary canon and of the omission of women and of gender analysis from so-called mainstream curricula; however, they are sometimes less conscious of the marginalization of ethnic and sexual minorities in women's studies, especially if the students are white, heterosexual, and middle-class. Consequently, I foreground for the students my method of constructing the syllabus, explaining why I included certain authors and texts and according to what criteria. I identify myself as a feminist teacher and scholar but clarify that my intention in the course is not necessarily to encourage them to embrace feminism but to help them learn to think critically about literature and the world they live in. (Although Women's Literature is almost always cross-listed in the women's studies program, I clarify this because many of the students enroll in the class to fulfill a general education requirement and so are not—and probably never will be—self-identified feminists.) However, I do explain that most of the interpretive strategies they learn during the semester will be informed by feminist theories, which I later introduce to them in brief, accessible essays by such writer-critics as Adrienne Rich, Virginia Woolf, Alice Walker, and bell hooks. Finally, I announce the goals of the class, which, I explain, derive from the larger enterprise of feminist literary criticism: to introduce them to a women's literary canon, yet all the while to keep them aware of the politics of canon formation; to compel them to define women's literary traditions, cautioning them against essentializing all women's experiences from the lives of white middle-class women; and to get them to think about how we measure the aesthetic value of literary works, especially those by women who do not fit the traditional androcentric criteria for great literature. To make these abstract comments about canon and course construction more concrete, I often assign on the second day reviews of *The Norton Anthology of Literature by Women* so that students will see that even their primary textbook is not a ready-made package of knowledge but is itself the object of much scholarly debate.

Because self-reflexivity is an important process that I model and hope to inculcate in students, I was disappointed in students' answers to an exam question I gave in Women's Literature at the University of New Orleans, a public urban commuter school, in 1998. These results would change my approach to teaching such white-authored feminist classics as Charlotte Perkins Gilman's "The Yellow Wall-Paper." I included in the syllabus almost exclusively North American and European authors. The class consisted of all women, mostly white and middle-class and, I would guess, mostly heterosexual. Although the university attracts a large number of nontraditional students, only one returning student was enrolled along with one Latina and two African Americans. All were non-English majors, and only a few had had women's studies courses. Because many were taking the course to fulfill their general education literature requirement, they were not experienced at literary analysis. Nevertheless, I gave them a final-exam question that would challenge them to be thoughtful about the formation of the feminist literary canon and that would engage them in textual analysis. Ultimately, the question would implicate them in the perils of constructing and producing knowledge, specifically in what Annette Kolodny calls "the minefield" of feminist literary criticism ("Dancing").

The question required students to choose one work from the semester's readings that they thought was indispensable to a women's literature syllabus. Then, with the director of women's studies posited as their hypothetical audience, they were asked to explain why they believed this work to be mandatory reading in a women's literature class. In their answers, they were expected to consider how well the work represented women's literary traditions and how well it engaged differences in women's class backgrounds, ethnic and racial heritages, and sexual orientations. Out of this class, the most popularly chosen texts were white-authored fiction like Kate Chopin's *The Awakening*, Charlotte Perkins Gilman's "The Yellow Wall-Paper," and Margaret Atwood's *The Handmaid's Tale*, although the students had also read Zora Neale Hurston's *Their Eyes Were Watching God* and Harriet Jacobs's *Incidents in the Life of a Slave Girl*. Among the reasons for one student's choosing "The Yellow Wall-Paper" was its history of publication, its rediscovery by 1970s feminists, and its recovery by critics as an exemplary feminist text. Another student chose *The Handmaid's Tale*, concluding that it was a universal voice for all women. She added that Atwood did not disclose the race of any of her characters, that in fact race was not important, for Atwood was focusing on gender oppression only, not racial oppression. This student obviously overlooked the fact that in Atwood's futuristic Gilead, the children of Ham were exported, leaving only those of European descent. In other words, the student overlooked the intersections of racism, sexism, and classism in Gilead's totalitarian theocracy, which is founded on a dominant subjectivity that represses difference. While one of the African American students selected *Jane Eyre*, the other chose *Incidents in the Life of a Slave Girl*. Unlike her classmates, who inadvertently essentialized all women's experiences from European models, this student took the risk of arguing for the universality of the African American narrator's struggles for freedom and autonomy.

What I learned from these exam answers is that not only had most of the students failed to understand the politics of canon formation, but they had also fallen prey to defining white middle-class women's experience as normative. But their uncritical selections of white authors was less of a problem than their failure to bring an analysis of race to their discussions, as in fact the exam question required. While I had intended this exercise to teach students, in part, about the challenges faced in canon formation, I had to admit that it also implicated them in the very claims to universality that I wanted them to interrogate. I determined to adjust my pedagogical approach to these texts, and my new plan made "The Yellow Wall-Paper" central in my grouping of *Incidents in the Life of a Slave Girl* and *Jane Eyre*. My proposed lesson would invite students to contrast Brontë's and Gilman's uses of the metaphor of slavery to represent nineteenth-century white women's confinement in patriarchy with Jacobs's use of the reality of slavery to protest black women's exploitation. In particular, this new focus would compel students to evaluate the ethics of white authors' appropriation of slavery as a trope. This process would necessarily engage them in a discussion of larger issues extending beyond the texts. These would include how Eurocentric biases, which construct those who are different as racial others, can be reproduced not only in the classroom but also in feminist literary criticism and how the invisibility of whiteness as a social construct can affect scholars' judgments of the presumed universality of texts and, in turn, shape canon formation.

In revising my approach, I was, of course, aware that most of my students had made the same mistake committed by the early feminist critics, who established a canon of authors mirroring their white middle-class identities, however inadvertently. That is, most of the students had failed to move out of the insular, narcissistic way of thinking produced by white dominant cultural values. In fact, it is to this white narcissism that Susan S. Lanser attributes the canonization of "The Yellow Wall-Paper" in feminist criticism. As she suggests in her 1990 essay "Feminist Criticism, 'The Yellow Wall-Paper,' and the Politics of Color in America," scholars' interpretations of Gilman's story, like her protagonist's readings of the wallpaper, "may have reduced the text's complexity to what we need most: our own image reflected back to us" (420). Because, she argues, "all feminist discourse on 'The Yellow Wall-Paper' has come from white academics," it has not questioned "the story's status as a universal woman's text" (423). Paralleling Gilman's protagonist with the critics who read her, Lanser adds that "the white, female, intellectual-class subjectivity which Gilman's narrator attempts to construct, and to which many feminists have also been committed perhaps unwittingly, is a subjectivity whose illusory unity, like the unity imposed on the paper, is built on the repression of difference" (435). To interrogate this narcissistic critical discourse, Lanser introduces a discussion of difference in the text, in which she links the image of the wallpaper to what she calls a discourse of racial anxiety, presumably experienced by many white Americans, including Gilman, during the heavy immigration years at the turn of the twentieth century. Although I knew I could not engage my introductory students in an analysis as sophisticated as Lanser's, I determined to come up with a pedagogical approach that would encourage them to think about the politics of difference and "The Yellow Wall-Paper," not so much in relation to theme, historical context, or Gilman's biography as in relation to genre.

First, I decided to pair more overtly "The Yellow Wall-Paper" with Harriet Jacobs's *Incidents in the Life of a Slave Girl*, published in 1861, thirty-one years before Gilman's story. These two nineteenth-century American works share the distinction of being rediscovered feminist classics. They also share an interest in autobiographical forms and women's authorship and agency, and they explore the themes of female embodiment and of captivity and escape. A juxtaposition of these two texts allows students to see Gilman's indebtedness to the slave narrative tradition and to consider how both black and white women of the nineteenth century used the condition of slavery to articulate their concerns about women's oppressions in the white dominant patriarchy. It also compels them to think about the ethics of nineteenth-century white women writers using the literal experience of slavery as a trope for their own entrapment. Finally, pairing *Incidents* with "The Yellow Wall-Paper" invites students to recognize the circumstances of Gilman's story as a historically contingent experience of a white woman of the upper class—to name the whiteness of the narrator, so to speak—so that they will be thoughtful about constructing the white middle-class heroine as normative or the story as a universal women's text.

Because most scholarship has classified "The Yellow Wall-Paper" within the Gothic tradition, it has overlooked the story's indebtedness to the slave narrative tradition. In fact, these two traditions are not unrelated, as Kari J. Winter suggests in her study *Subjects of Slavery, Agents of Change: Women and Power in Gothic Novels and Slave Narratives, 1790–1865*. Gothic fiction emerged in England during the same years that American slavery became a full-fledged system, between 1790 and 1830 (Winter 2). As Winter points out, "although Gothic novels and slave narratives were written within the very different literary conventions of fantasy and 'facticity,' both genres focus on the horrifying aspects of patriarchal cultures" (53). These interrelated genres, then, provide students with a critical basis for linking not only *Incidents in the Life of a Slave Girl* and "The Yellow Wall-Paper" but also other African American and Anglo feminist classics, including Charlotte Brontë's *Jane Eyre*, published over fifty years before Gilman's story; Jean Rhys's *Wide Sargosso Sea* (1966); Alice Walker's *The Color Purple* (1982); Margaret Atwood's *The Handmaid's Tale*, (1985); and Toni Morrison's *Beloved* (1987). Within the constraints of this essay, I concentrate on pedagogical strategies for relating Brontë's, Jacobs's, and Gilman's texts.

Both Jacobs and Gilman appealed to a similar audience—a white New England readership—and both had pedantic purposes: Jacobs to rally white northern women around the abolitionist cause, and Gilman to warn women like herself (and her former physician Dr. S. Weir Mitchell, too) of the deleterious effects of the popular rest cure. While Gilman uses the rest cure as her central paradigm for the nineteenth-century upper-class white woman's helplessness in the hands of a paternalistic patriarchy, she describes this experience using a rhetoric of slavery prominent in both abolitionist and feminist discourse of the mid- to late-nineteenth century. Gilman, of course, was quite familiar with this rhetoric. She was the great-niece of the abolitionist novelist Harriet Beecher Stowe, whom Harriet Jacobs had approached, with disappointing results, about publishing her narrative before securing the aid of Lydia Maria Child and Amy Post. Many of Gilman's feminist predecessors, writers like Elizabeth Cady Stanton, Angelina Weld Grimké, and Margaret Fuller, used slavery as an analogy to describe white women's ownership by their husbands. As Elaine R. Hedges explains in her afterword to the Feminist Press's 1973 edition of "The Yellow Wall-Paper," Gilman herself evokes a rhetoric of slavery in *Women and Economics: A Study of the Economic Relation between Men and Women as a Factor in Social Evolution* (56-58), which she published six years after "The Yellow Wall-Paper."

Before my students discuss *Incidents* and "The Yellow Wall-Paper," they read *Jane Eyre*, noticing how Brontë uses Gothicism and the condition of slavery to configure her white lower-middle-class protagonist's self-development. This prepares them later for their comparison of Jacobs's and Gilman's texts. My approach to teaching these elements in *Jane Eyre* is informed primarily by two contrasting interpretations: Sandra M. Gilbert and Susan Gubar's *The Madwoman in the Attic* and Carl Plasa's article "'Silent Revolt': Slavery and the Politics of Metaphor in *Jane Eyre*."

For the sake of our later analysis of Jacobs's and Gilman's works, we devote much of our discussion to the turning point in this Gothic novel—Jane's encounter with the captive Creole Bertha, which Gilbert and Gubar claim is Jane's confrontation with "her own imprisoned 'hunger, rebellion, and rage,' a secret dialogue of self and soul on whose outcome [. . .] the novel's plot, Rochester's fate, and Jane's coming-of-age all depend" (338). The problem with this interpretation of Bertha is that she is cast as Jane's dark double, and thus a Eurocentric bias, which renders those who are different as objectified racial others, is reproduced in the literary criticism and, in turn, in the classroom. To bring students to consciousness about this racial binarism, I focus on Bertha's story, illuminating how Brontë intersects the history of England's colonization of the West Indies, where slavery was finally abolished in 1834, with Bertha's imprisoning marriage to the imperialistic Rochester. (Certainly, the assignment of *Wide Sargosso Sea* is also effective in getting students to understand both the colonialist subtext of *Jane Eyre* and the extent to which Bertha is deprived of a subjectivity in order to serve as an alter ego to the developing subjectivity of Jane.) Then students see how Jane's final achievement of a presumably equal partnership with the redeemed though maimed Rochester depends on Bertha's revolt and apocalyptic destruction of herself and Thornfield Hall, the symbol of Victorian English patriarchy. Once the students have become aware of Brontë's simultaneous use of Bertha's captivity with a rhetoric of slavery to configure Jane's own servitudes and escapes, I then pose a question raised by

Plasa that is relevant to a later analysis of "The Yellow Wall-Paper." As Plasa points out, although Brontë's novel inscribes a "critique of gender- and class-ideology" by means of a "metaphorics of enslavement and mastery," not once does it refer literally to the institution of British slavery or to the colonialism with which Victorian readers in 1847 would have identified the West Indies (67). The danger of this figurative language, he suggests, is that it falsifies the real meaning, the literality, of slavery; like Brontë herself, he claims, white feminist critics (until the late 1970s) have also evaded the issue of slavery, colonialism, and race in *Jane Eyre* (69). As he concludes:

> The deployment of a metaphorics of slavery as a way of representing domestic oppression is, from one perspective, both a rhetorically powerful and politically radical maneuver. Yet from another perspective, that precisely of those who are or have been enslaved, [who have] *experienced* the metaphor, as it were—such a strategy can only be viewed as deeply problematic.   (67–68)

Having joined their analysis of gender and class with an analysis of race in *Jane Eyre*, the class is next prepared to consider similar components in Jacobs's and Gilman's works. *Jane Eyre* is subtitled "An Autobiography" to demonstrate the protagonist's assertion of a subject position within the male-dominated public life-writing tradition of Victorian English letters. In contrast, Jacobs's narrative is a true autobiography, which nevertheless appropriates conventions from the sentimental and seduction novel to appeal to its white northern female readership. Just as Brontë makes clear the distinction between herself and her fictional narrator, Jane Eyre, so Jacobs creates a persona, Linda Brent, to tell her story. Published fourteen years after *Jane Eyre* and two years before the Emancipation Proclamation in America, Jacobs's narrative literally represents slavery, which had been primarily metaphorical in Brontë's novel. Reversing her cultural positioning in the antebellum South as a racial other, Jacobs asserts her full personhood by writing her story in New York during her employment as a domestic servant for Nathaniel P. Willis and his second wife and then finally publishing it with editorial guidance from Lydia Maria Child. Jacobs's process of writing is secretive (for she suspects Nathaniel Willis to be proslavery), which anticipates the forbidden writings of Gilman's narrator as well as Offred in Atwood's *The Handmaid's Tale*. Having students read Jacobs's narrative in conjunction with Gilman's helps "shift the center," to use a term coined by Margaret L. Andersen and Patricia Hill Collins, changing their perspective "from the White, male-centered forms of thinking that have characterized much of Western thought, helping [them] understand the intersections of race, class, and gender in the experiences of all groups, including those with privilege and power" (15).

While students gained only partial knowledge of Bertha's captivity, filtered through the Eurocentric eyes of Jane and other characters in Brontë's novel, they now have access to the complete story of what Sandra Gilbert and Susan Gubar call the "woman in the attic"—of Harriet Jacobs, confined in her grandmother's garret—on her own terms. Unlike Jane Eyre's disembodied narration, where the Victorian English heroine projects her denied corporeal experiences onto the racially othered Bertha, Jacobs foregrounds her physicality and thus makes palpable the literal experience of slavery. Unlike that of Bertha and Gilman's protagonist, her concealment, of seven years, is paradoxical—it is both voluntary and a mandatory consequence of her master's abuse. Enfolded in total darkness in a hot garret that is only nine feet long and seven feet wide, she is "tormented by hundreds of little insects [. . .] that pierced through her skin, and produced an intolerable burning" (175). At one point, during her second winter, her limbs become so numb with cold that even her face and tongue become paralyzed, and she "[loses] the power of speech" (185). So cramped is her body that she fears becoming a cripple for life (192).

While much of Jacobs's content foregrounds the physicality of the captive's existence, the point of view she constructs truly "shifts the center." Having fashioned a peephole from a gimlet left in the roof of her attic retreat, Jacobs "uses to her advantage all the power of the voyeur" (V. Smith 32), keeping watch over her children and the devious efforts of her master to reclaim her. In fact, to deflect her position as object in the antebellum South and to claim her status as subject, Jacobs reverses the visual hierarchy mandated between blacks and whites during the period of slavery. To give students an interpretive strategy for understanding the relation between her gaze and her subject position—a technique that will later prove useful in their analysis of the writing practices of Gilman's nameless protagonist—I assign bell hooks's essay "Representations of Whiteness in the Black Imagination." Hooks's essay is doubly valuable because it is at once critical and pedagogical, linking the process of reading the representations of whiteness in black-authored texts to the dynamics of discussing race in the classroom.

As hooks suggests, in literary criticism as well as in the classroom "the absence of recognition" of whiteness as an object of study "is a strategy that facilitates making a group the Other" (167). In fact, understanding the mystery of whiteness has been a survival mechanism for African Americans, although many white students, as hooks points out, express surprise at the possibility that black people may observe them with "a critical 'ethnographic' gaze" (167). Tracing these looking relations back to slavery, she remembers, "black slaves [. . .] could be brutally punished for looking, for appearing to observe the whites they were serving, as only a subject can observe, or see"; thus many black people assumed a "mantle of invisibilty, to erase all traces of their subjectivity during slavery" (169). Students may easily apply hooks's theory of looking relations to Linda Brent's gaze in *Incidents in the Life of a Slave Girl*. Protected in her hiding place, Brent is able to remain invisible to her master, Dr. Flint, yet render him the object of her watchful gaze so that she may outwit his plans to capture her. Tellingly, the first person she sees after creating her peephole is Dr. Flint (175). To use hooks's words, her choice "to look directly" constitutes "an assertion of subjectivity, equality" (168). Indeed, her ability to scrutinize her white master influences the outcome of her trials—her ultimate securement of her and her children's freedom. As she concludes, seeming to echo the ending of *Jane Eyre*, "Reader, my story ends with freedom; not in the usual way, with marriage" (302).

Having brought an analysis of gender and race to their discussions of *Jane Eyre* and *Incidents in the Life of a Slave Girl*, the students are then equipped for a discussion of difference in their approach to "The Yellow Wall-Paper." Just as Jacobs invents Linda Brent to tell her tale of slavery, Gilman creates a fictional diarist to relate her own mental breakdown and sense of captivity within patriarchy. Jacobs uses her real experience of slavery to demonstrate how institutionalized racism prevented enslaved women from embodying the Victorian ideal of True Womanhood, an argument she knew would win the attention of her northern white female readers, who aspired toward this ideology of femininity. Unsettling the dominant racist hierarchy that denied the capacity of reasoning in people of African descent and so deprived them of the right to be considered human beings, Jacobs, like many of her fellow slave narrators, uses words to demonstrate her intellectual capabilities and thus her humanity. Gilman, like Brontë, uses a metaphorics of slavery to demonstrate how gender and class categories prevented white middle-class women from achieving their full human potential (although such categories did acknowledge their basic humanity). Just as Jacobs evokes the familiar nineteenth-century image of the woman in the house to expose enslaved women's degradation, Gilman uses the figure to expose white middle-class women's dehumanization by a patriarchal ideology that insists on elevating them as "Angels of the House." What Gilman, like many of her feminist contemporaries, suggests is that the degraded slave and the revered angel are two sides of the same patriarchal coin. For both Jacobs's and Gilman's protagonists, the forbidden act of writing is the road to personal freedom, yet the two narrators write autobiographically for different reasons: Linda Brent to recover her role as mother and to create a domestic space and home for her displaced family, and Gilman's character to eschew her maternal role and escape the domestic ideology that oppresses her.

To get students to think about the generic similarities between these two texts and to evaluate Gilman's use of the slavery metaphor, I quote from such nineteenth-century white feminists as Angelina E. Grimké, who declared, "The investigation of the rights of the slave has led me to a better understanding of my own" (114). While acknowledging that the oppression of white women could not be totally equivalent to the brutality of the slaves' existence, I remind students of the material realities of many nineteenth-century white women's lives: the husband's legal ownership of his wife's person, property, and children; the woman's lack of control of her own sexuality; the woman's inability to divorce; the denial of her access to education and to the vote. Students then analyze the fairly obvious rhetoric of slavery in Gilman's story. The protagonist is nameless, suggesting the subsumption of her identity under the patronym, not unlike the erasure of slaves' family names. She is confined in the nursery of a Gothic "colonial mansion" (9) where the windows are barred (12) and the bed is nailed down (19). Her gatekeeper is not a loving family member, as in Jacobs's narrative, but her paternalistic physician-husband, who has prescribed the rest cure that ironically exacerbates her postpartum depression. Complicit in his plan is the narrator's foil, her sister-in-law Jennie, who resembles Jane Eyre in her embodiment of the ideals of white Victorian womanhood and for whom the protagonist may function, like Bertha, as the rebellious other. The protagonist is deprived of all those things that she knows enhance her well-being—work, social interactions, and writing, her favorite creative outlet. Just as Linda Brent, during her concealment, watches the actions of her enemy, thereby exerting her gaze and agency, Gilman's narrator attempts to continue to write, surreptitiously. However, as Kolodny indicates, it is at the point at which John's opposition to her writing makes the effort "greater than the relief" that the protagonist begins her obsession with the wallpaper and her descent into madness. As Kolodny suggests, she "gives up her attempt to *record* her reality and instead begins to *read it*" ("Map" 156), and what she sees is "her own psyche write large" until she is "totally surrendered to what is quite literally her own text— or, rather, her self as text" (157). Of course, she projects her own feelings of oppression onto the wallpaper, imagining a woman there trapped behind bars and trying to get out. That Gilman intends this figure to represent the domestic imprisonment of nineteenth-century upper-middle-class white women is indicated by the narrator's remark that behind the wallpaper "sometimes I think there are a great many women" (30). Gilman concludes her story echoing the clichéd cry of the slave narrator, "free at last!" As the protagonist tears off the wallpaper, freeing the imagined woman and wresting a kind of freedom for herself in her madness, she exclaims, " I've got out at last" (36). Gilman implies that it is the nineteenth-century white woman's isolation on her pedestal, and not just her enshrinement in the cult of domesticity, that leads to the dissolution of her self. In contrast, the slave Linda Brent, who keeps a grip on her sanity to save her children, is ensconced in a support system of family and friends.

The juxtaposition of Jacobs's and Gilman's works invites students to fulfill the goals of a women's literature course: to define women's literary traditions, to understand the politics of canon formation, and to question the standards by which we measure artistic merit, especially the notion of universality. First, they understand the indebtedness of nineteenth-century European American authors to African American slave narrators and consider the ethics of their appropriation of slavery as a metaphor. Second, they become aware of how white feminist critics have assumed whiteness to be invisible and normative and how this has led to a canon of predominantly white authors, including such authors as Charlotte Perkins Gilman. Finally, by bringing an analysis of difference to their understandings of literary texts and their world, they are compelled to discover the commonalities among women as well as the dissimilarities.

Teaching "The Yellow Wall-Paper" in a Class on Women's Autobiography

Kara Virginia Donaldson

When students read "The Yellow Wall-Paper" in my Women's Autobiography class, our discussion of its form and content, Gilman's life, and her intent as a writer leads them to explore enthusiastically the meaning and uses of autobiography for women. Since I ask students to consider whether "The Yellow Wall-Paper" is an autobiography or merely autobiographical, I also assign Elaine R. Hedges's afterword; excerpts from Gilman's autobiography, *The Living of Charlotte Perkins Gilman*; and Domna Stanton's article "Autogynography: Is the Subject Different?" Students read chapter 7, "Love and Marriage"; chapter 8, "The Breakdown"; and, chapter 9, "Pasadena," from Gilman's autobiography. These chapters describe Gilman's marriage to Charles Walter Stetson; her depression, treatment by Dr. S. Weir Mitchell, and subsequent breakdown; her realization that separating from her husband will alleviate her mental agony; and her move to Pasadena and the writing and publishing of "The Yellow Wall-Paper." (*Writing Women's Lives*, edited by Susan Cahill, provides a useful introduction to Gilman and ten succinct pages from these chapters that follow the events in "The Yellow Wall-Paper.") Of course, students immediately find correspondences between the story and the autobiography and show consternation that some details are greatly altered. The disjunctions between Gilman's two life stories help us discuss the internal conflicts between fact and fiction as well as form and experience in both the story and autobiography. I ask my students, does an autobiography depend on being autobiographical? Where, I ask, does the truth lie in both *The Living* and "The Yellow Wall-Paper"—in the biographical details or somewhere else?

Although I ask whether or not "The Yellow Wall-Paper" is autobiography in an autobiography class, this question could also be asked in a women's literature class or American literature survey class. My discussion here both describes how "The Yellow Wall-Paper" can be taught in an autobiography class and provides some theoretical background on autobiography for instructors interested in raising these issues in another class. While my students begin the semester by reading Georges Gusdorf's "Conditions and Limits of Autobiography" and then read Stanton's article in conjunction with "The Yellow Wall-Paper," another instructor could let students' understanding of autobiography develop through their reading and discussion of Gilman. Pairing "The Yellow Wall-Paper" with *The Living* encourages students to think critically about diaries and autobiographies as well as the short story and about why so many nineteenth-century women utilized these genres when they sat down to write.

Hedges's afterword, with its mix of analysis and biography, prompts readers to ask if "The Yellow Wall-Paper" is a true story. It sends readers, particularly less practiced readers, like many of my students, back to the text as biographical critics. While it may seem that having the students read *The Living of Charlotte Perkins Gilman* would encourage the impulse to discover whether the events of "The Yellow Wall-Paper" are true, one reason I choose this text is to help my students avoid biographical criticism. Stanton's article helps place our discussion relative to these concerns and the genre of autobiography. Stanton claims that the term *autobiographical* has been used historically to indicate that women's writing cannot transcend the personal, private details of the self and that decoding women's writing as autobiographical devalues it. With Stanton's comments, I turn my students away from their desire to find the real details of Gilman's life—away from mining "The Yellow Wall-Paper" for biographical details or reading *The Living* as a transparent re-creation of the writer's life. Instead, I ask students to study the deviations between Gilman's two accounts to locate the autobiographical intent. I want students to consider autobiography not only as a genre but also as a mode of self-reflection for both writer and reader. Furthermore, this grouping of texts challenges them to see this mode not as a method of transcending the divided self but rather as an acknowledgment that this division is the human condition.

We begin this task by comparing and contrasting the form of the story and the autobiography. "The Yellow Wall-Paper" is both a short story and a diary. As a diary with a narrating "I," the short story appears to be autobiographical. The students recognize immediately, however, that there is no beginning—"I was born . . ."—and that the story opens in the middle when the diarist is already trapped in "ancestral halls" (1). This is not a narrative with beginning, middle, and end orchestrated by a reflective "I" narrator looking back over her life but rather a series of hurried, secretive, and immediate responses creating an incremental buildup of events, moments, and suspense over the twelve entries. When we discuss *The Living*, we make similar discoveries; it is both an autobiography and a diary. While the convention is that autobiography tells a story in which the narrator "I" and the protagonist "I" are the same, Gilman's references to and reliance on the diaries she kept as her autobiography's source graphically demonstrate the distance in time and place between narrator and protagonist. As with "The Yellow Wall-Paper," Gilman constructs the narrative of *The Living* through diary entries. Reading both diaries allows students to question the genre and what Gilman could and could not do in both the short story and the autobiography.

During this discussion, a student might remark that the title is *The Living*, not *The Life*, and that the verbal form also suggests action rather than the retrospective clarity that characterizes a finished life. The title also suggests that Gilman is countering the typical female narrative and expressing her desire "to earn [her] own living" (106). Such points help us avoid reifying *The Living* as the ultimate truth of Gilman's life as we compare and contrast the different ways Gilman represents her experience in fiction and in autobiography and as we then reconsider those categories.

Gilman's reliance on the diary form and her mix of genres advance the question of the diary's relation to more formal life writing. Margo Culley claims that both women's "periodic life-writing" and autobiographies written for a public audience arise from the same desire: "the urge to give shape and meaning to life with words and to endow this meaning-making with a permanence that transcends time" (xi). The shape given to lives in diaries has changed over time. Not until the late nineteenth century did the diary become the "arena of the 'secret' inner life" (3). As the diarist stopped simply recording events and became the diary's subject, the form became associated with women. The perceived split between public and private sphere strengthened this divide between the public lives and *Lives* of men and the private lives of women. The diary entries in "The Yellow Wall-Paper" relate a woman's life story but one that does not conform to accepted female narratives that continue happily ever after. Culley and Stanton both reject claims that women's autobiographies are formally different from men's, as they are neither more fragmentary nor more inscribed through others' lives. And yet, in "The Yellow Wall-Paper," the diary's traditional association with women and privacy shapes how the story functions. Our class discussion of these matters leads us to ask, What does it mean when women write?

To answer this question we analyze the opening passages in which the narrator of "The Yellow Wall-Paper" assesses her desire and struggle to write. I ask my students, What kind of relationship does she have with her husband, John? What kind of relationship does she have with her implied reader? While the narrator claims, "I would not say it to a living soul, of course, but this is dead paper and a great relief to my mind," she situates the reader as "this dead paper" (9–10). All diaries, secret or not, presuppose a listener, a confidante, or another type of audience: "that presence becomes a powerful 'thou' to the 'I' of the diarist" (Culley 12). The diarist creates the listener she needs because she can only say to John what he wants to hear. When she speaks her truth, he contradicts her: "You see he does not believe I am sick! And what can one do?" (10) The narrator creates the reader as "you" at the same time that she creates the "I" for herself. Her writing is an act of self-assertion because, as her sentence shows through its content and structure, John will not allow her the position of the "I" as subject of her own life story; she must conform to his interpretation of her life story. Yet by writing, she can claim an audience for her own story. With the second person, the narrator conjures up a reader who can "see" that John does not "see" her. With the shift in point of view to "one," which refers to both herself and the reader she addresses, the diarist pulls the reader into the positions she inhabits both as John's creation and as a woman writer and demonstrates the intertextuality of life and *Life*. She writes to create herself and to maintain her own sanity despite the social and cultural dominance of John's text. John fears that her writing will lead her to develop a self that cannot be happy in her role as wife and mother; she will become a self that needs expression. He does not recognize that she is already that self.

At this point I ask students to find passages in Stanton's article that could explain or describe the narrator's desire and anxiety. Stanton claims that the act of writing itself is for women an act of "fundamental deviance" (13): "the

graphing of the *auto* was an act of self-assertion that denied and reversed
woman's status" as other (14). Fulfilling this need, despite the injunctions not
to, exhausts Gilman's narrator: "I did write for a while in spite of them; but it
does exhaust me a good deal—having to be so sly about it, or else meet with
heavy opposition" (10). Having already discussed why the narrator feels she has
to be "so sly," I ask my students why the narrator is so exhausted. Is it because
the female writer recognizes that she is a "contradiction to the dominant definition of woman and [. . . a] usurper of male prerogatives" (Stanton 13)? From
this subordinate position, the "speaking 'I' constituted the reading 'you' as the
representation of society's view of women and thus as the personification of the
writing interdiction" (13). According to Stanton's paradigm Gilman should construct the reader as the interdictor, but she does not. I ask my students if the
writing interdiction is in Gilman's "diary." Yes, they say, but not as the reader,
who is "one" with her. In "The Yellow Wall-Paper," Gilman displaces this writing interdiction from the reader, whom she hopes will read her text sympa-
thetically, and personifies it in the character of her husband, John.

Now I ask my students, Why does Gilman make the narrator's husband a
doctor even though her real-life husband was an artist? We contrast passages
describing the husbands' responses to their wives' illnesses in *The Living* and
"The Yellow Wall-Paper." We examine the diarist's reflection about her husband as doctor:

> If a physician of high standing, and one's own husband, assures friends
> and relatives that there is really nothing the matter with one but tempo-
> rary nervous depression—a slight hysterical tendency—what is one to
> do?   (10)

Students notice that her husband is the subject-actor in the sentence and that
he acts first as a physician—a well-known one—rather than as a husband. They
comment on his *public* assertions of her state within his (medicalized) narrative of women's roles and nature and how he *author*izes certain behaviors while
rejecting others. The narrator repeatedly conjures up again her new listener,
"one," whose subject position and position in marriage are akin to hers. Representing the reader on the page reinforces the narrator's everywoman status
by drawing the reader into the narrator's subject position. Constituting these
three figures in the same sentence, the narrator's desire for this reader seems
intricately linked to Gilman's construction of the narrator's husband as a doctor who doesn't listen to his patient-wife.

What about Gilman's husband? What do we learn about him from Gilman in
The Living? We reread the following account in class:

> My diary is full of thankfulness for happiness and prayers for deserving
> it, full of Walter's constant kindness and helpfulness in the work when I
> was not well [. . .].

I think Walter was happy. A most successful exhibition [of his work] in Boston had established him more favorably and enabled him to meet domestic expenses [. . .].

A lover more tender, a husband more devoted, woman could not ask. He helped in the housework more and more as my strength began to fail [. . .].

And then Gilman quotes from her diary:

"Feel sick and remain so all day." "Walter stays home and does everything for me." "Walter gets breakfast." October 10th: "I have coffee in bed mornings while Walter briskly makes fires and gets breakfast." "O dear! That I should come to this!" By October 13th the diary stops altogether. [. . .] "March 23rd, 1885. This day, at about five minutes to nine in the morning, was born my child, Katharine." [. . .]

We had attributed all my increasing weakness and depression to pregnancy, and looked forward to prompt recovery now. All was normal and ordinary enough, but I was already plunged into an extreme of nervous exhaustion which no one observed or understood in the least.   (87–89)

Students notice the double portrait of Walter embedded in *The Living*: one reflecting the retrospective autobiographical narrative and one relying on the diary that was a near contemporary of "The Yellow Wall-Paper." Students quickly shift their interest to the diary's Walter, noticing how Gilman contrasts her inability to act with her "brisk" and efficient husband. This discrepancy provokes another discussion of women's use of the diary and other forms of autobiography and their claim to report the truth.

I ask my students again why Gilman transformed Walter into John. Usually a student will volunteer the comment that if Gilman wrote about her supportive husband, her readers would not be very sympathetic. Another might say that Gilman wanted to represent a more typical marriage. We might at this point need to discuss the students' disapproval of Gilman and the modern concept of postpartum depression. Such comments and discussion give me an opening to reassert John's role as the "personification of the writing interdiction" and how that construction helps the reader identify with the narrator as a woman who is trying to write her own life, rather than have it written for her.

John the doctor is a more typical husband than Walter Stetson and perhaps more extreme than the average husband in his expectations that the narrator can "for his sake [. . .] use [her] will and self-control and not let any silly fancies run away with [her]" (22). By changing her husband—by making the narrator's husband and doctor the "personification of the writing interdiction"—Gilman conveys the truth of her experience to her reader. To show that this interdiction pervades not only the narrator's text but the narrator's life—and by extension the reader's and writer's life—Gilman names a real person who represents the most extreme example of the cultural writing inter-diction, Dr. S. Weir Mitchell:

> John says if I don't pick up faster he shall send me to Weir Mitchell in the fall.
> But I don't want to go there at all. I had a friend who was in his hands once, and she says he is just like John and my brother, only more so!
> (18–19)

Students wonder who this friend is: it has not seemed as if the narrator had someone with whom to discuss what John is like. Sometimes a student wonders if this friend could be Gilman; that is, if a narrative slippage reveals an autho-rial intent to comment on Weir Mitchell and husbands' and doctors' control of women's bodies and minds. The last sentence's conversational tone reinforces this reading. After all, Gilman is claiming that John and the narrator's brother are like Weir Mitchell. My students claim that John is definitely not Walter; he is Weir Mitchell.

We discuss what students learned about this doctor from *The Living* and Hedges's afterword and how he treated prostrate women. In the autobiography Gilman reports that Weir Mitchell diagnosed her as having a tendency toward hysteria and proposed this cure: "Live as domestic a life as possible. [. . .] And never touch pen, brush or pencil as long as you live" (96). After this treatment Gilman describes behaving the most like the woman in her story: she would "crawl into closets and under beds" (96). So for Gilman, her husband, Walter, did not appear to be enforcing the writing interdiction, but marriage, mother-hood, and the medicalized narrative of appropriate female behavior did.

After these discussions, my students are ready to argue that autobiography is not just "the attempt and the drama of a *man* struggling to reassemble *him-self* in *his* own likeness at a certain moment of *his* history" (Gusdorf 43; my emphasis); it also recounts the writer's specific material and historic location. The writer, particularly if she is a woman, may not be, as Gusdorf claims, the "essential agent" of both "his" life and *Life* (37). Rather, women's autobiogra-phy "dramatize[s] the fundamental alterity and non-presence of the subject, even as it asserts itself discursively and strives toward an always impossible self-possession" (Stanton 14). My students realize that the disjunction between and within the two texts not only illustrates a woman's life in a historical moment and contains a specific social and political intent but also shows the woman writer's struggle to represent herself as the subject of her own narrative.

Gilman claims that "the real purpose of the story was to reach Dr. S. Weir Mitchell, and convince him of the error of his ways" (*Living* 121). Yet she man-ages to displace his position as intended reader through her portrayal of a doc-tor in the text. Whether it was reaching Mitchell that prompted her to write or whether it was the "relief" of writing down "what [she] feel[s] and think[s] in some way" as it was for the narrator of "The Yellow Wall-Paper" (21), Gilman argues that women need real work. This real work often is, as Stanton claims, "to constitute the female subject" (14). By the end of our discussion of Gilman's writing, my class comes full circle questioning the genre of autobiography itself and problematizing the acceptance of the biographical details as the authentic elements of an autobiography. The autobiography's truth, some students now argue, is "a likeness no longer of things but of the person" (Gusdorf 44); or, rather, the likeness here is no longer even of the person but of her social and historical location. Changing the autobiographical details makes the story more true because the narrator is not Gilman but an everywoman figure. In "The Yellow Wall-Paper," Gilman does what Emily Dickinson, another nineteenth-century woman writer, suggests: "Tell all the Truth but tell it slant" (506).

On the midterm examination, I give students the opportunity to make their own assessment about the story with this essay question: "Is 'The Yellow Wall-Paper' autobiography?" Invariably, some students decide that "The Yellow Wall-Paper" is autobiography; others insist that it is autobiographical. In either case, approaching the story in this context is an effective strategy and sharpens the critical skills that students can bring to their reading of fiction, autobiography, women's literature, and American literature.

Teaching *Herland*
in an American Literature Course

Joanne B. Karpinski

The broad reach of an American literature course makes it logistically practical to teach only one representative work for each author considered. In this context, I prefer to teach *Herland* rather than "The Yellow Wall-Paper," even though the story is artistically superior to the novel. *Herland* fits well into an American literature course because it either exemplifies or problematizes the fundamental issues such a course will discuss: literary history, genre, style, theme, plot structure, setting, characterization, and the role of gender in constructing them all.

Teaching *Herland* with respect to the history of American literature deconstructs the oppositional hierarchy through which that history has been traditionally expressed: a white male mainstream with an undertow of writing by women and minorities. Elizabeth Ammons's *Conflicting Stories* encapsulates this model in its title and provides a "remarkably simple" (3) sketch of the evolution of the American literary canon:

> American literature came of age in the early nineteenth century [. . .] and then exploded into brilliant creativity at midcentury in the [. . .] "American Renaissance." Fictive literature after the Civil War then underwent a change from romanticism to realism. [. . .] The nation's literature then descended into a valley at the turn of the century before erupting in a second brilliant outpouring of talent, akin to that of the American Renaissance, in the 1920s.
>
> At its crudest this portrait, which only recognizes white writers, [. . .] also defines the romance, narrative that turns away from realistic depiction of social and cultural issues, as the nation's best and most important form. (3)

Students who have internalized this historical outline may need permission to revise it. Ammons destabilizes this "resolutely white and masculine" tradition (17) by problematizing its institutional history. Within American universities during the early decades of the twentieth century, Ammons argues,

> American literature as a field [. . .] and the profession of professor as it is now understood emerged at the same time in American history; and that time, *which was when women writers of the Progressive Era wrote* was [. . .] a period of mounting white male anxiety in the academy about the feminization of literature. (15–16; my emphasis)

Ammons points out that only after "the profession of professor in the United States opened up at least a little to people of color and white women in the

1960s and seventies would the model drawn in the reactionary twenties begin to receive widespread, revisionary scrutiny" (17).

When Gilman's writings are taught from this institutional perspective, it becomes perfectly clear why her work was backwatered from the 1920s onward: even the reputations of her more successful male contemporaries William Dean Howells, Edward Bellamy, and Joaquin Miller declined when the academy became the predominant arbiter of literary worth. Gilman's aversion to modernism as a style as well as her dislike of the New Woman's over-enthusiasm for suffrage and sexual liberation only compounded these large-scale historical reasons for her eclipse (Karpinski 1–3). Such "revisionary scrutiny" envisions a cultural role for the novel that differs from the mainstream focus on the creation of a distinctively American style. Cathy N. Davidson observes:

> Given both the literary insularity of many novel readers and the increasing popularity of the novel, the new genre necessarily became a form of education, especially for women. Novels allowed for a means of entry into a larger literary and intellectual world and a means of access to social and political events from which many readers (particularly women) would have been otherwise largely excluded.   (10)

Davidson sees the education provided by novels as subversive of traditional sources of authority, compounding the transfer of religious education and religious authority in nineteenth-century America from church and father to home and mother:

> [The novel] required, in fact—from reader and writer—virtually no traditional education or classical erudition since, by definition, the novel was new, novel. Furthermore, the novel was, formalistically, voracious. It fed upon and devoured more familiar literary forms [. . .]. Psychologically, the early novel embraced a new relationship between art and audience, writer and reader, a relationship that replaced the authority of the sermon or Bible with the enthusiasms of sentiment, horror, or adventure, all of which relocated authority in the individual response of the reading self.   (13–14)

Viewed from this perspective, Gilman's *Herland* emerges—and should be taught—not as an isolated monument of feminist *bricolage* but as a work fully grounded in the practices that developed the novel in America. Hitherto slighted subgenres like didactic, sentimental, and domestic fiction emerge as legitimate traditions, and teaching *Herland* situates these forms with respect to the mainstream genres of prose romance, realism, and naturalism.

Both student taste and traditional American literary history tend to disdain the didactic. But considered within a tradition of didactic literature that not only includes the "high" genre of the bildungsroman but also "encompass[es] such diversity as the classical Aesop's Fables and the medieval morality play *Everyman*, as well as much United States fiction written in the nineteenth century" (Donawerth and Kolmerten xv), Gilman's didactic prose gains dignity from the company it keeps. Within the didactic paradigm, the flat characters that fail aesthetically for tastes grounded emotionally in romanticism and psychologically in realism develop strategic value; they embody "Socratic questions; that is ideas, not [the] characters, are well rounded" (Donawerth and Kolmerten xvi). Thus "in *Herland* the differing [but static] characters of Gilman's visitors matter, representing as they do radically different possible interactions between the values" of *Herland* and the male-dominant society (Ferns 31–32). The narrator, Van, adheres to the norm of the visitor to utopia whose consciousness mediates the differences between this new world and his point of origin; Terry embodies close-minded opposition; and Jeff wholeheartedly embraces the new system precisely because it does not require him to change his uncritical idealization of women. When Gilman's *Herland* is situated within a venerable tradition of didactic writings, the novel takes on new dimensions for students, and they realize that didacticism does not negate literary value. A writing assignment that facilitates this realization asks students to compare the function of literary types in *Herland* and Mark Twain's *Huckleberry Finn*. Through this exercise they can discover that, like Van's, Huck's ethical education advances through encounters with characters who, although more colorfully described and more realistically localized than Gilman's teaching figures, nevertheless play similar didactic roles.

I tell my students that given the enormous volume of utopian literature produced in the United States at the turn of the century (at least 160 works in the years 1888–1900 alone), the utopian novel might briefly have trumped the prose romance or realistic fiction for consideration as the true "National Novel" (Roemer 9). Prominent male and female writers both produced utopian fiction, but a gendered difference in focus emerges between them:

> Where United States utopias by men stress as ends in themselves matters of public policy, be they political, economic, or technological, women's utopias are more likely to include these matters primarily as they provide a means to the social end of fully developed human capacity of all people. Typically, women make issues of family, sexuality and marriage more central than do men.   (Donawerth and Kolmerten xxi)

By reintroducing the centrality of the marriage plot, the female utopia connects the form more closely to mainstream American fiction. After writing a comparison of *Herland* to Sinclair Lewis's *Babbitt* or Theodore Dreiser's *An American Tragedy*, for example, students should come to realize that Gilman's work transforms the marriage plot from a narrative to an analytical device by stratifying its three pairs of lovers in terms of conventional romance, social contract, and eroticized power struggle.

Herland also models for students the way in which female utopian fiction draws on the conventions of the sentimental novel, the most popular form of early American fiction, in order to make it easier to negotiate its brave new worlds. Readers of utopian fiction would have recognized sentimental patterns such as the centrality of the marriage plot and the domestic setting, and such recognition would make it easier for readers to absorb variations on these themes (Pfaelzer 8). In *Herland*, these familiar tropes would help contain Gilman's subversion of the redemptive heroine figure and the expansion of the domestic sphere into the entire ecosystem. Gilman's use of a male narrator to recount a feminist utopian experience similarly plays with genre expectations:

> The male narrator situates the reader at the conscious center of dominant power relationships and, hence, at the center of the process of change. Further, the male narrator is socially buffered from the madness which Gilman's female narrator suffers in "The Yellow Wallpaper" as she analyzes and expresses her subjective reality.
>
> (Marsha Smith, qtd. in Pfaelzer 9)

There are other connections to make with students. The novel's connection of right feeling to right action (even including the miracle of parthenogenesis!) echoes the sentimental code of *Uncle Tom's Cabin*, written by Gilman's great-aunt Harriet Beecher Stowe, but it refuses to sacrifice its right-thinking, right-acting women to the project of redeeming male protagonists—a fate such women frequently suffer in sentimental fiction and mainstream literature as well.

Utopian fiction necessarily makes use of the conventions of realism as well; as Anne Cranny-Francis points out, realism is the narrative mode employed to naturalize ideology into the lives of readers (137). Gilman, says Carol Farley Kessler, uses the realistic mode to "dislodge traditional ideology by presenting alternative, 'realizable' possibilities for more egalitarian gender roles" ("Consider" 129). *Herland*, however, in its project to alter basic premises of the predominant American ideology, seeks to diminish the tension between outer and inner self that is traditionally regarded as the hallmark of the realistic style. The transformative realism of *Herland* acts as a counterpoint both to the naturalistic ideology of determinism and to the romantic ideology of individual self-realization and thus provides ample reasons for the novel's inclusion on an American literature survey syllabus.

Like the literary naturalists, Gilman believed that social and especially economic forces (rather than psychological necessities) are the primary drivers of human behavior; however, *Herland* explicitly rejects the naturalist precepts that instinct invariably triumphs over reason and that biology is destiny. By developing a comparison of *Herland*'s female protagonists with those of Dreiser's *Sister Carrie* or Stephen Crane's *Maggie: A Girl of the Streets*, students can work out a trajectory of female growth toward self-sufficiency that does not entail physical denigration or moral compromise. The assignment also enables students to assess the aesthetic cost of Gilman's commitment to reason over instinct. In *Herland* victory over the id is a precondition of species survival; this enforced curtailment of libidinal energy deprives the novel of subtext, a factor that diminished the novel's impact in the era of modernism.

Literary transcendentalism inaugurated a gendered hierarchy in the conception of American literature traditionally considered mainstream: male protagonists developed their rugged individual consciousness by opposing civilizing conventions conventionally inscribed as female. This trope permeates the high tradition passing from Emerson through Thoreau and Whitman as well as the pulp fiction popularized by writers such as Edgar Rice Burroughs and H. P. Lovecraft. Gilman deconstructs this hierarchy in *Herland* to both didactic and comic effect, making her novel an excellent counterpoint to more canonical works on the syllabus.

By insisting that individuals develop a broader spectrum of their potential by contributing to the fabric of a community, *Herland* problematizes *Huckleberry Finn*'s thesis that self-actualization demands that the individual "light out for the Territory" (366). Students can investigate for themselves the gendered contrast in the narrative approach to civilization and its discontents by writing a comparison of the social structure and function of Gilman's all-female community with the all-male community that Herman Melville sets afloat on the *Pequod*. The ending of *Herland* makes it clear that Gilman hoped such a community could eventually incorporate both genders in full equality; the gender-bonded community that forms the basis for self-realization should evolve, rather than suffer the violent dissolution of *Moby-Dick*'s fraternity of isolates. *Herland* also destabilizes the masculine quest monomyth by portraying Terry as a kind of male Emma Bovary, forlornly trying to impose the tropes of the quest on a resisting cultural text. Terry's adventures with his two companions initially seem to fulfill the expectations of the genre, but thanks to the non-hierarchical, noncompetitive structure of Herland, Terry's insistence on acting out the paradigm results in his ejection from the community he sought first to save and then to dominate.

Unfortunately, Gilman is not so critical of another staple of the quest paradigm: its elitism. She perpetuates the stereotype of natural aristocracy through the character of Jeff, a southern gentleman who is both a scientist and a poet. Jeff's belief in women's innate moral superiority makes him the most successful transplant to Herland and allows him alone to get his wife pregnant. That the normal process of reproduction is reintroduced into Herland by such a benign chauvinist is an irony of which Gilman seems unaware.

Discussing the defect of elitism in Herland leads students to see the issue as a broader problem in American literature, however—a problem that troubles not only pulp fiction but also the reform novels that provide a generally more positive model for Gilman's work and even the great novels of the mainstream tradition. If students compare Gilman's southern aristocrat with one of Faulkner's or

Gilman's elegant indigenes with Hemingway's Hispanic characters, they are prompted to consider how some authors with multigenerational American roots responded to the influx of immigrants from eastern and southern Europe as well as to the internal emigration of African Americans from the Deep South. Such authors expressed a desire to preserve the traditional values of the republic, whether by presenting fantasies of violent heroism or paradigms for the improvement of education and social welfare or by withdrawing into a realm of aesthetic contemplation.

As the previous paragraph suggests, any discussion of *Herland* moves easily from the realm of American literature to that of American studies. Gilman explicitly made the connection between her writing and the work of reshaping American culture: "One girl reads this, and takes fire! I write for her" (Gilman, *Diaries* 2: 855). Moreover, Gilman embarked on her public career as a writer and lecturer for the Nationalist movement, itself inspired by a work of utopian fiction—Bellamy's *Looking Backward*.

Teaching *Herland* provides the opportunity for students to discuss the likely efficacy of educational reforms hypothesized by Horace Greeley and John Dewey and to forecast the results of systematic attention to land-use management or industrial safety. But the aspect of American culture that *Herland* most radically addresses is its topography of desire, which opens the way for discussion of the influence of Thorstein Veblen and Sigmund Freud.

In *Women and Economics*, Gilman castigated the sexuo-economic relation that kept women in such subjection to men that even getting the vote would not make a significant difference to their lives, but in *Herland* she even rejects the erotic nature of the redemptive influence that sentimental fiction had assigned to women. Van discovers that loving "up" is the only way to approach Ellador, and Terry learns that marital rape is a felony. Only Jeff's idealizing love is fruitful; mere erotic desire is sterile and is met with rejection. This explicitly anti-Freudian account of the relation of eros to civilization can offer students a standpoint from which to discuss the universalizing tendency of the Freudian model.

It is not only the libidinous desire of the American male that Gilman holds to account in *Herland* but also the acquisitive desire and conspicuous consumption of the American leisure class, which makes the novel a good companion to the study of Veblen. Many of Van and Ellador's conversations satirize the shortcomings of wretched excess predicated on an unequal distribution of goods. Inverting the overblown descriptions of wealth and splendor that characterize the lost worlds of male adventure fantasies, Gilman describes an ecosystem groomed to produce plenty without spoil in the primarily agrarian Herland. She refers to the industry of Herland without ever actually describing it, thus leaving the reader to imagine it more as a quality of the Herlanders' characters than as actual physical plants consuming resources and producing wastes. Gilman's attitude toward technology is somewhat ambivalent; in the inverted order of Herland, machines reduce physical drudgery and increase the availability of lower-cost goods and services, which distracts attention from their potential to threaten such yeoman livelihoods as Herland depends on and to create dehumanizing, unequal relationships between owners, producers, and consumers. In *Herland*, class struggle and alienated labor have been eliminated without benefit of Marx. Since the novel was produced at a time when Marxist revolution was a live option among America's workers, it usefully counterpoints a discussion of the American labor movement.

Student writing can consider whether the conversion from the capitalist acquisition-consumption cycle achieved in *Herland* can be a permanent one. Since only Terry clings to the primitive acquisition perspective, Gilman seems to be suggesting that the Herlander way of life can be chosen; and since Jeff and Celis achieve heterosexual union within the Herlander ethos, she implies that utopian evolution is natural and inevitable. Nevertheless, Terry's perspective violently enforces itself, and Terry is expelled from Herland. This pessimistic conclusion could be accounted for in purely literary terms, as Gilman's bow to the conventions of the utopian genre, or more usefully, as an incorporation of the sentimental convention by which the true end of the novel takes place in the reader's sensibilities. An American studies perspective might conclude, however, that by utterly eliminating the wilderness either as a habitat for the id or as a frontier for the economy, Herland had become terminally idyllic—its benign claustrophobia verging on fascism. Celis's child and Ellador's travels will provide the place with the hybrid vigor that Gilman's sequel, *With Her in Ourland*, exhibits.

Like Kate Chopin's *The Awakening*, *Herland* works well in an American literature course "less for its capacity to define distinctive periods than for its textual power to pose questions about those periods and their relations" (Bonner 103). With both its strengths and its weaknesses, *Herland* can provoke lively discussion of major themes in American literature and major movements in American culture—and provoking lively discussion was Gilman's strong suit, after all.

Teaching "The Yellow Wall-Paper" in the Context of American Literary Realism and Naturalism

Cynthia J. Davis

When I began teaching at my university in 1994, I inherited a number of responsibilities from my predecessor. Among these were two courses entitled American Literary Realism and Naturalism, one offered at the undergraduate and the other at the graduate level. There is enough demand for these courses that I am usually asked to offer them both annually. Staying true to the titular emphasis, however, can tie the hands of someone interested in expanding offerings beyond the white male trinities of the realists William Dean Howells, Henry James, and Mark Twain and the naturalists Stephen Crane, Theodore Dreiser, and Frank Norris. How to sneak in a few women and minorities while still remaining focused on the literary movements at hand?

One of the authors I have most successfully integrated into these courses is Charlotte Perkins Gilman (1860–1934). The obvious justification for teaching Gilman in such a course is chronological. After all, Gilman produced many of her most influential works during the heyday of literary realism and naturalism in America, and it behooves students to recognize that there were other, different voices speaking at the same time. One might easily rationalize Gilman's presence on the syllabus by situating her particular brand of optimistic reform within the era's emergent progressivism and invoking the comparable sympathies of writers including Howells, Hamlin Garland, and Upton Sinclair. Allowing students access to more didactic writings enables them to debate the potential benefits of telling as opposed to James's mandated showing and to consider by contrast the limitations of more mimetic modes of representation.

Yet it is not as an alternative voice that I have most frequently presented Gilman. In fact, I have been most successful in introducing her ideas when I couch them as consistent with realistic and naturalistic tenets. Of course, Gilman's "The Yellow Wall-Paper" (1892) is regularly interpreted as a work of psychological realism, but this harrowing tale is also rightly seen as the exception to Gilman's didactic rule, and Gilman herself is seldom if ever identified with either of these literary movements. So while Walter Benn Michaels and numerous feminist critics have pointed to realistic or naturalistic tendencies in the story, rarely is a search conducted for similar tendencies in its author. The strategy I want to recommend here entails presenting Gilman as a naturalist with a twist. In my experience, reading her short story "The Yellow Wall-Paper" alongside several of her nonfiction treatises including *Women and Economics* (1898) produces riveting discussions of Gilman's fictional and nonfictional takes on determinism and their alignment with the bleaker portraits of the literary naturalists. As a result, students can come to a new understanding of the determinisms popular in the Gilded Age and a new awareness of their possibilities and problems.

The first time I encountered Gilman's chilling tale I was a sophomore in college, enrolled in an introductory survey of American literature. The context was the story's fit within the course's overarching theme, American Dreams, American Nightmares. "The Yellow Wall-Paper" was hailed as a representative nightmare, compared with the darker tales of Edgar Allan Poe and Nathaniel Hawthorne before it and referred to later when discussing such disturbing documents of oppression as Ralph Ellison's "The Battle Royale" or Maxine Hong Kingston's *The Woman Warrior*. I was to read it one more time as an undergraduate in a senior-level women's literature seminar, where the emphasis was on Gilman's biography, the story's depiction of patriarchal oppression, and the narrator's defiant, mad resistance.

Now that I find myself on the other side of the lectern, I most frequently teach "The Yellow Wall-Paper" in a course on American women writers, organized around the intersection of gender and genre. This course aims to assess how an author's gender identity influences generic output, though I often find myself devoting class time to questions of literary value. This is certainly true whenever I teach any of Gilman's works other than "The Yellow Wall-Paper," arguably the most literary of her literary productions.

When I last offered this course, I decided to confront the issue of aesthetics head on and included in my course pack not only "The Yellow Wall-Paper" but also two other Gilman tales, "If I Were a Man" and "The Unnatural Mother," each with the author's name concealed. Before class I asked students to compare and contrast the three tales and to guess the gender of each story's author (purposefully allowing two erroneous assumptions: that at least one was by a man and that they each had different authors). This assignment launched a spirited discussion of the gender politics informing each story and the gender identity of each author. There were heated debates over whether any of these stories could have been written by a man. Students soon realized that they automatically gendered female any story that preached a message, any story, to reverse James, that told rather than showed. When I asked why preaching and teaching were necessarily feminine qualities, the students recognized that they had bought into the gendering process emergent in Gilman's lifetime, when James and others were involved in assessing didactic, emotionally wrought writing—so often the domain of women—as less aesthetically pleasing and their own more indirect, ambiguous works as aesthetically superior.

I also historicize such assessments as they arise when I teach Gilman alongside James and others in my realism and naturalism courses. But there my intent in introducing other works by Gilman is not to confuse the students but to clarify Gilman's belief system, which in significant ways overlaps with the realists'. To facilitate discussions of Gilman's particular stance toward evolution and literature, I assign readings from *Women and Economics* and her later study *The Man-Made World* (1911). Sections of these works reveal Gilman's debt to such thinkers as Edward Bellamy and Lester Ward and her enthusiastic embrace of Darwinian evolutionary theory as explanatory force. We discuss the fact that Gilman viewed human life—both individual and collective—as an organic entity and regarded all its forms, for so long as they were duly governed by natural laws, to be not only constantly evolving but clearly improving. In her view, since biology dictates that "all the tendencies of a living organism are progressive in their development" (*Women* 59), all that does not lend itself to the organism's development must be intrinsically alien to it. As Gilman insists in her preface to *Women and Economics*, "some of the worst evils under which we suffer, evils long supposed to be inherent and ineradicable in our natures, are but the result of certain arbitrary conditions of our own adoption, and [. . .] by removing those conditions, we may remove the evils resultant" (xxxix). If nature was left to its own devices, both male and female would continue to flourish over time.

I ask my students how Gilman would have answered the question of why women especially had not flourished. On the basis of the assigned readings, they join her in pointing to environmental forces, which she believed inhibited our inherent evolutionary tendencies. According to Gilman, despite our best efforts and natural impulses to improve, extrinsic factors including climate, habitat, nourishment, and other people both "form and limit" a given creature ("Our Excessive Femininity" 4). The word "limit" seems to be crucial to Gilman's brand of determinism: if it is natural for humans to evolve, then environmental circumstances typically operate as devolutionary, degenerative forces. For Gilman, as I summarize for my students, the natural is not reduced to or replaced by the social; it is retained as a relatively plastic category that, for all its naturalness, is still capable of being altered through its functions, dysfunctions, and interactions.

Once Gilman's reform Darwinism has been elucidated, I ask students in my graduate-level courses to compare it with the social Darwinism of Herbert Spencer, and I go to the blackboard to chart the similarities and differences. An article by Lois Magner is very helpful in eliciting this comparison and worth assigning at the graduate level. In brief, Spencer's fervent belief in the the survival of the fittest at the social level led him to object to attempts to improve the lot of the less unfortunate—hence his opposition to vaccinations and even fire departments. By contrast, Gilman, whose defining organism was the social, not the individual, body, believed it was each individual's obligation as part of the collectivity to intervene. Reading Darwin through divergent moral valences and from different epistemological standpoints, Spencer and Gilman disagreed about what lay at the essence of evolution. Where Spencer saw combat, struggle, and self, Gilman saw growth, change, and selflessness.

The next question we confront in both classes is whether Gilman might properly be called a naturalist. The answer students seem most satisfied with is maybe. For as we've discovered together, Gilman preached evolutionary views not to reflect Hobbesian understanding of life but to show readers how inherently unnatural such nastiness and brutishness were. In essence, Gilman resists naturalism's prerequisite moral ambiguity and manipulates naturalistic doctrines so that they teach, and at times even preach, a lesson in human progress. Perhaps nowhere is the twist Gilman gives to naturalism made clearer than in her literary theory, and here is where the selections from *The Man-Made World* come in handy. According to Gilman, "great literature" is that which relinquishes its focus on the androcentric past, transcends sex, and encompasses all of life (*Man-Made World* 100). This latter qualification may remind students of the impulses behind realism and naturalism, but contra these movements, Gilman's literary theory explicitly links realism and didacticism. Truthful fiction, she argued, should "teach us life easily, swiftly, truly; *teach not by preaching but by truly re-presenting*; and we should grow up becoming acquainted with a far wider range of life in books than could even be ours in person. Then meeting life in reality we should be wise—and not be disappointed" (*Man-Made World* 101; my emphasis). It is worth discussing with students the way that Gilman, in this telling quotation, links representation (*re*-presentation) not to mimeticism but to didacticism or, rather, renders the latter two typically opposed practices virtually synonymous.

Turning from her literary theory to her literary production, we examine whether Gilman practiced what she preached, or, rather, taught. "The Yellow Wall-Paper" may be a difficult test case, as it is surely Gilman's most subtle and complex literary work. It is also the one piece of fiction by Gilman that most warrants the label naturalistic. At this point, I typically ask my students how "The Yellow Wall-Paper" might fit within the rubric of literary naturalism, and they are usually quick to supply evidence. Aside from its psychological realism, it follows naturalistic plot lines in casting its protagonist as a woman ensnared by circumstances—a woman who, to borrow from Dreiser's description of Sister Carrie, is finally more written than she writes (although she writes copiously, frenetically). Certainly, the story's ending, where the once-articulate, upper-class narrator is reduced to an atavistic creature crawling about the room on all fours, remains one of the creepier fictional representations of devolution.

In my graduate classes, I like at this point to provide a brief synopsis of the critical debate surrounding the story's ambiguous thematics. Classic feminist interpretations of the tale—beginning with Elaine Hedges's afterword in the 1973 Feminist Press reissue—read as an allegory, in which the protagonist as Everywoman is driven mad by a wallpaper symbolic of patriarchy's script, which as it envelops the heroine both represents and causes her subjectification (see also Gilbert and Gubar, *Madwoman*, and Kolodny, "Map," for additional representatives of this argument). Psychoanalytic literary critics typically invert this pattern, suggesting that the heroine projects her madness outward and writes her hysteria large on her surroundings (Berman; Haney-Peritz; Herndl; Jacobus; Johnson; and Veeder each provide psychoanalytic readings of the tale). Also divergent are interpretations of the story's maddening (both literally and critically speaking) conclusion. While some have read it as defeat, others (including Gilbert and Gubar; Fetterley; Kennard; and Treichler, "Escaping") attempt to mitigate the tale's severity and wrest a degree of agency for the protagonist by suggesting that the conclusion represents a kind of triumph—the only sane, imaginative response to an insane world.

These divergent interpretations of "The Yellow Wall-Paper"—helpfully overviewed in Hedges's "'Out at Last'?"—demonstrate that if the story was meant to teach, its lesson remains murky. And yet, as I inform my students, Gilman confided to her friend Alexander Black that she wrote the story "to preach. If it is literature, that just happened" (Black 39). A similar intent is also conveyed in her essay "Why I Wrote 'The Yellow Wallpaper'?," where Gilman maintains that the story was "not intended to drive people crazy, but to save people from being driven crazy." So if we take Gilman at her word, what precisely was she preaching about, and what exactly was it that was driving her and others crazy?

Clearly, there are a number of specified and unspecified causes for the speaker's illness. And yet, as I have argued elsewhere, there is provocative textual and contextual evidence to suggest that the house's pathogenic role has been neglected. Throughout her career, Gilman espoused a sort of domestic determinism, a theory emanating from her belief that environmental forces tend to impede natural progress. A handout of quotes detailing Gilman's anti-domestic ideology helps students gloss the determining force of the story's own haunted house.

In her 1903 work *The Home*, Gilman pinpoints domesticity as the root of women's ills. For example, comparing two statues on display at the World's Fair—one male and the other female and each based on the mean average of a collection of college students' measurements—Gilman attributes the female statue's evident inferiority to women's confinement within the home: "the figure of the man is far and away more beautiful than that of the woman," she writes. "We are softer and whiter *for our long housing*; but not more truly beautiful" (210–11; my emphasis). Gender differences, Gilman infers, are the result not so much of biology as of domesticity. Her point is clarified in a 1903 article that appeared in *Success* magazine: "The effect of the home *and nothing else* upon women," Gilman avows, "has been precisely what it would have been on men—cramping, dwarfing, blinding, choking, keeping down the higher human instincts" ("Home" 411). If the situation were reversed and men were secluded in the house and women set free upon the world, men would develop "women's brains" and women "men's": "We have called the broader, sounder, better balanced, more fully exercised brain 'a man's brain,' and the narrower, more emotional and personal one 'a woman's brain'; whereas the difference is merely that between the world and the house" (*Home* 274). Gilman's analogy nicely conveys her conviction that for most women geography, not anatomy, is destiny.

Believing that, especially in men's eyes, "the woman and the home [had become] one and indivisible" (*Home* 22), Gilman takes this supposed symbiosis and renders its stultifying effects symbolically. Thus in her poem "In Duty Bound," she likens the traditional housewife trapped in the home to the soul imprisoned in that housewife's body:

> A house with roof so darkly low
> The heavy rafters shut the sunlight out;
> One cannot stand erect without a blow;
> Until the soul inside
> Cries for a grave—more wide.   (rpt. in *Living* 77)

Just as the woman cannot move within such a home, the soul cannot move within such a domesticated, feminine body: both are unhealthy, confining.

Most students are eager to explore the connection between the author's critique of traditional domestic structures and her unhappy childhood, and they are especially interested to learn of her father's abandonment and her mother's distressingly distanced method of child rearing. We also discuss how domesticity's negative connotations intensified for Gilman in the wake of her marriage to Walter Stetson, during which, she later confided, she "was well while away and sick while *at home*" (*Living* 95; my emphasis). Is it any wonder, then, that "The Yellow Wall-Paper" is less a work of domestic fiction than an exposé of the fictions concerning domesticity? Indeed, I encourage students to read the story as an early, fictional attempt to articulate the domestic determinism she expounds repeatedly in her later expository prose. That in 1892 her deterministic theories were still emergent and provisional may help to explain the story's own inarticulateness concerning the etiology of the dis-ease it so visibly enacts.

In that now famous moment in 1887 when Gilman sought out Dr. S. Weir Mitchell for treatment, she was informed by him that his rest cure depended, in Gilman's telling paraphrase, on the patient's leading "as domestic a life as possible" (*Living* 96). As Gilman reveals in her autobiography, "I went home, followed those directions rigidly for months, and came perilously near to losing my mind" (96). Gilman's transcription of Mitchell's words is significant because it pinpoints the pivotal role of domesticity in inducing her mental collapse. If, as my students discover from their handout, it is true that she wrote the story to convince Mitchell of "the error of his ways" (*Living* 121), then, given that Mitchell's "ways" were frequently guided by his belief that woman was and should be both the "source and center of the home" (*Wear* 55), we can read "The Yellow Wall-Paper" at its most conscious level as a fictional attempt to demonstrate the errors of such a view.

But the story can also be read as documenting the pernicious truths of its reverse—that is, of the possibility that the home may, unnaturally, be the source of the woman. I recommend that rather than view woman as homemaker, students explore the extent to which the story posits the home as woman maker. The very first "character" we meet is, after all, the house, variously described as an "ancestral hall," "a colonial mansion," "a hereditary estate" (9), "the most beautiful place" (11). In many respects, the house is more fleshed out than any of its inhabitants: we get more detailed description of it than of anything or anybody else—even its furniture and furnishings seem animated (16–17). This anthropomorphism may simply signify that the narrator, starved for creative activity, is projecting her personality onto the inanimate objects surrounding her. Yet Gilman's already outlined domestic determinism prompts a counterreading, one in which the house's personality might be seen as literally contouring the impressionable protagonist's rather than the reverse.

It is in the story's early pages, when we first meet the still nameless "I" who tells the tale, that she appears the most lucid, the most sane. And it is there that she performs her diagnosis of what ails her, insisting that "there is something strange about the house—I can feel it" (11). Her objection to the fact that the house "stood so long untenanted" (9) is by no means unwarranted, nor is her concern over its secluded location—"it is quite alone, standing well back from the road, quite three miles from the village" (11). Throughout the story, the narrator's idea of a cure necessitates removal not just from the room that torments her but from the house itself, as shown when she begs John to take her away (23) and even when she at one point "seriously" contemplates "burning the house" (29). We see this desire expressed as well through the protagonist's persistent, yearning glances from her attic window at the outlying gardens and enticing lane, areas soon declared off-limits by her doctor-husband. The bars on the windows, the bolted-down bed, the gate at the stairs, the rings on the walls, all suggest that this home has served as a place of incarceration, perhaps a madhouse: it thus makes sense given Gilman's domestic determinism that someone enclosed therein would go mad.

Few contemporary readers may have taken this point about the story's domestic message—being more likely to read it as a harrowing Gothic tale than to grasp its latent critique of domesticity. Yet as I hope to have shown—to both my students and my readers—it is possible to make a case for the story as a document of determinism and hence for its presence on the syllabus of courses on American literary realism and naturalism. It is important to stress, however, that unlike many other deterministic stories, "The Yellow Wall-Paper" attempts to teach about, and to warn against, deterministic processes, rather than merely to reflect them as status quo. Horace Scudder may have rejected the story for the *Atlantic Monthly*, claiming that "I could not forgive myself if I made others as miserable as I have already made myself." Yet Gilman intended not to spread misery but instead to alleviate it, by spelling out, in graphic detail, the misery that domestic confinement could cause. Conrad Shumaker ("Realism") has argued that the story is in fact brutally realistic about bourgeois women's lot in life but that at the time of its publication readers were not willing to accept its realism, opting instead to write it off as the stuff of fantasy and thereby failing to face up to women's real suffering. One benefit of teaching the story as realistic today is that students—who, after all, have benefited from two waves of feminist movement—are usually more willing to confront and accept the truths it presents or teaches about (remembering that for Gilman these two terms are often synonymous). That its truths have proven over the years so hard to grasp suggests that more mimetic modes may not be the best vehicles for getting an author's message across. It seems important to close discussions of Gilman as a realist-naturalist by reminding students of the story's anomalous status in the author's canon, of her decision thenceforth to use more clear-cut didactic forms. While Gilman may not qualify as a bona fide literary realist or naturalist, including her in such a course teaches us a good deal about both literary movements and the reasons why not everyone writing at the time might have embraced their tenets firmly and forever.

NOTE

Parts of this essay are adapted from chapter 4 in *Bodily and Narrative Forms: The Influence of Medicine on American Literature* by Cynthia J. Davis, © 2000 by the Board of Trustees of the Leland Stanford Jr. University, and are printed here by permission of Stanford University Press, www.sup.org.

NOTES ON CONTRIBUTORS

Mary C. Carruth is a faculty member and assistant director of women's studies at the University of Georgia, Athens. With interests in women's studies, early American women writers, and autobiography, she is currently editing a feminist critical collection on early American literature and culture to 1830.

Priscilla Ferguson Clement is professor of history and women's studies at Penn State University, Delaware County Campus. She is the author of *Growing Pains: Children in the Industrial Age, 1850–1890* (1997) and *Welfare and the Poor in the Nineteenth-Century City, Philadelphia, 1800–1854* (1985) and coeidtor of *Boyhood in America: An Encyclopedia* (2001).

Cynthia J. Davis is associate professor of English at the University of South Carolina, Columbia. She is the author of *Bodily and Narrative Forms: The Influence of Medicine on American Literature, 1845–1915* (2000) and the coauthor of *Women Writers in the United States: A Timeline of Social, Cultural, and Literary History* (1996). Her current project is a biography of Charlotte Perkins Gilman.

Melanie V. Dawson is visiting assistant professor at the College of William and Mary. With Susan Harris Smith she edited *The American 1890s: A Cultural Reader* (2000). She is the author of articles on Edith Wharton and Henry James. Her current projects are a book on literature and nineteenth-century entertainment practices, tentatively titled "Spectacles of Agency," and a study on configuring identification in a mass-culture age.

Kara Virginia Donaldson is a lecturer in English and women's studies at Rutgers University. She is the author of "Alisoun's Language: Body, Text, and Glossing in Chaucer's 'Miller's Tale'" (1992) and "Harriet Beecher Stowe, Gender Relations, and Reform in New York City, 1871–75," a working paper from the Institute of Research on Women (1999), and contributing editor to *Women Memoirists II, L–Z* (1998). She organized the 2001 Teaching Literature Conference at Rutgers University and is currently at work on a study of the fallen woman in nineteenth-century American literature.

David Faulkner is a visiting instructor at the State University of New York, Cortland. He is the author of essays on Charles Dickens and Matthew Arnold, and his current projects include articles on Rudyard Kipling and Oscar Wilde and on Dickens's *A Tale of Two Cities*.

Janet Gabler-Hover is professor of English at Georgia State University. She is author of *Truth in American Fiction: The Legacy of Rhetorical Idealism* (1990); "The North-South Reconciliation Theme and the 'Shadow of the Negro' in *Century Illustrated Magazine*," in *Periodical Literature in Nineteenth-Century America* (1995); and *Dreaming Black/Writing White: The Hagar Myth in American Cultural History* (2000). Her articles have appeared in *Philological Quarterly*, *Henry James Review*, and *Texas Studies in Literature and Language*.

Lisa Ganobcsik-Williams is a lecturer in the Department of English and Comparative Literary Studies at the University of Warwick. She is the author of "The Intellectualism of Charlotte Perkins Gilman: Evolutionary Perspectives on Race, Ethnicity, and Class" (1999) and "Charlotte Perkins Gilman and the *Forerunner*: A New Woman's Changing Perspective on American Immigration" (2001). Her research interests include late-nineteenth- and early-twentieth-century American literature and expository writing.

Catherine J. Golden is professor of English at Skidmore College. She is the editor of *Book Illustrated: Text, Image, and Culture, 1770–1930* (2000) and *The Captive Imagination: A Casebook on "The Yellow Wallpaper"* (1992) and coeditor, with Joanna S. Zangrando, of *The Mixed Legacy of Charlotte Perkins Gilman* (2000) and, with Denise D. Knight, of Gilman's *Unpunished* (1997). Her essays and reviews have appeared in *Victorian Studies*, *Victorian Poetry*, *Profession 95*, and *Studies in American Fiction*. Her current project, "Lives between the Pages: The Figure of the Woman Reader in Text and Illustration in Victorian British and American Literature," is a book-length study examining fictional and illustrative depictions of the woman reader.

Judith Harris is assistant professor of English at George Washington University. She is the author of *Atonement* (2000), *Song of the Moon* (1982), and *Poppies* (1981). Her work has appeared in *After Confession: Poetry as Autobiography* (2001) and in *South Atlantic Quarterly*, *AWP*, *American Scholar*, *Tikkun*, *Storming Heaven's Gate: Women's Writing*, *Her Face in the Mirror*, *Prairie Schooner*, *Antioch Review*, *Poetry Northwest*, *English Journal*, *New York Quarterly*, *Women's Review of Books*, *JAMA*, *Southern Humanities Review*, and numerous anthologies and book collections. Her current project is "Signifying Pain: Constructing and Healing the Self through Writing," forthcoming from State University of New York Press.

Guiyou Huang is associate professor and chair of the English Department at Kutztown University. He is the author of *Whitmanism, Imagism, and Modernism in China and America* (1997); "Asian, Asian American, American: Texts in Between" (forthcoming); and editor of *Asian American Autobiographers: A Bio-bibliographical Critical Sourcebook* (2001) and *Asian American Poets: A Bio-bibliographical Critical Sourcebook* (2002). He is the author of thirty articles, and his current project is a book titled "The Columbia Guide to Asian American Literature."

Joanne B. Karpinski is associate professor of English at Regis University. She is the editor of *Critical Essays on Charlotte Perkins Gilman* (1992); coeditor, with David Mogen and Scott Sanders, of *Frontier Gothic* (1993); and author of "When the Marriage of True Minds Admits Impediments: Charlotte Perkins Gilman and William Dean Howells" (1988) and "The Economic Conundrum in the Life Writing of Charlotte Perkins Gilman" (2000). Her current project is an edition of Gilman's lectures.

Carol Farley Kessler is professor emerita of English, American studies, and women's studies at Penn State University, Delaware County Campus. She is the editor of two editions of *Daring to Dream* (1984, 1995); Elizabeth's Stuart Phelps's 1877 *The Story of Avis* (1985); and coeditor, with Kathryn M. Grossman, of a special issue on utopias of *Journal of General Education* (1984). She is the author of *Elizabeth Stuart Phelps* (1982) and *Charlotte Perkins Gilman: Her Progress toward Utopia, with Selected Writ-*

ings (1995). Her current research project is an edition of Mary Griffith's 1836 utopia, *Three Hundred Years Hence*.

Michael J. Kiskis is professor of American literature at Elmira College. He is the editor of *Mark Twain's Own Autobiography: The Chapters from the* North American Review (1990) and the coeditor, with Laura Skandera-Trombley, of *Constructing Mark Twain: New Directions in Scholarship* (2001) as well as essays on Mark Twain and American women writers of the nineteenth century. He is past editor of *Studies in American Humor* and current editor of *Modern Language Studies*. His current projects include a book-length study of Twain's autobiographical writing.

Denise D. Knight is professor of English at the State University of New York, Cortland, and president of the Charlotte Perkins Gilman Society. She is author of *Charlotte Perkins Gilman: A Study of the Short Fiction* (1997) and editor of Herland, *"The Yellow Wall-Paper," and Selected Writings of Charlotte Perkins Gilman* (1999); *The Abridged Diaries of Charlotte Perkins Gilman* (1998); *Nineteenth-Century American Women Writers: A Bio-Bibliographical Critical Sourcebook* (1997); *The Later Poetry of Charlotte Perkins Gilman* (1996); a two-volume critical edition of *The Diaries of Charlotte Perkins Gilman* (1994); and *"The Yellow Wall-Paper" and Selected Stories of Charlotte Perkins Gilman* (1994). Her work has appeared in numerous essay collections and journals. Her current project is a critical edition of Wharton's *Ethan Frome* and *Summer*.

Lisa A. Long is assistant professor of English and chair of the Gender and Women's Studies Program at North Central College. She is the editor of Paul Laurence Dunbar's *The Fanatics* (2001) and author of "The Post-bellum Reform Writings of Rebecca Harding Davis and Elizabeth Stuart Phelps" (2001); "Charlotte Forten and the Quest for 'Genius, Beauty, and Deathless Fame'" (1999); "Imprisoned in/at Home: Criminal Culture in Rebecca Harding Davis's *Margret Howth: A Story of Today*" (1998); and "'The Corporeity of Heaven': Rehabiliating the Civil War Body in *The Gates Ajar*" (1997), which won the 1997 Norman Foerster Prize from *American Literature*. Her current project is a book on representations of the American Civil War, health, and history.

Michelle A. Massé is associate professor at Louisiana State University, Baton Rouge. She is author of *In the Name of Love: Woman, Masochism, and the Gothic* (1992) and essays on psychoanalysis, feminism, and fiction. She is editor of the State University of New York Press's Feminist Theory and Criticism series and is currently working on a study of Louisa May Alcott.

Michelle N. McEvoy is a lecturer in English at the University of California, Los Angeles. She is author of "Envisioning/Revisioning Woolf: Filming Her Fiction at the End of the Century" (2000) and "Powers of Horror and Peace: Abjection and Community in Virginia Woolf's *Between the Acts*" (1999). Her teaching and research interests include twentieth-century British literature, women's writing and feminist theory, narrative, cultural studies, intertextuality, and film adaptation. Her current project is a study of issues of internationalism and antialienism in twentieth-century British literature.

Wendy Ripley is associate professor of English at Columbia Union College. She is author of "Wife of Bath: Advocate of Sovereignty or Equality?" (1988). Her research and teaching interests include nineteenth-century American women writers, women's studies, American literature, and American studies. Her current project, "Women Working at Writing: Achieving Professional Status in Nineteenth-Century America," is a book-length study of the professionalization of American women writers from 1850 to 1875.

Gary Scharnhorst is professor of English at the University of New Mexico. His publications include *Charlotte Perkins Gilman* (1985), *Charlotte Perkins Gilman: A Bibliography* (1985), and *Bret Harte: Opening the American Literary West* (2000). He is editor of *American Literary Realism* and editor in alternating years of *American Literary Scholarship*.

Gary Totten is assistant professor of English at Concordia College. He is the author of articles on Edith Wharton, Theodore Dreiser, and Simone de Beauvoir. He is currently editing an essay collection on the significance of material culture in Edith Wharton's life and work.

Mark W. Van Wienen is associate professor of English at Augustana College. He is author of *Partisans and Poets: The Political Work of American Poetry in the Great War* (1997) and editor of *Rendezvous with Death: American Poems of the Great War* (2002). His current project is a study of reform socialist literature in the United States between 1890 and 1940.

CONTRIBUTORS AND SURVEY PARTICIPANTS

The following scholars and teachers of Gilman's works contributed essays for this volume, made valuable suggestions, or participated in the survey that preceded and provided materials for the preparation of this book:

Dale M. Bauer, *University of Kentucky*
Susan Blake, *Lafayette College*
Mary C. Carruth, *University of Georgia*
Priscilla Ferguson Clement, *Penn State University, Delaware County*
Cynthia J. Davis, *University of South Carolina, Columbia*
Melanie V. Dawson, *College of William and Mary*
Mary Jo Deegan, *University of Nebraska, Lincoln*
Kara Virginia Donaldson, *Rutgers University, New Brunswick*
David Faulkner, *State University of New York, Cortland*
Janet Gabler-Hover, *Georgia State University*
Lisa Ganobcsik-Williams, *University of Warwick*
Catherine J. Golden, *Skidmore College*
Judith Harris, *George Washington University*
Michael R. Hill, *Iowa Western Community College*
Tammy Horn, *University of West Alabama*
Guiyou Huang, *Kutztown University*
Joanne B. Karpinski, *Regis College*
Eileen Kenney, *University of Nebraska, Omaha*
Carol Farley Kessler, *Penn State University, Delaware County*
Michael J. Kiskis, *Elmira College*
Denise D. Knight, *State University of New York, Cortland*
Lisa A. Long, *North Central College*
Jean M. Lutes, *Manhattan College*
Michelle A. Massé, *Louisiana State University, Baton Rouge*
Michelle N. McEvoy, *University of California, Los Angeles*
Charlotte Rich, *Eastern Kentucky University*
Wendy Ripley, *Columbia Union College*
Gary Scharnhorst, *University of New Mexico, Albuquerque*
Shawn St. Jean, *State University of New York, Brockport*
Gary Totten, *Concordia College*
Ellen Tsagaris, *Quest College*
Jennifer S. Tuttle, *University of New England*
Mark W. Van Wienen, *Augustana College*
Joanna Schneider Zangrando, *Skidmore College*

WORKS CITED

"The Yellow Wall-Paper" and Herland: Paperback Editions and Anthologies (in Chronological Order)

The Yellow Wall-Paper. Afterword Elaine R. Hedges. 1973. 2nd ed. New York: Feminist, 1996. Corr. ed. 2000.

Herland. Ed. Ann J. Lane. New York: Pantheon, 1979.

The Charlotte Perkins Gilman Reader. Ed. and introd. Ann J. Lane. New York: Pantheon, 1980.

"The Yellow Wallpaper" and Other Writings by Charlotte Perkins Gilman. Introd. Lynne Sharon Schwartz. New York: Bantam, 1989.

———. *The Captive Imagination: A Casebook on "The Yellow Wallpaper."* Ed. and introd. Catherine Golden. New York: Feminist, 1992.

Herland and Selected Stories by Charlotte Perkins Gilman. Ed. and introd. Barbara H. Solomon. New York: Signet, 1992.

The Yellow Wallpaper. Ed. and introd. Thomas L. Erskine and Connie L. Richards. New Brunswick: Rutgers UP, 1993.

"The Yellow Wall-paper" and Selected Stories of Charlotte Perkins Gilman. Newark: U of Delaware P, 1984.

"The Yellow Wall-Paper" and Other Stories. Ed. and introd. Robert Shulman. New York: Oxford UP, 1995.

"The Yellow Wallpaper" and Other Stories. Mineola: Dover, 1997.

Herland. Mineola: Dover, 1998.

The Yellow Wallpaper. Ed. Dale M. Bauer. Boston: Bedford, 1998.

Charlotte Perkins Gilman's "The Yellow Wall-paper" and the History of Its Publication and Reception. Ed. Julie Bates Dock. University Park: Pennsylvania State UP, 1998.

Herland, "The Yellow Wall-Paper," and Selected Writings. Ed. and introd. Denise D. Knight. New York: Penguin, 1999.

"The Yellow Wall-Paper" and Other Writings. Introd. Alexander Black. New York: Modern Lib., 2000.

Books and Articles

Achebe, Chinua. *Things Fall Apart*. 1959. New York: Anchor, 1994.

Allen, Polly Wynn. *Building Domestic Liberty: Charlotte Perkins Gilman's Architectural Feminism*. Amherst: U of Massachusetts P, 1988.

Ammons, Elizabeth. *Conflicting Stories: American Women Writers at the Turn into the Twentieth Century*. New York: Oxford UP, 1991.

Andersen, Margaret L., and Patricia Hill Collins, eds. *Race, Class, and Gender.* 4th ed. Belmont: Wadsworth/Thomson, 2001.

Arnold, Matthew. Culture and Anarchy *and Other Writings.* New Haven: Yale UP, 1994.

Asher, Robert, and Charles Stephenson, eds. *Labor Divided: Race and Ethnicity in United States Labor Struggles, 1835–1960.* Albany: State U of New York P, 1990.

Barnes, Elizabeth. *States of Sympathy: Seduction and Democracy in the American Novel.* New York: Columbia UP, 1997.

Bassuk, Ellen L. "The Rest Cure: Repetition or Resolution of Victorian Women's Conflicts?" *The Female Body in Western Culture: Contemporary Perspectives.* Ed. Susan Rubin Suleiman. Cambridge: Harvard UP, 1986. 130–51.

Bauer, Dale M., ed. *The Yellow Wallpaper.* Boston: Bedford, 1998.

Beard, George Miller. *American Nervousness; Its Causes and Consequences: A Supplement to Nervous Exhaustion.* New York: Arno, 1972.

Bederman, Gail. *Manliness and Civilization: A Cultural History of Gender and Race in the United States, 1880–1917.* Chicago: U of Chicago P, 1995.

Beecher, Catharine E. *Letters to the People on Health and Happiness.* New York: Harper, 1856.

———. *Physiology and Calisthenics for School and Family.* New York: Harper, 1856.

Beecher, Catharine E., and Harriet Beecher Stowe. *The American Woman's Home, or Principles of Domestic Science.* New York: Ford, 1869.

Beer, Janet. *Kate Chopin, Edith Wharton, and Charlotte Perkins Gilman: Studies in Short Fiction.* New York: St. Martin's, 1997.

Beilharz, Peter. *Labour's Utopias: Bolshevism, Fabianism, Social Democracy.* New York: Routledge, 1992.

Beilharz, Peter, and Chris Nyland, eds. *The Webbs, Fabianism and Feminism: Fabianism and the Political Economy of Everyday Life.* Aldershot: Ashgate, 1998.

Bellamy, Edward. *Looking Backward, 2000–1887.* 1888. New York: Viking-Penguin, 1986.

———. "Socialism and Nationalism." *New Nation* 27 Jan. 1894: 38.

———. "Talks on Nationalism." *New Nation* 18 Apr. 1891: 191–92.

Bennett, Michael, and Vanessa D. Dickerson, eds. *Recovering the Black Female Body: Self-Representations by African American Women.* New Brunswick: Rutgers UP, 2001.

Berkin, Carol Ruth. "Private Woman, Public Woman: The Contradictions of Charlotte Perkins Gilman." Karpinski 17–42.

Berman, Jeffrey. *The Talking Cure: Literary Representations of Psychoanalysis.* New York: New York UP, 1985.

———. "The Unrestful Cure: Charlotte Perkins Gilman and 'The Yellow Wallpaper.'" Golden, *Imagination* 211–41.

Bérubé, Michael. "Aesthetics and the Literal Imagination." Richter 391–97.

Black, Alexander. "The Woman Who Saw It First." *Century* 107 (1923): 33–42. Rpt. in Karpinski 56–66.

Blicksilver, Edith, ed. *The Ethnic American Woman: Problems, Protests, Lifestyle.* 5th ed. Atlanta: Blicksilver, 1997.

Bonner, Thomas, Jr. "*The Awakening* in an American Literature Survey Course."

Approaches to Teaching Chopin's The Awakening. Ed. Bernard Koloksi. New York: MLA, 1988. 99–103.

Boston Women's Health Book Collective. *Our Bodies, Ourselves for the New Century: A Book for and by Women*. Rev. ed. New York: Simon, 1998.

Brontë, Charlotte. Jane Eyre: *Authoritative Text, Backgrounds, and Criticism*. 2nd ed. New York: Norton, 1987.

Butler, Judith. *Bodies That Matter: On the Discursive Limits of 'Sex.'* London: Routledge, 1993.

Cahill, Susan, ed. and introd. *Writing Women's Lives: An Anthology of Autobiographical Narratives by Twentieth-Century American Women Writers*. New York: Harper, 1994.

Cain, William E. "A Literary Approach to Literature: Why English Departments Should Focus on Close Reading, Not Cultural Studies." *Chronicle of Higher Education* 13 Dec. 1996: B4–5.

Ceplair, Larry, ed. *Charlotte Perkins Gilman: A Nonfiction Reader*. New York: Columbia UP, 1991.

Chopin, Kate. "The Story of an Hour." *Literature: Reading, Reacting, Writing*. Ed. Laurie G. Kirszner and Stephen R. Mandell. 4th ed. Fort Worth: Harcourt, 2000. 71–73.

Cixous, Hélène. "The Laugh of the Medusa." Trans. Keith Cohen and Paula Cohen. *Signs* 1 (1976): 875–93.

Clarke, Edward H. *Sex in Education: A Fair Chance for Girls*. Boston: Osgood, 1874.

Cofer, Judith Ortiz. "The Story of My Body." Crawford and Unger 47–54.

Commager, Henry Steele, ed. *Lester Ward and the Welfare State*. Indianapolis: Bobbs, 1967.

Conrad, Joseph. *The Heart of Darkness*. New York: St. Martin's, 1989.

Crane, Stephen. *Prose and Poetry*. New York: Lib. of Amer., 1984.

Cranny-Francis, Anne. *Feminist Fiction: Feminist Uses of Generic Fiction*. New York: St. Martin's, 1990.

Crawford, Mary, and Rhoda Unger, eds. *In Our Own Words: Readings on the Psychology of Women and Gender*. New York: McGraw, 1997.

Crawford, Mary Caroline. *The College Girl of America and the Institutions Which Make Her What She Is*. Boston: Page, 1904.

Crewe, Jonathan. "Queering 'The Yellow Wallpaper': Charlotte Perkins Gilman and the Politics of Form." *Tulsa Studies in Women's Literature* 14 (1995): 415–51.

Culley, Margo, ed. and introd. *A Day at a Time: The Diary Literature of American Women from 1764 to the Present*. New York: Feminist, 1985.

Darwin, Charles. *Descent of Man and Selection in Relation to Sex*. 2 vols. New York: Appleton, 1871.

———. *The Voyage of the Beagle*. 1839. New York: Penguin, 1989.

Davidson, Cathy N. *Revolution and the Word: The Rise of the Novel in America*. New York: Oxford UP, 1986.

Davis, Cynthia J. *Bodily and Narrative Forms: The Influence of Medicine on American Literature*. Stanford: Stanford UP, 2000.

Deegan, Mary Jo. Introduction. Gilman, With Her in Ourland 1–57.

DeKoven, Marianne. "Gendered Doubleness and the 'Origins' of Modernist Form." Erskine and Richards 209–23.

DeLamotte, Eugenia C. "Male and Female Hysteria in 'The Yellow Wallpaper.'" *Legacy: A Journal of Nineteenth-Century American Women Writers* 5 (1988): 3–14.

Dickinson, Emily. "Tell all the Truth but tell it slant." Poem 1129. *The Complete Poems of Emily Dickinson*. Ed. Thomas H. Johnson. Boston: Little, 1960. 506–07.

Dock, Julie Bates, comp. and ed. *Charlotte Perkins Gilman's "The Yellow Wall-paper" and the History of Its Publication and Reception*. University Park: Pennsylvania State UP, 1998.

Dock, Julie Bates, et al. "'But One Expects That': Charlotte Perkins Gilman's 'The Yellow Wallpaper' and the Shifting Light of Scholarship." *PMLA* 111 (1996): 52–65.

Donawerth, Jane L., and Carol A. Kolmerten, eds. *Utopian and Science Fiction by Women: Worlds of Difference*. Syracuse: Syracuse UP, 1994.

Doskow, Minna. Introduction. *Charlotte Perkins Gilman's Utopian Novels:* Moving the Mountain, Herland, *and* With Her in Ourland. Ed. Doskow. Madison: Fairleigh Dickinson UP, 1999. 1–29.

Drinka, George Frederick. *The Birth of Neurosis: Myth, Malady, and the Victorians*. New York: Simon, 1984.

Eagleton, Terry. "The Rise of English." *Literary Theory: An Introduction*. Minneapolis: U of Minnesota P, 1983. 17–53.

Eastlake, Charles. *Hints on Household Taste in Furniture and Upholstery and Other Details*. Boston: Osgood, 1872.

Ehrenreich, Barbara, and Deirdre English. *For Her Own Good: 150 Years of the Experts' Advice to Women*. Garden City: Anchor, 1978.

Engels, Friedrich. *The Origin of the Family, Private Property, and the State*. Ed. Eleanor Burke Leacock. 1942. New York: International, 1972.

Erskine, Thomas L., and Connie L. Richards, eds. *The Yellow Wallpaper*. New Brunswick: Rutgers UP, 1993.

Feldstein, Richard. "Reader, Text, and Ambiguous Referentiality in 'The Yellow Wallpaper.'" Feldstein and Roof 269–79. Rpt. in Golden, *Imagination* 307–18.

Feldstein, Richard, and Judith Roof, eds. *Feminism and Psychoanalysis*. Ithaca: Cornell UP, 1989.

Ferns, Chris. "Rewriting Male Myths: *Herland* and the Utopian Tradition." Gough and Rudd 24–37.

Fetterley, Judith. "Reading about Reading: 'A Jury of Her Peers,' 'The Murders in the Rue Morgue,' and 'The Yellow Wallpaper.'" Golden, *Imagination* 253–60.

———. "Reading about Reading: 'The Yellow Wallpaper.'" Erskine and Richards 181–89.

Figes, Eva. *Patriarchal Attitudes*. Greenwich: Fawcett, 1970.

Findlay, Barbara. "Lester Frank Ward as a Sociologist of Gender: A New Look at His Sociological Work." *Gender and Society* 13 (1999): 251–65.

Fleenor, Juliann E. "The Gothic Prism: Charlotte Perkins Gilman's Gothic Stories and Her Autobiography." *The Female Gothic*. Ed. Fleenor. Montreal: Eden, 1983. 227–41.

Ford, Karen. "'The Yellow Wallpaper' and Women's Discourse." *Tulsa Studies in Women's Literature* 4 (1985): 309–14.

Foucault, Michel. "Of Other Spaces." *Diacritics* 16 (1986): 22–27.

Freeman, Mary Wilkins. "The Revolt of 'Mother.'" *The Short Fiction of Sarah Orne Jewett and Mary Wilkins Freeman*. Ed. Barbara H. Solomon. New York: Modern American Lib., 1979. 418–52.

Freud, Sigmund. *The Aetiology of Hysteria*. 1886. Freud, *Reader* 96–112.

———. "Fragment of an Analysis of a Case of Hysteria ('Dora')." Freud, *Reader* 172–239.

———. *The Freud Reader*. Ed. Peter Gay. New York: Norton, 1989.

Freud, Sigmund, and Josef Breuer. "On the Psychical Mechanism of Hysterical Phenomena: Preliminary Communications." 1893. *Studies in Hysteria*. New York: Avon, 1966. 37–52.

Friedan, Betty. *The Feminine Mystique*. New York: Norton, 1963.

Fuller, Margaret. Woman in the Nineteenth Century *and Other Writings*. Ed. Donna Dickenson. New York: Oxford UP, 1994.

Garvey, Ellen Gruber. *The Adman in the Parlor: Magazines and the Gendering of Consumer Culture, 1880s to 1910s*. Oxford: Oxford UP, 1996.

Gilbert, Sandra, and Susan Gubar. "'Fecundate! Discriminate!': Charlotte Perkins Gilman and the Theologizing of Maternity." Rudd and Gough 199–216.

———. *The Madwoman in the Attic: The Woman Writer and the Nineteenth-Century Literary Imagination*. New Haven: Yale UP, 1979.

Gilman, Charlotte Perkins. "As to Purposes." *Forerunner* 1 (1909): 32. Rpt. in Ceplair 195.

———. "Comment and Review." *Forerunner* 1 (Oct. 1910): 26–27.

———. "Comment and Review." *Forerunner* 4 (June 1913): 166.

———. *The Diaries of Charlotte Perkins Gilman*. Ed. Denise D. Knight. 2 vols. Charlottesville: UP of Virginia, 1994.

———. "Editorial Notes." *Impress* 1 (June 1894): 1.

———. "Feminism or Polygamy." *Forerunner* 5 (1914): 260–61.

———. *Forerunner*. 7 vols. (1909–16). New York: Greenwood, 1968.

———. "The Giant Wisteria." Gilman, Herland 154–62.

———. "Girls of To-day." Gilman, *In This Our World* 36–37.

———. Herland, *"The Yellow Wall-Paper," and Selected Writings*. Ed. Denise D. Knight. New York: Penguin, 1999.

———. "The Holy Stove." Gilman, *In This Our World* 54–55.

———. "The Home as an Environment for Women." *Success* July 1903: 411–12.

———. *The Home: Its Work and Influence*. New York: McClure, 1903.

———. *"In This Our World" and Other Poems*. 1893. San Francisco: Barry, 1895.

———. *In This Our World*. 3rd ed. Boston: Small, 1898.

———. Letter to Martha Luther Lane. 27 July 1890. Rhode Island Historical Soc.

———. Letter to Lester Ward. 28 Nov. 1900. John Hay Lib., Brown U.

——. Letter to Lester Ward. 20 Jan. 1904. John Hay Lib., Brown U.

——. Letter to Lester Ward. 15 Mar. 1906. John Hay Lib., Brown U.

——. *The Living of Charlotte Perkins Gilman: An Autobiography*. Fwd. Zona Gale. New York: Appleton, 1935. Madison: U of Wisconsin P, 1990.

——. *The Man-Made World; or, Our Androcentric Culture*. 1911. New York: Source, 1970. Excerpts. Knight, *Study* 116–24.

——. "On Human Nature." Three Lectures on Nationalism. 1890. Gilman Papers, Schlesinger Lib., Radcliffe Inst.

——. "Our Domestic Duties." Twelve Talks for Class Series. Oct. 1891–Feb. 1892. Gilman Papers, Schlesinger Lib., Radcliffe Inst.

——. "Our Excessive Femininity." Lectures from the 1890s. Gilman Papers, Schlesinger Lib., Radcliffe Inst.

——. "Reasonable Resolutions." *Forerunner* 1 (1910): 1.

——. "She Walketh Veiled and Sleeping." Gilman, *In This Our World* 35.

——. "Similar Cases." Gilman, *In This Our World* 72–76.

——. "A Suggestion on the Negro Problem." 1908. Rpt. in Ceplair 176–83.

——. "A Summary of Purpose." *Forerunner* 7 (1916): 286–90.

——. "Thoughts and Figgerings." Excerpts. Knight, *Study* 114–15.

——. "Through This." *Kate Field's Washington* 13 Sept. 1893: 166.

——. "The Way Up." Twelve Talks for Class Series. Oct. 1891–Feb. 1892. Gilman Papers, Schlesinger Lib., Radcliffe Inst.

——. "We, as Women." Gilman, *In This Our World* 42–43.

——. "What the People's Party Means." Five Lectures. 1890s, n.d. Gilman Papers, Schlesinger Lib., Radcliffe Inst.

——. "What We Are Doing." *Impress* 13 Oct. 1894: 1–2.

——. "Why Cooperative Housekeeping Fails." *Harper's Bazaar* July 1907: 625–29.

——. "Why I Wrote 'The Yellow Wallpaper'?" *Forerunner* 4 (Oct. 1913): 271.

——. "Why We Honestly Fear Socialism." *Forerunner* 1 (1909): 7–10.

——. With Her in Ourland: *Sequel to* Herland. Ed. Mary Jo Deegan and Michael R. Hill. Westport: Greenwood, 1997.

——. *Women and Economics: A Study of the Economic Relation between Men and Women as a Factor in Social Evolution*. 1898. Ed. Carl N. Degler. New York: Harper Torchbook, 1966.

——. *The Yellow Wall-Paper*. 1899. Afterword by Elaine Hedges. New York: Feminist, 1996.

"Gilman Inducted into National Women's Hall of Fame." *Charlotte Perkins Gilman Newsletter* 5 (1995): 1.

Glaspell, Susan. *Trifles*. 1916. *Norton Anthology of Literature by Women: The Traditions in English*. Ed. Sandra M. Gilbert and Susan Gubar. 2nd ed. New York: Norton, 1996. 1351–60.

Goffman, Erving. "The Insanity of Place." *Psychiatry* 32 (1969): 357–88.

Golden, Catherine, ed. *The Captive Imagination: A Casebook on "The Yellow Wallpaper."* New York: Feminist, 1992.

————. "'Written to Drive Nails With': Recalling the Early Poetry of Charlotte Perkins Gilman." Rudd and Gough 243–66.

Golden, Catherine J., and Joanna Schneider Zangrando, eds. *The Mixed Legacy of Charlotte Perkins Gilman*. Newark: U of Delaware P, 2000.

Goodheart, Eugene. *Does Literary Studies Have a Future?* Madison: U of Wisconsin P, 1999.

Goodwyn, Lawrence. *Democratic Promise: The Populist Movement in America*. New York: Oxford UP, 1976.

Gorsline, Douglas. *What People Wore: A Visual History of Dress from Ancient Times to Twentieth-Century America*. New York: Viking, 1952.

Gough, Val. "Lesbians and Virgins: The Motherhood in *Herland*." *Anticipations: Essays on Early Science Fiction and Its Precursors*. Ed. David Seed. Syracuse: Syracuse UP, 1995. 195–215.

Gough, Val, and Jill Rudd, eds. *A Very Different Story: Studies on the Fiction of Charlotte Perkins Gilman*. Liverpool: Liverpool UP, 1998.

Graff, Gerald, and James Phelan. "Why Study Critical Controversies?" *Adventures of Huckleberry Finn*. Ed. Graff and Phelan. Boston: Bedford, 1995. 1–15.

Green, Harvey. *Fit for America: Health, Fitness, Sport, and American Society*. Baltimore: Johns Hopkins UP, 1986.

Grimké, Angelina E. *Letters to E. Beecher, in Reply to an Essay on Slavery and Abolition, Addressed to A. E. Grimke*. Boston: Knapp, 1838.

Grob, Gerald N. *Mental Institutions in America: Social Policy to 1875*. New York: Free, 1973.

Gubar, Susan. "*She* in *Herland*: Feminism as Fantasy." Meyering 191–202.

Gusdorf, Georges. "Conditions and Limits of Autobiography." 1956. Ed. and trans. James Olney. *Autobiography: Essays Theoretical and Critical*. Princeton: Princeton UP, 1980. 28–48.

Hale, Edward Everett. "Susan's Escort." Smith and Dawson 412–25.

Haney-Peritz, Janice. "Monumental Feminism and Literature's Ancestral House: Another Look at 'The Yellow Wallpaper.'" *Women's Studies* 12 (1986): 113–28. Rpt. in Golden, *Imagination* 261–76.

Harding, Sandra. *The Science Question in Feminism*. Ithaca: Cornell UP, 1986.

Hare-Mustin, Rachel T., and Patricia Broderick. "The Myth of Motherhood: A Study of Attitudes toward Motherhood." *Psychology of Women Quarterly* 4 (1979): 114–28.

Hare-Mustin, Rachel T., and Jeanne Maracek, eds. *Making a Difference: Psychology and the Construction of Gender*. New Haven: Yale UP, 1990.

Harris, Susan K. *Nineteenth-Century American Women's Novels: Interpretive Strategies*. Cambridge: Cambridge UP, 1990.

Hayden, Dolores. *The Grand Domestic Revolution: A History of Feminist Designs for American Homes, Neighborhoods, and Cities*. Cambridge: MIT P, 1981.

Hedges, Elaine R. Afterword. *The Yellow Wall-Paper*. New York: Feminist, 1973. 37–63.

————. "'Out at Last'? 'The Yellow Wallpaper' after Two Decades of Feminist Criticism." Golden, *Imagination* 319–33; Karpinski 222–33.

Hedrick, Joan D. *Harriet Beecher Stowe: A Life*. New York: Oxford UP, 1994.

Heller, Scott. "Wearying of Cultural Studies, Some Scholars Rediscover Beauty." *Chronicle of Higher Education* 4 Dec. 1998: A15.

Herman, Judith Lewis. *Trauma and Recovery: The Aftermath of Violence from Domestic Abuse to Political Terror*. New York: Basic, 1992.

Herndl, Diane Price. *Invalid Women: Figuring Feminine Illness in American Fiction and Culture, 1840–1940*. Chapel Hill: U of North Carolina P, 1995.

——. "The Writing Cure: Charlotte Perkins Gilman, Anna O., and 'Hysterical' Writing." *NWSA Journal* 1 (1988): 52–74.

Hill, Mary A. *Charlotte Perkins Gilman: The Making of a Radical Feminist, 1860–1896*. Philadelphia: Temple UP, 1980.

——, ed. *Endure: The Diaries of Charles Walter Stetson*. Philadelphia: Temple UP, 1985.

——, ed. *A Journey from Within: The Love Letters of Charlotte Perkins Gilman, 1897–1900*. Lewisburg: Bucknell UP, 1995.

hooks, bell. *Black Looks: Race and Representation*. Boston: South End, 1994.

——. "Representations of Whiteness in the Black Imagination." Hooks, *Black Looks* 165–78.

——. *Teaching to Transgress: Education as the Practice of Freedom*. New York: Routledge, 1994.

Howells, William Dean. *The Altrurian Romances*. Bloomington: Indiana UP, 1968.

Hunter Coll. Women's Studies Collective. *Women's Realities, Women's Choice: An Introduction to Women's Studies*. 2nd ed. New York: Oxford UP, 1995.

Huxley, Aldous. *Brave New World*. 1932. New York: Harper Perennial, 1969.

Irigary, Luce. "This Sex Which Is Not One." Trans. Claudia Reeder. *New French Feminisms*. Ed. Elaine Marks and Isabelle De Courtivron. New York: Schocken, 1981. 99–106.

Jacobs, Harriet. *Incidents in the Life of a Slave Girl*. 1861. New York: Oxford UP, 1988.

Jacobus, Mary. "An Unnecessary Maze of Sign-Reading." Golden, *Imagination* 277–95.

Jameson, Fredric. *The Political Unconscious: Narrative as a Socially Symbolic Act*. Ithaca: Cornell UP, 1981.

Jeffries, Sheila. *The Spinster and Her Enemies: Feminism and Sexuality, 1880–1930*. London: Pandora, 1985.

Jespersen, Otto. *Essentials of English Grammar*. Tuscaloosa: U of Alabama P, 1981.

Johnson, Barbara. "Is Female to Male as Ground Is to Figure?" Feldstein and Roof 255–68.

Karnezis, George. Letter. *Chronicle of Higher Education* 15 Jan. 1999: B3+.

Karpinski, Joanne, ed. *Critical Essays on Charlotte Perkins Gilman*. New York: Hall, 1992.

Kasmer, Lisa. "Charlotte Perkins Gilman's 'The Yellow Wallpaper': A Symptomatic Reading." *Literature and Psychology* 36.3 (1990): 1–15.

Katzenbach, Lois, and William Katzenbach. *The Practical Book of American Wallpaper*. Philadelphia: Lippincott, 1951.

Keller, Evelyn Fox. *A Feeling for the Organism: The Life and Works of Barbara McClintock*. New York: Freeman, 1983.

Kennard, Jean E. "Convention Coverage; or, How to Read Your Own Life." *New Literary History* 13 (1981): 69–88. Rpt. in Golden, *Imagination* 168–90.

Kessler, Carol Farley. "Charlotte Perkins Gilman." *Modern American Women Writers*. Ed. Elaine Showalter et al. New York: Collier-Macmillan, 1993. 97–108.

——. *Charlotte Perkins Gilman: Her Progress toward Utopia and Selected Writings*. Syracuse: Syracuse UP, 1995.

——. "Consider Her Ways: The Cultural Work of Charlotte Perkins Gilman's Pragmatopian Stories, 1908–1913." Donawerth and Kolmerten 126–36.

Kett, Joseph F. *Rites of Passage: Adolescence in America, 1790 to the Present*. New York: Basic, 1977.

Kilcup, Karen L. "Bigger Is Not Always Better: Teaching Medium-Length and Shorter Works in Diverse Genres." *Heath Anthology of American Literature Newsletter* 21 (2000): 3–6.

Kirkbride, Thomas S. *Construction, Organization, and General Arrangements for Hospitals for the Insane*. 1880. New York: Arno, 1973.

Knight, Denise D. "Charlotte Perkins Gilman and the Shadow of Racism." *American Literary Realism* 32 (1999): 159–69.

——. *Charlotte Perkins Gilman: A Study of the Short Fiction*. New York: Twayne, 1997.

——. Introduction and a Note on the Text. *"The Yellow Wall-Paper" and Selected Stories of Charlotte Perkins Gilman*. Newark: U of Delaware P, 1994. 9–33.

——. *The Later Poetry of Charlotte Perkins Gilman*. Newark: U of Delaware P, 1996.

——. "The Reincarnation of Jane: 'Through This'—Gilman's Companion to 'The Yellow Wall-Paper.'" *Women's Studies* 20 (1992): 287–302.

Kolodny, Annette. "Dancing through the Minefield: Some Observations on the Theory, Practice, and Politics of a Feminist Literary Criticism." Showalter, *New Feminist Criticisms* 144–67.

——. "A Map for Rereading; or, Gender and the Interpretation of Literary Texts." *New Literary History* 11 (1980): 451–67. Rpt. in Golden, *Imagination* 149–67.

Kumar, Krishan. *Utopia and Anti-utopia in Modern Times*. New York: Blackwell, 1987.

Lacan, Jacques. "Seminar on the 'Purloined Letter.'" *The Purloined Poe: Lacan, Derrida, and Psychoanalytic Reading*. Ed. John P. Muller and William J. Richardson. Trans. Jeffrey Mehlman. Baltimore: Johns Hopkins UP, 1988. 28–54.

——. "The Signification of the Phallus." *Ecrits: A Selection*. Trans. Alan Sheridan. New York: Norton, 1977. 281–91.

Lane, Ann J. *To Herland and Beyond: The Life and Work of Charlotte Perkins Gilman*. New York: Pantheon, 1990.

Lanser, Susan S. "Feminist Criticism, 'The Yellow Wallpaper,' and the Politics of Color in America." *Feminist Studies* 15 (1989): 415–41. Rpt. in Erskine and Richards 225–56.

Lawrence, D. H. "The Rocking-Horse Winner." *Literature: Reading, Reacting, Writing*. Ed. Laurie G. Kirszner and Stephen R. Mandell. 4th ed. Fort Worth: Harcourt, 2000. 318–30.

Lears, T. J. Jackson. *Fables of Abundance: A Cultural History of Advertising in America*. New York: Basic, 1994.

Lengermann, Patricia Madoo, and Jill Niebrugge-Brantley, eds. *The Women Founders: Sociology and Social Theory, 1830–1930*. New York: McGraw, 1998.

Levine, George. "Introduction: "Reclaiming the Aesthetic." *Aesthetics and Ideology*. Ed. Levine. New Brunswick: Rutgers UP, 1994. 1–28.

Lewis, R. W. B. *The American Adam: Innocence, Tragedy, and Tradition in the Nineteenth Century*. Chicago: U of Chicago P, 1955.

Lubin, David M. *Act of Portrayal: Eakins, Sargent, James*. New Haven: Yale UP, 1985.

Lutz, Tom. *American Nervousness, 1903: An Anecdotal History*. Ithaca: Cornell UP, 1991.

MacPike, Loralee. "Environmental and Psychological Symbolism in 'The Yellow Wallpaper.'" *American Literary Realism* 8 (1975): 286–88.

Magner, Lois N. "Darwinism and the Woman Question: The Evolving Views of Charlotte Perkins Gilman." Karpinski 115–28.

Mankiller, Wilma, et al., eds. *The Reader's Companion to U.S. Women's History*. Boston: Houghton, 1998.

Marchalonis, Shirley. *College Girls: A Century in Fiction*. New Brunswick: Rutgers UP, 1995.

Marx, Karl, and Frederick Engels. *The Communist Manifesto*. New York: Norton, 1988.

———. *The Marx-Engels Reader*. 2nd ed. Ed. Robert C. Tucker. New York: Norton, 1978.

Massé, Michelle. "Things That Go Bump in the Night: Husbands, Horrors, and Repetition." *In the Name of Love: Women, Masochism, and the Gothic*. Ithaca: Cornell UP, 1992. 10–39.

Meyering, Sheryl L., ed. *Charlotte Perkins Gilman: The Woman and Her Work*. Ann Arbor: UMI, 1989.

Michaels, Walter Benn. *The Gold Standard and the Logic of Naturalism: American Literature at the Turn of the Century*. Berkeley: U of California P, 1987.

Mill, John Stuart. *On Liberty*. Mill, On Liberty *and Other Writings* 1–115.

———. On Liberty *and Other Writings*. Ed. Stefan Collini. Cambridge: Cambridge UP, 1989.

———. *The Subjection of Women*. Mill, On Liberty *and Other Writings* 117–217.

Mitchell, S. Weir. *"The Autobiography of a Quack" and "The Case of George Dedlow."* New York: Century, 1900.

———. *Doctor and Patient*. 1888. New York: Arno, 1972.

———. *Fat and Blood*. Philadelphia: Lippincott, 1877.

———. *In War Time*. 1884. New York: Century, 1912.

———. *Lectures on the Diseases of the Nervous System, Especially in Women*. Philadelphia: Lea's, 1881.

———. *Wear and Tear; or, Hints for the Overworked*. Philadelphia: Lippincott, 1871.

Moers, Ellen. *Literary Women*. Garden City: Doubleday, 1976.

Moi, Toril. *Sexual/Textual Politics: Feminist Literary Theory*. London: Routledge, 1985.

Neely, Carol Thomas. "Alternative Women's Discourse." *Tulsa Studies in Women's Literature* 4 (1985): 315–21.

Ohmann, Richard. *Selling Culture: Magazines, Markets, and Class at the Turn of the Century*. New York: Verso, 1996.

Packard, E. P. W. *Modern Persecution; or, Insane Asylums Unveiled*. 1875. New York: Arno, 1973.

Painter, Nell Irvin. *Standing at Armageddon: The United States, 1877–1919*. New York: Norton, 1987.

Parker, Rozsika, and Griselda Pollock. *Old Mistresses: Women, Art, and Ideology*. London: Routledge, 1985.

Patmore, Coventry. *The Angel in the House*. London: Parker, 1854.

Peyser, Thomas Galt. "Reproducing Utopia: Charlotte Perkins Gilman and *Herland*." *Studies in American Fiction* 20 (1992): 1–16.

———. *Utopia and Cosmopolis: Globalization in the Era of American Literary Realism*. Durham: Duke UP, 1998.

Pfaelzer, Jean. "American Utopias: Texts and Contexts." *American Transcendental Quarterly* 3.1 (1989): 1–10.

Plasa, Carl. "'Silent Revolt': Slavery and the Politics of Metaphor in *Jane Eyre*." *The Discourse of Slavery: Aphra Behn to Toni Morrison*. Ed. Plasa and Betty J. Ring. New York: Routledge, 1994. 64–93.

Poirier, Suzanne. "The Weir Mitchell Rest Cure: Doctor and Patients." *Women's Studies* 10 (1983): 15–40.

Power, Susan. *The Ugly-Girl Papers; or, Hints for the Toilet*. New York: Harper, 1874.

Rich, Adrienne. "Compulsory Heterosexuality and Lesbian Existence." *Signs Reader*. Ed. Elizabeth Abel and Emily K. Abel. Chicago: U of Chicago P, 1983. 139–68.

———. *Of Woman Born: Motherhood as Experience and Institution*. New York: Norton, 1976.

Richter, David H., ed. *Falling into Theory: Conflicting Views on Reading Literature*. 2nd ed. Boston: Bedford–St. Martin's, 2000.

Robinson, Lillian. "Treason Our Text: Feminist Challenges to the Literary Canon." Richter 153–66.

Roemer, Kenneth M. *The Obsolete Necessity: American Utopian Writings, 1888–1900*. Kent: Kent State UP, 1976.

Rossi, Alice, ed. *The Feminist Papers: From Adams to Beauvoir*. Boston: Northeastern UP, 1988.

Rothman, David J. *The Discovery of the Asylum: Social Order and Disorder in the New Republic*. Boston: Little, 1971.

Rudd, Jill, and Val Gough, eds. *Charlotte Perkins Gilman: Optimist Reformer*. Iowa City: U of Iowa P, 1999.

Ruedy, August. "Interesting Letters from Charlotte Perkins Gilman." *Amerikanische Turnzeitung* 8 (1935): 9–10.

Ruth, Sheila, ed. *Issues in Feminism: An Introduction to Women's Studies*. 4th ed. Mountain View: Mayfield, 1997.

Sanday, Peggy Reeves. *Female Power and Male Dominance: On the Origins of Sexual Inequality*. New York: Cambridge UP, 1981.

Sanger, Margaret. *Woman and the New Race*. New York: Brentano's, 1920.

Sapiro, Virginia. *Women in American Society: An Introduction to Women's Studies*. 4th ed. Mountain View: Mayfield, 1998.

Scharnhorst, Gary. *Charlotte Perkins Gilman*. Boston: Twayne, 1985.

———. *Charlotte Perkins Gilman: A Bibliography*. Metuchen: Scarecrow, 1985.

Schneider, Dorothy, and Carl J. Schneider. *American Women in the Progressive Era, 1900–1920*. New York: Anchor, 1993.

Scholes, Robert. "A Fortunate Fall." Richter 111–19.

Schwartz, Ruth Cowan. *More Work for Mother: The Ironies of Household Technology from the Open Hearth to the Microwave*. New York: Basic, 1983.

Scudder, Horace. Letter to Charlotte Perkins Gilman. 18 Oct. 1890. Charlotte Perkins Gilman Papers, Schlesinger Lib., Radcliffe Inst.

Seidenberg, Robert. "The Trauma of Eventlessness." *Psychoanalytic Review* 59 (1972): 95–108.

Severa, Joan L. *Dressed for the Photographer: Ordinary Americans and Fashions, 1840–1900*. Kent: Kent State UP, 1995.

Shakespeare, William. *The Tempest*. New York: Washington Square, 1961.

Showalter, Elaine. *A Literature of Their Own: British Women Novelists from Brontë to Lessing*. Princeton: Princeton UP, 1977.

———, ed. *The New Feminist Criticism: Essays on Women, Literature, and Theory*. New York: Pantheon, 1985.

Shumaker, Conrad. "Realism, Reform, and the Audience: Charlotte Perkins Gilman's Unreadable Wallpaper." *Arizona Quarterly* 47 (1991): 81–93.

———. "'Too Terribly Good to Be Printed': Charlotte Perkins Gilman and 'The Yellow Wallpaper.'" Golden, *Imagination* 242–52.

Sicherman, Barbara. "The Uses of a Diagnosis: Doctors, Patients, and Neurasthenia." *Journal of the History of Medicine and Allied Sciences* 32 (1977): 33–54.

Smith, Barbara Herrnstein. "Contingencies of Value." Richter 147–52.

Smith, Valerie. *Self-Discovery and Authority in Afro-American Narrative*. Cambridge: Harvard UP, 1987.

Smith, Susan Harris, and Melanie Dawson, eds. *The American 1890s: A Cultural Reader*. Durham: Duke UP, 2002.

Smith-Rosenberg, Carroll. *Disorderly Conduct: Visions of Gender in Victorian America*. New York: Oxford UP, 1985.

———. "The Hysterical Woman: Sex Roles and Role Conflict in Nineteenth-Century America." Smith-Rosenberg, *Conduct* 197–216.

Smith-Rosenberg, Carroll, and Charles E. Rosenberg. "The Female Animal: Medical and Biological Views of Woman and Her Role in Nineteenth-Century America." *Journal of American History* 60 (1973): 332–56.

Soderholm, James, ed. *Beauty and the Critic: Aesthetics in an Age of Cultural Studies.* Tuscaloosa: U of Alabama P, 1997.

Stanton, Domna C. "Autogynography: Is the Subject Different?" *The Female Autograph.* Ed. Stanton. New York: New York Literary Forum, 1984. 3–20.

Stevenson, Louise L. *The Victorian Homefront: American Thought and Culture, 1860–1880.* New York: Twayne, 1991.

St. Jean, Shawn. "Renovating 'The Yellow Wall-Paper': A Dual-Text Critical Edition." Unpublished ms.

Stowe, Harriet Beecher. *The Oxford Harriet Beecher Stowe Reader.* Ed. Joan D. Hedrick. New York: Oxford UP, 1999.

Thomas, Heather Kirk. "'A Kind of "Debased Romanesque" with Delirium Tremens': Late-Victorian Wall Coverings and Charlotte Perkins Gilman's 'The Yellow Wallpaper.'" Golden and Zaugrando 189–206.

Thoreau, Henry David. "Resistance to Civil Government." Walden *and "Resistance to Civil Government."* 2nd ed. Ed. William Rossi. New York: Norton, 1992. 226–45.

Tortora, Phyllis G., and Keith Eubank. *Survey of Historic Costume: A History of Western Dress.* 3rd ed. New York: Fairchild, 1998.

Treichler, Paula A. "Escaping the Sentence: Diagnosis and Discourse in 'The Yellow Wallpaper.'" *Tulsa Studies in Women's Literature* 3 (1984): 61–77. Rpt. in Golden, *Imagination* 191–210.

———. "The Wall behind the Yellow Wallpaper: Response to Carol Neely and Karen Ford." *Tulsa Studies in Women's Literature* 4 (1985): 323–30.

Twain, Mark. *The Adventures of Huckleberry Finn.* New York: Harper, 1987.

———. *Pudd'nhead Wilson.* 1894. New York: Signet, 1964.

Tyson, Lois. *Critical Theory Today: A User-Friendly Guide.* New York: Garland, 1999.

Veblen, Thorstein. 1899. *Theory of the Leisure Class.* New York: Penguin, 1979.

Veeder, William. "Who Is Jane? The Intricate Feminism of Charlotte Perkins Gilman." *Arizona Quarterly* 44 (1988): 40–79.

Ward, Lester Frank. "Our Better Halves." *Forum* 6 (1888): 266–75.

———. *Pure Sociology: A Treatise on the Origin and Spontaneous Development of Society.* New York: Macmillan, 1903.

Welter, Barbara. "The Cult of True Womanhood, 1820–1860." *American Quarterly* 18 (1966): 151–74.

The Whole Family: A Novel by Twelve Authors. Durham: Duke UP, 2001.

Williams, Raymond. *Keywords: A Vocabulary of Culture and Society.* New York: Oxford UP, 1985.

Winter, Kari J. *Subjects of Slavery, Agents of Change: Women and Power in Gothic Novels and Slave Narratives, 1790–1865.* Athens: U of Georgia P, 1992.

Wollstonecraft, Mary. 1792. *A Vindication of the Rights of Women.* Troy: Whitston, 1982.

The Woman's Book, Dealing Practically with the Modern Conditions of Home-Life, Self-Support, Education, Opportunities, and Everyday Problems. New York: Scribner, 1894.

The Woman's Book: Contains Everything a Woman Ought to Know. London: Jack, 1911.

Wood, Ann Douglas. "'The Fashionable Diseases': Women's Complaints and Their Treatment in Nineteenth-Century America." *Journal of Interdisciplinary History* 4 (1972): 25–52. Rpt. in Golden, *Imagination* 110–19.

Woolf, Virginia. "The Mark on the Wall." Woolf, *Reader* 151–59.

———. "Professions for Women." Woolf, *Reader* 276–82.

———. *A Room of One's Own.* New York: Harcourt, 1929.

———. *The Virginia Woolf Reader.* Ed. Mitchell A. Leaska. San Diego: Harcourt, 1984.

Yamada, Mitsuye. "Invisibility Is an Unnatural Disaster." Crawford and Unger 165–69.

Audiovisual Materials

Gattaca. Dir. Andrew Niccol. Perf. Ethan Hawke, Uma Thurman, and Jude Law. Columbia Tristar, 1997.

The Handmaid's Tale. Screenplay by Harold Pinter. Dir. Volker Schlondorff. Perf. Natasha Richardson, Faye Dunaway, and Aidan Quinn. HBO, 1990.

The Matrix. Dir. Andy Wachowski and Larry Wachowski. Perf. Keanu Reeves, Carrie-Anne Moss, and Laurence Fishburne. Warner, 1999.

Pink Floyd.: The Wall. Dir. Alan Parker. MGM, 1982.

The Wizard of Oz. Dir. Victor Fleming. Perf. Judy Garland, Frank Morgan, and Ray Bolger. 1939. Videocassette. MGM/United Artist, 1998.

The Yellow Wall-Paper. Dir. John Clive. Perf. Julia Watson and Stephen Dillon. WGBH Educ. Foundation, 1989.

The Yellow Wall-Paper. Dir. John Robbins. Perf. Eda Seasongood. Internat. Instructional Television, 1978.

The Yellow Wall-Paper. Dir. Tony Romain. Perf. Rachael Lillis and Michael Slayton. Tony Romain / Vision Films, 1996.

The Women. Dir. George Cukor. Perf. Norma Shearer, Joan Crawford. MGM, 1939.

INDEX

Achebe, Chinua, xvi, 40, 43, 46
Addams, Jane, 7, 88, 89
Allen, Polly Wynn, 8, 10, 11, 72, 113
Ammons, Elizabeth, 10, 159–60
Andersen, Margaret L., 148
Anderson, Sherwood, 135
Anna O. (Bertha Pappenheim), 76
Aristotle, 114
Arnold, Matthew, xvi, 40, 41, 42
Asher, Robert, 35
Atwood, Margaret, 135, 144, 146, 148

Barnes, Elizabeth, 9
Bassuk, Ellen L., 86
Bauer, Dale M., 5, 8, 9, 12, 18, 26, 29, 71
Beard, George, 7, 9, 131
Bederman, Gail, 9
Beecher, Catharine E., 7, 12
Beer, Janet, 12
Beilharz, Peter, 36, 39
Bellamy, Edward, 8, 32, 33, 37, 101, 106,
    107, 110, 119, 160, 164, 168
Bennett, Michael, 94
Berkin, Carol Ruth, 10
Berman, Jeffrey, 75, 76, 80, 86, 169
Berkin, Carol Ruth, 10
Bérubé, Michael, 27
Black, Alexander, xi, 6, 10, 170
Blackwell, Antoinette Brown, 88, 89
Blackwell, Henry B., 27
Blicksilver, Edith, 85
Bonner, Thomas, Jr., 165
Broderick, Patricia, 86
Brönte, Charlotte, 145, 146, 147–49, 150
Bruce, Dr. Emily, 73
Bryan, William Jennings, 36
Burroughs, Edgar Rice, 163
Butler, Judith, 94

Cahan, Abraham, 110
Cahill, Susan 152
Cain, William, 27
Cather, Willa, 110, 135
Ceplair, Larry, 9
Chamberlin, Dorothy Stetson, 72
Chamberlin, Walter Stetson, 72
Channing, Grace Ellery, 20, 21, 72
Charcot, Jean-Martin, 76
Child, Lydia Maria, 147, 148
Chopin, Kate, 8, 12, 18, 95, 133, 134, 138,
    139, 144, 165

Cixous, Hélène, 91, 92–93, 94, 96
Clarke, Edward H., 7, 9, 18
Clive, John, 11, 68, 69, 73
Cofer, Judith Ortiz, 87
Collins, Patricia Hill, 148
Commager, Henry Steele, 121
Conrad, Joseph, xvi, 40, 43, 45, 46, 135
Crane, Stephen, 118, 162, 166
Cranny-Francis, Anne, 162
Crawford, Mary Caroline, 13
Crewe, Jonathan, 8, 11
Cukor, George, 12
Culley, Margo, 153, 154

Darwin, Charles, xvi, 40, 43, 44, 45, 88, 113,
    118, 119, 120, 121, 127, 130, 168
Davidson, Cathy N., 160
Dawson, Melanie, 98
Deegan, Mary Jo, 8, 11, 122
Degler, Carl N., 3
DeKoven, Marianne, 27
DeLamotte, Eugenia C., 86
Dewey, John, 164
Dickens, Charles, 135, 140
Dickerson, Vanessa D., 94
Dickinson, Emily 158
Dock, Julie Bates, 5, 8, 11, 26, 27, 32
Donawerth, Jane L., 161
"Dora," 75, 76, 77–79, 81, 82 See also
    Freud
Doskow, Minna, 8, 11, 100
Dreiser, Theodore, 161, 162, 166, 169
Drinka, George Frederick, 9
Durkheim, Emile, 7

Eagleton, Terry, 28
Eakins, Thomas, 12
Eastlake, Charles, 12
Ehrenreich, Barbara, 7, 9
Ellison, Ralph, 167
Emerson, Ralph Waldo, 163
Engels, Friedrich, 36, 37, 38, 40, 45
English, Deirdre, 7, 9
Erskine, Thomas L., 4, 26
Eubanks, Keith, 72, 73

Faulkner, William, 12, 134, 163
Feldstein, Richard, 8, 11, 26, 91, 93
Fetterley, Judith, 8, 11, 27, 170
Figes, Eva, 9
Fleenor, Juliann, 11

Flower, B. O., 98
Ford, Karen, 91, 94–95
Foucault, Michel, 8
Freeman, Mary Wilkins, 8, 12, 102, 103, 104
Friedan, Betty, 7
Freud, Sigmund, 7, 75, 76–79, 81, 82, 94, 136, 164
Fuller, Margaret, 40, 43, 44, 47, 147

Garland, Hamlin, 166
Garvey, Ellen, 98
Gilbert, Sandra, 7, 8, 10, 11, 91, 122, 147, 149, 169, 170
Gilman, George Houghton, 25, 72, 121
Glaspell, Susan, 8, 64, 135
Goffman, Erving, 8, 86
Golden, Catherine J., 3, 4, 7, 10,12, 26, 48, 86
Goodheart, Eugene, 27
Goodwyn, Lawrence, 34
Gorsline, Douglas, 72
Gough, Val, 7, 8, 10, 11, 100
Graff, Gerald, 26
Greeley, Horace, 164
Green, Harvey, 98
Grimké, Angelina Weld, 147, 150
Grob, Gerald N., 70
Gubar, Susan, 7, 8, 10, 11, 91, 97, 122, 124, 147, 149, 169, 170
Gusdorf, Georges, 152, 157, 158

Hale, Edward Everett, 102–03, 104
Haney-Peritz, Janice, 11, 91, 93, 95, 169
Harding, Sandra, 130
Hare-Mustin, Rachel T., 86
Harris, Susan K., 10
Hatfield, Jo H., 11
Hawthorne, Nathaniel, 135, 167
Hayden, Dolores, 8
Hedges, Elaine R., xv, 3, 8, 11, 19, 27, 53, 86, 87, 91, 147, 152, 169, 170
Hedrick, Joan D., 12
Heller, Scott, 27
Hellman, Lillian, 12
Hemingway, Ernest, 126, 164
Herman, Judith Lewis, 76
Herndl, Diane Price, 7, 86, 169
Hill, Mary A., 6, 8, 10, 20, 21, 22, 32, 34, 86
hooks, bell, 42, 47, 143, 149
Howe, Harriet, 10
Howells, William Dean, 6, 8, 26, 32, 39, 103, 160, 166
Hunt, Isaac H., 70
Hurston, Zora Neale, 143
Huxley, Aldous, xvi, 40, 46

Ibsen, Henrik, 135
Irigary, Luce, 94

Jackson, Shirley, 12
Jacobs, Harriet, 144, 146, 147, 148, 149–50, 151
Jacobus, Mary, 11, 26, 169
James, Henry, 26, 103, 166, 167
Jameson, Fredric, 26, 30
Jeffries, Sheila, 9
Jespersen, Otto, 57
Johnson, Barbara, 169

Kafka, Franz, 135
Karnezis, George, 26
Karpinski, Joanne B., 7, 10, 160
Kasmer, Lisa, 8, 11, 91, 93, 95–96
Katzenbach, Lois, 73, 74
Katzenbach, William 73, 74
Keller, Evelyn Fox, 7, 131
Kelley, Florence, 7
Kellogg, Dr. John Harvey, 18, 100
Kennard, Jean E., 27, 91, 170
Kessler, Carol Farley, 8, 10, 38, 85, 86, 100, 162
Kett, Joseph F., 99
Kilcup, Karen, 84
Kingston, Maxine Hong, 85, 86, 87, 167
Kirkbride, Thomas S., 71
Knight, Denise D., 6, 9, 10, 11, 34, 50, 86, 87
Kolmerten, Carol A., 161
Kolodny, Annette, 8, 11, 91, 144, 151, 169
Kumar, Krishan, 39

Lacan, Jacques, 91, 93, 94, 95–96
Lane, Ann J., 4, 5, 6, 8, 10, 11, 72, 86
Lanser, Susan S., 8, 11, 34, 86, 145
Larsen, Nella, 110
Lawrence, D. H., 134, 139
Lears, T. J. Jackson, 98
Lengermann, Patricia Madoo, 11
Levine, George, 27
Lewis, R. W. B., 43
Lewis, Sinclair, 161
Lovecraft, H. P., 163
Lubin, David M., 12
Luther, Martha [Lane], 19, 20, 24
Lutz, Tom, 74

MacPike, Loralee, 11
Magner, Lois N., 113, 116, 168
Mankiller, Wilma, 10
Maracek, Jeanne, 86
Marchalonis, Shirley, 102
Martineau, Harriet, 7
Marx, Karl, xvi, 7, 36, 37, 38, 40, 43, 45, 165
McClintock, Barbara, 7, 131
Mead, Herbert, 7
Melville, Herman, 163
Meyering, Sheryl L., 7, 10

Michaels, Walter Benn, 11, 166
Mill, John Stuart, xvi, 7, 40, 41, 42, 44, 45, 47
Miller, Arthur, 135
Miller, Joaquin, 160
Mitchell, Dr. S. Weir, 8, 11, 17, 18, 19, 20, 21, 24, 67, 68, 72, 74, 75, 76, 81, 83, 86, 90, 128–29, 131, 132, 146, 152, 157–58, 171
Moers, Ellen, 10
Moi, Toril, 93
Morris, William 74
Morrison, Toni, 146

Neely, Carol Thomas, 91
Niebrugge-Brantley, 11
Norris, Frank, 166
Nyland, Chris, 36

Oates, Joyce Carol, 135
Ohmann, Richard, 98
Olsen, Tillie, 110

Packard, E. P. W., 71
Packard, Mrs. E. P. W., 71
Painter, Nell Irvin, 34
Pappenheim, Bertha See Anna O.
Parker, Rozsika, 12
Patmore, Coventry, 7
Peck, Thurston, 6
Peyser, Thomas Galt, 8, 11, 34, 37
Pfaelzer, Jean, 162
Phelps, Elizabeth Stuart, 103
Pherlan, James, 26
Plasa, Carl, 147, 148
Plato, 114
Poe, Edgar Allan, 12, 135, 167
Poirier, Suzanne, 8, 11, 86
Pollock, Griselda, 12
Post, Amy, 147
Power, Susan, 18
Previn, Dorrie, 11

Ray, Isaac, 70
Rhys, Jean, 146
Rich, Adrienne, 86, 130, 143
Richards, Connie L., 4, 26
Richter, David H., 27
Robbins, John, 67, 69
Robinson, Lillian S., 27
Roemer, Kenneth N., 161
Romain, Tony, 69
Rosenberg, Charles E., 7
Rossi, Alice, 88
Rothman, David J., 69, 79
Rudd, Jill, 7, 8, 10, 11, 100
Ruedy, August, 122
Ruth, Sheila, 85

Sanday, Peggy Reeves, 89
Sandoz, Mari, 7
Sanger, Margaret 7, 101, 129
Sapiro, Virginia, 85, 88, 89
Sargent, John Singer, 12
Scharnhorst, Gary, 6, 9, 10, 32, 36, 121
Schneider, Carl J., 18
Schneider, Dorothy, 18
Scholes, Robert, 47
Schwartz, Lynne Sharon, 4
Schwartz, Ruth Cowan, 7
Scudder, Horace, 32, 172
Seidenberg, Robert, 86
Severa, Joan L., 72
Shakespeare, William, 46, 47, 135
Showalter, Elaine, 10
Shulman, Robert, 4
Shumaker, Conrad, 11, 172
Sicherman, Barbara, 8, 86
Sinclair, Upton, 166
Soderholm, James, 27
Solomon, Barbara H., 5
Smith, Barbara Hernnstein, 27
Smith, Marsha, 162
Smith, Susan Harris, 98
Smith, Valerie, 149
Smith-Rosenberg, Carroll, 7, 9, 86
Soderholm, James, 27
Spencer, Herbert, 88, 113, 116, 121, 168
Stanton, Domna, 152, 153, 154, 155, 157, 158
Stanton, Elizabeth Cady, 147
Stein, Gertrude, 126
Steinbeck, John, 135
Stephenson, Charles, 35
Stetson, Charles Walter, 8, 10, 11, 19, 20, 21, 22, 23, 24, 67, 71, 72, 86, 152, 156, 171
Stetson, Katharine, 20, 21, 23, 72, 86, 155–56, 157
Stevens, Wallace, 136
Stevenson, Louise L., 102
St. Jean, Shawn, 5
Stowe, Harriet Beecher, 12, 147, 162

Thomas, Heather Kirk, 74
Thomas, W. I., 7
Thoreau, Henry David, 40, 163
Tortora, Phyllis G., 72, 73
Treichler, Paula A., 8, 11, 26, 54, 55, 91, 170
Twain, Mark, 40, 103, 163, 166
Tyson, Lois, 28

Unger, Rhoda, 87

Veblen, Thorstein, 7, 9, 164
Veeder, William 11, 82, 87, 169

Vega, Suzanne, 11
Vonnoh, Robert William, 72

Walker, Alice, 143, 146
Ward, Lester Frank, xii, xvi, 7, 119, 120–21, 122–24, 168
Webb, Beatrice, 7, 36
Webb, Sidney, 7, 36
Weber, Max, 7
Wellington, Amy, 10
Welter, Barbara, 7
Wharton, Edith, 8, 74, 96
Whitman, Walt, 122, 163

Williams, Raymond, 35, 100
Willis, Nathaniel P., 148
Winter, Kari J., 146
Wollstonecraft, Mary, 7
Wood, Ann Douglas, 7, 86
Woolf, Virginia, 7, 12, 143
Wright Orville, 13
Wright, Wilbur, 13

Yamada, Mitsuye, 87

Zangrando, Joanna Schneider, 7, 10

Modern Language Association of America

Approaches to Teaching World Literature

Joseph Gibaldi, series editor

Achebe's Things Fall Apart. Ed. Bernth Lindfors. 1991.
Arthurian Tradition. Ed. Maureen Fries and Jeanie Watson. 1992.
Atwood's The Handmaid's Tale *and Other Works*. Ed. Sharon R. Wilson,
     Thomas B. Friedman, and Shannon Hengen. 1996.
Austen's Pride and Prejudice. Ed. Marcia McClintock Folsom. 1993.
Balzac's Old Goriot. Ed. Michal Peled Ginsburg. 2000.
Baudelaire's Flowers of Evil. Ed. Laurence M. Porter. 2000.
Beckett's Waiting for Godot. Ed. June Schlueter and Enoch Brater. 1991.
Beowulf. Ed. Jess B. Bessinger, Jr., and Robert F. Yeager. 1984.
Blake's Songs of Innocence and of Experience. Ed. Robert F. Gleckner and
     Mark L. Greenberg. 1989.
Boccaccio's Decameron. Ed. James H. McGregor. 2000.
British Women Poets of the Romantic Period. Ed. Stephen C. Behrendt and
     Harriet Kramer Linkin. 1997.
Brontë's Jane Eyre. Ed. Diane Long Hoeveler and Beth Lau. 1993.
Byron's Poetry. Ed. Frederick W. Shilstone. 1991.
Camus's The Plague. Ed. Steven G. Kellman. 1985.
Cather's My Ántonia. Ed. Susan J. Rosowski. 1989.
Cervantes' Don Quixote. Ed. Richard Bjornson. 1984.
Chaucer's Canterbury Tales. Ed. Joseph Gibaldi. 1980.
Chopin's The Awakening. Ed. Bernard Koloski. 1988.
Coleridge's Poetry and Prose. Ed. Richard E. Matlak. 1991.
Conrad's "Heart of Darkness" *and* "The Secret Sharer." Ed. Hunt Hawkins and
     Brian W. Shaffer. 2002.
Dante's Divine Comedy. Ed. Carole Slade. 1982.
Dickens' David Copperfield. Ed. Richard J. Dunn. 1984.
Dickinson's Poetry. Ed. Robin Riley Fast and Christine Mack Gordon. 1989.
Narrative of the Life of Frederick Douglass. Ed. James C. Hall. 1999.
Eliot's Middlemarch. Ed. Kathleen Blake. 1990.
Eliot's Poetry and Plays. Ed. Jewel Spears Brooker. 1988.
Shorter Elizabethan Poetry. Ed. Patrick Cheney and Anne Lake Prescott. 2000.
Ellison's Invisible Man. Ed. Susan Resneck Parr and Pancho Savery. 1989.
English Renaissance Drama. Ed. Karen Bamford and Alexander Leggatt. 2002.
Dramas of Euripides. Ed. Robin Mitchell-Boyask. 2002.
Faulkner's The Sound and the Fury. Ed. Stephen Hahn and Arthur F. Kinney. 1996.
Flaubert's Madame Bovary. Ed. Laurence M. Porter and Eugene F. Gray. 1995.
García Márquez's One Hundred Years of Solitude. Ed. María Elena de Valdés and
     Mario J. Valdés. 1990.

Gilman's "The Yellow Wall-Paper" and Herland. Ed. Denise D. Knight and
    Cynthia J. Davis
Goethe's Faust. Ed. Douglas J. McMillan. 1987.
Hebrew Bible as Literature in Translation. Ed. Barry N. Olshen and
    Yael S. Feldman. 1989.
Homer's Iliad *and* Odyssey. Ed. Kostas Myrsiades. 1987.
Ibsen's A Doll House. Ed. Yvonne Shafer. 1985.
Works of Samuel Johnson. Ed. David R. Anderson and Gwin J. Kolb. 1993.
Joyce's Ulysses. Ed. Kathleen McCormick and Erwin R. Steinberg. 1993.
Kafka's Short Fiction. Ed. Richard T. Gray. 1995.
Keats's Poetry. Ed. Walter H. Evert and Jack W. Rhodes. 1991.
Kingston's The Woman Warrior. Ed. Shirley Geok-lin Lim. 1991.
Lafayette's The Princess of Clèves. Ed. Faith E. Beasley and Katharine Ann
    Jensen. 1998.
Works of D. H. Lawrence. Ed. M. Elizabeth Sargent and Garry Watson. 2001.
Lessing's The Golden Notebook. Ed. Carey Kaplan and Ellen Cronan Rose. 1989.
Mann's Death in Venice *and Other Short Fiction.* Ed. Jeffrey B. Berlin. 1992.
Medieval English Drama. Ed. Richard K. Emmerson. 1990.
Melville's Moby-Dick. Ed. Martin Bickman. 1985.
Metaphysical Poets. Ed. Sidney Gottlieb. 1990.
Miller's Death of a Salesman. Ed. Matthew C. Roudané. 1995.
Milton's Paradise Lost. Ed. Galbraith M. Crump. 1986.
Molière's Tartuffe *and Other Plays*. Ed. James F. Gaines and
    Michael S. Koppisch. 1995.
Momaday's The Way to Rainy Mountain. Ed. Kenneth M. Roemer. 1988.
Montaigne's Essays. Ed. Patrick Henry. 1994.
Novels of Toni Morrison. Ed. Nellie Y. McKay and Kathryn Earle. 1997.
Murasaki Shikibu's The Tale of Genji. Ed. Edward Kamens. 1993.
Pope's Poetry. Ed. Wallace Jackson and R. Paul Yoder. 1993.
Shakespeare's Hamlet. Ed. Bernice W. Kliman. 2001.
Shakespeare's King Lear. Ed. Robert H. Ray. 1986.
Shakespeare's Romeo and Juliet. Ed. Maurice Hunt. 2000.
Shakespeare's The Tempest *and Other Late Romances.* Ed. Maurice Hunt. 1992.
Shelley's Frankenstein. Ed. Stephen C. Behrendt. 1990.
Shelley's Poetry. Ed. Spencer Hall. 1990.
Sir Gawain and the Green Knight. Ed. Miriam Youngerman Miller and
    Jane Chance. 1986.
Spenser's Faerie Queene. Ed. David Lee Miller and Alexander Dunlop. 1994.
Stendhal's The Red and the Black. Ed. Dean de la Motte and Stirling Haig. 1999.
Sterne's Tristram Shandy. Ed. Melvyn New. 1989.
Stowe's Uncle Tom's Cabin. Ed. Elizabeth Ammons and Susan Belasco. 2000.
Swift's Gulliver's Travels. Ed. Edward J. Rielly. 1988.
Thoreau's Walden *and Other Works*. Ed. Richard J. Schneider. 1996.

Vergil's Aeneid. Ed. William S. Anderson and Lorina N. Quartarone. 2002.
Voltaire's Candide. Ed. Renée Waldinger. 1987.
Whitman's Leaves of Grass. Ed. Donald D. Kummings. 1990.
Woolf's To the Lighthouse. Ed. Beth Rigel Daugherty and Mary Beth Pringle. 2001.
Wordsworth's Poetry. Ed. Spencer Hall, with Jonathan Ramsey. 1986.
Wright's Native Son. Ed. James A. Miller. 1997.